# Better Résumés

FOR

# Executives

AND

# Professionals

## THIRD EDITION

by
**Robert F. Wilson**
President, Wilson McLeran, Inc.
New Haven, Connecticut
and
**Adele Lewis**
Former President and Founder
Career Blazers Agency, Inc.

BARRON'S
BARRON'S EDUCATIONAL SERIES, INC.

© Copyright 1996 by Barron's Educational Series, Inc.
Prior editions © Copyright 1991 and 1983 by
Barron's Educational Series, Inc.

*All inquiries should be addressed to:*
Barron's Educational Series, Inc.
250 Wireless Boulevard
Hauppauge, New York 11788

Library of Congress Catalog Card No. 95-32118
International Standard Book No. 0-8120-9508-1

**Library of Congress Cataloging in Publication Data**

Wilson, Robert F.
     Better résumés for executives and professionals / by Robert F. Wilson
     and Adele Lewis.—3rd ed.
          p.     cm
     Includes bibliographical references (p.   ) and index.
     ISBN 0-8120-9508-1
     1. Résumés (Employment)   I. Lewis, Adele Beatrice, 1927–
II. Title.
HF5383.W485        1996                                                   95-32118
650.14— dc20                                                                CIP

PRINTED IN THE UNITED STATES OF AMERICA
     89      100      9876543

# Contents

## Introduction

Appendices: Corporate Information Directories; List of
Action Verbs

# Acknowledgments

Among those who contributed to the quality of this revision are Nancy Schuman, who suggested both excellent computer-related job-search sources and specifics for updating the technological résumés; and Warren Bratter, who led Barron's editorial team in making this edition the best reference work possible for executives and professionals working to change or upgrade their careers.

# Introduction

If you are reading these words in a bookstore or library, trying to decide whether this book is worth your time and money, let us help you telescope the decision-making process.

We assume that, having turned to this page, you are either an executive or a professional with an interest in improving or changing your career. We assume you know that a powerful, effective résumé is one essential tool toward accomplishing your goal.

We assume also that either you want to continue working in your current career area or you are changing career fields but know precisely in what new area you want to apply past career interests, skills, and accomplishments. (If you are less than sure of your next career move, you will find valuable tips in Chapter 5. You may want to read that chapter first and conduct further research on your own before using the rest of this book.)

From these assumptions we frame our entire universe of prospective readers, and we welcome you among them. Good luck in your new or improved career.

# Taking Care of Business Before You Write Your Résumé

Satisfied job holders don't need résumés and rarely feel the need to update their old ones. The rest of you—either unhappy in your current position or having just left your last job—should read on.

Even the best-written résumés and marketing plans won't by themselves propel job seekers into the best next job; other important issues must be considered and controlled to allow enough time and peace of mind for the actual job hunt. Those of you in either of the categories mentioned in the first paragraph will have to harness all of your concentration powers to launch a successful job search—without rushing the process. So before getting to the nuts and bolts of creating a résumé, every job seeker should be sure that three possible trouble areas are under total control:

- Job-loss stress
- Family communications
- Financial crunch

Having these problems under control, understand, is not necessarily the same as *eliminating* them. Complete solutions may not be possible without outside assistance—which obviously is beyond the scope of this book. What we can do, however, is suggest ways of dealing with these problems to minimize any interference with your paramount task—finding the best next job as quickly as possible.

## Job-loss Stress

If you have just lost your job or feel that termination is imminent, a sharp sensation just below your rib cage may be one of several constant reminders that all is not well. This minor discomfort, however, is the least of it.

The psychologist who compared job-loss-associated trauma with that of divorce or the death of a loved one was onto something. Knowing the seven stages illuminating the tortuous path through this nightmare can help to keep your feelings in sharp focus—even push you through the process more quickly. As delineated in a self-administered employment transition program called *Job-Bridge*, these stages can be identified as follows:

**1. Shock.** You probably don't know what hit you. More extreme cases include panic, confusion, and an inability to take positive action.

**2. Denial.** You may refuse to believe what has happened and think instead that a terrible mistake has been made.

**3. Relief.** If your dismissal releases you from pressures building weeks or months ago, you may view your newfound "freedom" as an opportunity that would have presented itself only if you had quit instead—to a timetable *you* created.

**4. Anger.** Some of those recently fired fantasize about getting even with former bosses or colleagues they perceive to be responsible. Others become angry with themselves for not correcting a situation that became intolerable. Still others—and don't feel guilty if you're one of them—do both.

**5. Bargaining.** Some people, in a futile and often panic-motivated attempt to "right a wrong," appeal to their employer for a second chance or possible reassignment. Actually, there is often justification for assignment to a more appropriate position elsewhere in the firm. In your case, however, the time for negotiating such an alternative has irrevocably passed.

**6. Depression.** When the reality of the lost job finally sinks in, this emotion is almost invariably the result. It can mean lost sleep, anxiety, or even a withdrawal from family and friends. Such depression usually lasts from a few days to three weeks. If it persists much longer than three weeks, it could mean *clinical* depression—in which case you should call a physician.

**7. Acceptance.** The time it takes to accept the loss of a job varies, but it will happen. Only at this point can you begin to think ahead and start to design your marketing plan in a comprehensive way. Understand, however, that if it takes longer than you think it should to find employment, mild depression probably will reappear. Knowing this may help you fight through it when it returns.[1]

## Family Communications

Two characteristics you'll require in significant quantity during a job transition period are energy and confidence. To be sure you can draw on both of these resources at will, you'll need the support of your family. A spouse, a brother or sister, an uncle—virtually any interested family members—can be a part of your best support team, provided they are up to speed on your progress and problems.

Many job seekers make the mistake of shielding their families from problems that, after all, affect everyone and not just the primary salary earner. Protecting one's family from some fairly tough truths (such as a possible loss of income for an indefinite period) helps nobody. Not only are potentially viable alternatives for bringing in supplementary income never considered, but carrying so great a burden alone tends to drain both energy and confidence at a time when they are needed desperately.

## Financial Crunch

Knowing you may be without a paycheck within the next few weeks or months should be the trigger for implementing an expense-cutting and resource-husbanding plan to get you through what could be a tough period. Start with the elimination of frivolous spending; cut everything but the essentials. Call a family meeting to be sure everyone is aware of the realities, and decide what measures are best for the entire family. Most importantly, get a commitment from everyone in the family for short- and long-term efforts to conserve. Consider what family resources can be converted to available cash for payment of unavoidable expenses as many as six to nine months down the road. Make it a rule to share any deteriorating financial condition with the bank that holds your mortgage, your credit card companies, and other major creditors who have more than a passing interest in your ability or willingness to make monthly payments. Most people think that keeping a low profile will cause creditors to somehow forget about them or overlook their indebtedness for an indefinite period. Quite the contrary. Such an attitude invariably is the prelude to disaster. The only solution is to communicate with those you owe. It is the

[1]*Job-Bridge. ©Wilson McLeran, Inc., New Haven, CT 06511*

only way to avoid the embarrassing phone calls, personal visits, and, finally, law-suits and liens against your personal holdings that all collection agencies reserve as their ultimate weapon.

## Career Direction

After these three areas have been dealt with to your satisfaction, one more impor-tant consideration remains. The focus of your résumé depends totally on the career you have chosen—more specifically, on the range of opportunities within it that both interest you and for which you are qualified.

If you still want a job like the one you just left or intend to leave soon, turn to page 239 for specific suggestions. If a new course is not clear to you, however, don't guess; consult an expert. Certified career counselors are available in most cities to help you decide how to proceed. Many counselors without accreditation are equally qualified to help, but they can be more difficult to find. In either case, don't rely so much on the initials after the name as on the names of references you can check to verify your counselor's effectiveness.

# In Search of the Perfect Résumé

Your next consideration—after dealing effectively with the possible trouble areas discussed in Chapter 1—is to attend to your image-building tools, your résumé being foremost among them.

A résumé is the single most important self-advertisement any executive or professional on the move can own. It is your advance communication to generate interviews. It is your minidossier, to be distributed among prospective colleagues for review, comment, and—the ultimate goal—recommendation to hire. It is your statement of self, which says as much to a potential boss about your tastes and values as it does about your responsibilities and accomplishments.

If you are not known to a prospective employer, a good résumé—or, under some circumstances, just a good letter of introduction—is essential to getting the interview. Without the opportunity of meeting a possible boss face to face, your chances of getting hired are nonexistent.

Some career counselors recommend withholding the résumé as a trump card in generating interviews. If asked, they advise, stall. The longer you can avoid showing your résumé, apparently, the better.

The supposition seems to be that once an employer has seen your résumé, all your weaknesses will have been exposed, putting you just moments away from rejection. Anyone as reluctant as this to use a résumé, though, must not know how effective a good one can be.

This is not to say that résumés should *always* be used. One legitimate reason for not using a résumé or for delaying its use as long as possible would be that you want to make a career change so drastic that previous experience bears no relationship whatsoever to the intended new direction.

For just about every other situation, however, we emphatically recommend the preparation, use, and occasional updating of the best-written and -designed résumé possible. If you are going after more than one kind of job, you may need more than one résumé. But you do indeed need a résumé. In today's business and professional world, the résumé is viewed as indispensable—almost as much so as the calling card.

Don't leave your old job without it.

## The Experts Rate Résumés

Résumés are used, for the most part, in only three kinds of situations:

1. to generate an interview for an open position,
2. to determine whether an opening exists—either immediately or in the near future,
3. as part of a presentation to *create* a position.

But no matter which of these situations applies to you, the only effective résumé is one that leads to interviews. The résumés you will see in this book—including the one you learn to write—are designed to generate interviews.

Several years ago we took a survey to find out how line and staff executives evaluated résumés. We interviewed the interviewers themselves: more than fifty corporate officers, line managers, and human resource executives in a wide variety of Fortune 500 and smaller companies. Here's what we asked them:

- How many résumés do you receive a day?
- How much time do you take to read each one?
- What determines how much time you spend on each one?
- How long do you believe a résumé should be ?
- What information do you think a résumé should convey?
- What résumé format do you prefer (chronological, functional, other)?
- How would you describe a "good" résumé?
- How would you describe a "bad" résumé?
- What do you think are the most frequent mistakes people make when writing résumés?
- What information do you think a cover letter should contain?

The point about which there was virtually unanimous agreement was this: *A résumé must communicate—totally and instantly.*

Let's say you're responding to an advertisement or have knowledge from other sources about a position known also to other candidates. By definition you are in competition with anywhere from several dozen to many hundreds of other men and women who want the job. Under these circumstances, our experts say, ten to twenty seconds is about all the time you have to persuade a prospective employer to read every word—or at least to absorb most of what you have to offer. It must be clear immediately, they say, that you know precisely where you are going with your career and that you have just the right background at your current level to qualify for the position.

Or let's say you're making a "cold call" on a company—either because you've heard there was an opening or because your capabilities and experience uniquely qualify you for an opening you've heard is likely to break. Here too a strong résumé, backed up by an equally strong cover letter, is the first step you need to get in the door.

# Chronological vs. Functional

Before getting to specific résumé components that help to achieve total communication, let's spend a few paragraphs comparing the two most common résumé formats: the chronological and the functional.

The basic difference between the two is that the chronological résumé stresses accomplishments and responsibilities tied closely to specific positions and employers, whereas the functional résumé stresses a profile of your experience based on professional strengths or skills groupings, irrespective of any particular jobs held while attaining them.

With few exceptions, the chronological résumé format was preferred by the corporate executives we interviewed as doing the best job of indicating an individual's direction, skills, accomplishments, and promotion record.

The only situations in which the chronological format should be modified or discarded in favor of the functional, say our experts, are these:

- You have a spotty work record—four jobs in six years, for example.
- You are reentering the corporate or professional world after several years of freelancing, consulting, homemaking, or unemployment.
- You are making a dramatic change of careers—from personnel management to computer sales, as an extreme and unlikely example.

One of our clients, the wife of a career diplomat, had done only volunteer work twelve years before returning to the United States. She wanted to use her premarital travel experience—with a tour company, an airline, and a trade association—in some way to get back into a salaried position in travel sales or sales promotion. As it turned out, after she had completed our questionnaire (parts of which are reprinted in Chapter 3) we had enough data—including her three years as president of the International Women's Club of Copenhagen and as business English lecturer at a Brussels secretarial school—for a résumé that led to an interview and subsequent promotion job for a major international hotel chain. As you can see from her résumé (all résumé identities in this book have been changed) on pages 186–187, she was able legitimately to list the magazine she founded and published for the women's club, including the thousands of dollars of advertising she sold to keep it going and the managerial experience she gained by supervising a staff of twelve.

A freelancer's accomplishments can be chronicled the same way; likewise for the consultant and the self-employed entrepreneur. An impressive client list, detailing specific accomplishments and an ability to bring projects in on time and to budget, can offset the stigma of a largely noncorporate work history. (See pages 22–23 for an example.) Similarly, a business sold for a profit is a rare phenomenon. If you can count it among your accomplishments, highlight it prominently.

If you've held too many jobs in too few years however, you face a more challenging problem; similarly so if you have not worked for some time—either for pay or in volunteer positions. In these instances you will be better off with either a functional résumé or no résumé at all.

The functional résumé stresses career-wide accomplishments, responsibilities, and skills, and it avoids a complete chronology of employment—with a list of employers and inclusive employment dates often the last entry.

Even though your reasons for going to the functional résumé are sound, you face a risk in using it. According to most of the corporate executives we surveyed, it raises more questions than it answers and makes many prospective employers suspicious. Functional résumés should be used only in situations where the "whole truth"—that is, an all-inclusive chronological format—will kill any chance of an interview.

# What Makes Good and Bad Résumés

To do its job—get you the interview—a résumé must clearly and forcefully make the best possible case for your ability to meet the needs of the targeted prospective employers. Obviously there are other factors to consider. One résumé cannot be an all-situation solution. Occasionally a specially written résumé is called for. An individual going after two different but related types of positions may want to distribute two or three variations of the same résumé. The list of individuals receiving the résumé, of course, is key, as is the letter that accompanies the résumé. These two stages we'll cover in Chapters 5 and 6, respectively.

None of this, however, takes away from the power of a well-written, well-designed résumé. Put in the form of negative example (and taken directly from responses to the corporate survey discussed earlier), let's imagine an employer "Hit List" of résumé characteristics, any one of which will ensure that a candidate is a candidate no more. For ease of discussion, we'll divide the characteristics into the categories of Appearance, Clarity, and Content. They break down like so:

## Appearance

- Tacky typing or reproduction job
- Poor paper quality
- Vibrant, bizarre, or otherwise offbeat paper color
- Typographical errors
- Gratuitous, attention-getting visual effects (wild or mixed type styles, brochure format, photographs)
- Paper size other than 8½ by 11 inches
- Length of more than two pages (with exceptions, of course; see Chapter 3)

## Clarity

- Description of jobs or accomplishments longer than four lines, causing difficult reading
- Position objective or experience summary not clearly stated
- Grammatical or syntactical errors or inconsistencies
- Personal data (name, address, phone numbers) not immediately identifiable
- Job history not stated in reverse chronological order

## Content

- Excessive space devoted to items not directly related to career (hobbies, detailed personal data, detailed descriptions of jobs related to former careers)
- Employment gaps not sufficiently played down or explained
- Sequence of major headings inappropriate to level (for example, education listed first for person with solid, career-related experience)
- Career-related volunteer experience not effectively treated or developed
- Accomplishments insufficiently treated or, where appropriate, not quantitatively stated

In Chapter 3 we'll go into more detail about these characteristics and the inevitable exceptions to the rule, take a look at predominant résumé types and styles, and determine when to use them.

# Résumé Nuts and Bolts

All successful authors write with a specific audience in mind. A successful résumé writer should be no less selective. Your target may be an individual hiring for the only position in the world for which you would consider leaving your present job. Or it could be every vice-president of marketing in the bottled water industry with sales exceeding $10 million in Southern California, Texas, and Florida. No matter. Know him, her, or them as well as you can, and write a résumé addressing specific needs.

An ability to write directly to needs rests on the mastery of three essential levels of information:

1.  knowledge of industry
2.  knowledge of company
3.  knowledge of position or function.

The simplest, most easily managed goal is to move up the ladder in a relatively straight line—assuming more or broader responsibilities in your function and staying within your industry. In this case, your job is to demonstrate—either directly or indirectly—your awareness of industry trends, problems, and promise. The "knowledge of company" level should be dealt with only in terms of your present company. Your awareness of the idiosyncrasies of other specific companies can be handled in the cover letter accompanying the résumé.

As to "knowledge of position," chances are the job you want is much like the one your boss has. In this case you need to be clear that your *prospective* boss can see which of your *current* boss's responsibilities you either have handled or can handle. This, we repeat, is the simplest, most easily managed challenge. Those of you changing functions, industries, or both will find it tougher, but the strategy remains the same.

Writing your best résumé requires the assemblage of all pertinent professional, personal, and educational data. Most good career counselors use a detailed questionnaire, completed by each client and augmented by a one-on-one "drawing-out" session based on responses to specific questionnaire questions.

# The Targeted Resume

Prospective employers with virtually identical openings can maintain sharply differing priorities with respect to their definitions of an "ideal" candidate. As you'll soon see from your research of specific companies—or even from a careful reading of several companies' openings for virtually identical jobs—a single résumé is not going to be enough. The alternative: a targeted résumé, adjusted to meet every job opportunity.

In these days of a personal computer in almost every office or den, this strategy is relatively easy to implement. First prepare a "master résumé" that you can adjust as necessary, situation by situation. You'll see how as we go through the résumé components one by one.

# Objective

After identifying yourself by name, address, and phone number at the top of page 1, the first item of information should be your immediate career objective. This and the entry that follows—the Summary—provide the direction, tone, and major emphasis of the entire résumé. The cumulative effect of any résumé is determined by these two components. For this reason the Objective and the Summary offer the greatest opportunity to customize your résumé for individual situations.

We ask each of our clients to identify both a short- and a long-term Objective on our questionnaire to determine whether enough thought has been given to career path. In some instances—particularly for you younger job seekers—it may be a good idea to write your immediate Objective in a way that incorporates both your immediate and your long-term goals ("Telemarketing Sales, Leading to Sales Management Position," for example).

In other instances it may be that a single, specific title will serve. If such an Objective thoroughly covers the job you want (and are qualified for—and exists), then you are lucky and this is all you should use. For example:

- Operations Vice-President
- Senior Corporate Counsel
- Foundation Executive Director

These have a certain crisp purity, don't they? Let's hope you're able to zero in on your Objective as precisely—but don't be surprised if doing so isn't quite this easy. If you have most recently held a vice-presidency, for example, a similar well-paying position of power may be perfectly right for you and yet not carry a company or corporate officership. Corporate structure can vary widely, even in two companies within the same industry. A vice-president in one company can be a senior manager in another and yet carry the same responsibilities. If this is true in your situation, broaden the Objective for your master résumé. Samples in this case:

- Senior Management—Sales/Merchandising
- Director of Healthcare Services
- Orchestral Conductor or Choral Director

If your field is relatively new or quickly evolving, you may need to cast your net wider still:

- Telecommunications Programming Management
- Director of Development, Major University
- Online or email Product Manager

No matter what your objective, state it broadly enough on your master résumé to embrace all acceptable closely related positions but not so broadly that you diffuse your focus and appear to be willing to accept anything out there. A prospective employer may infer lack of direction—or worse, that you're in a panic situation and will take anything you can get. A targeted résumé makes it possible to vary your Objective as often as the need arises.

# Summary

Whereas the purpose of the Objective is to succinctly describe the position you want by level, function, and/or industry, the Summary section (or "Background," or "Professional Highlights," if you prefer) is a companion entry indicating those achievements and skills that will verify and document your ability to handle the job you want. Together, these two entries will position you so completely that the impression a reader has will be conditioned almost entirely upon them.

Anywhere from two to five brief, powerful sentences will be enough, highlighting those aspects of your background of most appeal. The beauty of a Summary is that it offers the advantages of a functional résumé, with none of its disadvantages (for example, the absence of dates tied to specific accomplishments, an omission that often raises questions in the mind of the reader). You have the opportunity to combine and emphasize similar aspects of your work experience that may go back ten or twenty years.

One of our candidates had a strong financial background spanning three industries over eighteen years. Among his achievements was originating the airline credit card that was eventually imitated by every major airline. The problem was that his airline experience came immediately after his M.B.A. and would have been buried near the end of the résumé had it been treated chronologically. We decided to use a one-sentence general Summary, followed by a Highlights section that would cause selected accomplishments to "pop out" visually. [The complete résumé appears on pages 86–87.] It read like this:

**SUMMARY**      Fourteen years' experience in financial and business planning, marketing, and controller functions for a manufacturer, an airline, and a brokerage firm.

**HIGHLIGHTS**   • Conceived and implemented TWA's "Getaway," now the most popular of all airline credit card systems

               • Assisted in negotiating the transfer of TWA control away from the Hughes organization

               • As media liaison, used marketing and advertising to make general public aware of negotiability of industrial diamonds

               • Developed capacity for improving relations between factory and office workers to increase production and cut costs

               • As general manager, tightened financial controls and directed short- and long-term business planning

To write the best Summary—for *any* opportunity—go back over your career and list all the skills, repsonsibilities, and achievements you feel will qualify you for the position in question. Pare down your list to the top six or seven points, incorporating as many as possible that match the requirements of the opening. Then combine those that are similar in scope or function, so that you wind up with a brief narrative that has a little flow to it.

Choose your words carefully. If your Summary sustains the reader's interest, more likely than not the rest of the résumé will too. Don't be flowery. Your chances of getting the interview will not be improved by any records set in the use of adjectives or polysyllables. Make every word count. Rewrite your first drafts, striking out unnecessary words and phrases and tightening sentences until they say exactly what you mean. Then have one or more friends who know you well professionally read what you've written and suggest accomplishments you either have forgotten or perhaps have dismissed as unimportant.

If you are changing careers—even slightly—don't mention the function or industry *being* changed. One client with a strong sales and marketing background wanted to minimize the fact that his excellent record had been compiled for the past seven years in the catering industry, a field he wanted to leave. So although we went into considerable detail relating his experience in terms of specific employers later in the résumé, it was more effective to write the Summary stressing more generic skills and accomplishments as follows:

**SUMMARY:** Extensive experience in sales and service of major industrial and commercial accounts. Outstanding record in acquiring direct accounts and initiating client contact at top management levels. Comprehensive background conceptualizing and implementing advertising campaigns.

An industry-changing executive, then, can encourage a prospective employer to consider his or her "pure" strengths first—at the top of the résumé—before revealing that those strengths were attained in what might be viewed as an alien industry.

Such a Summary, in fact, can be used with two or more specific Objectives to provide résumés with as many differing orientations as opportunities warrant. Two used by the marketing executive whose Summary appears above are as follows:

- Executive Management, Hotel Industry
- Television Time Sales/Marketing Management

So in essence he has three résumés to be used for situations that have already come up, with the option of preparing others pointed toward slightly differing situations as needed.

For opportunities you discover that don't fall precisely under templates representing your one or more specific areas of interest, go back to your computer and craft a résumé that matches your background with the specs of the job. Recast your Objective and Summary in any way that will *legitimately* display your relevant, job-specific skills and accomplishments.

# Experience

The heart of the résumé is the organization and presentation of your job history. If you have selected the chronological format as the one best for you, your goal is to make as much as you can out of every position you have had. Describe your major responsibilities, to be sure, but concentrate most heavily on accomplishments you can legitimately own or share. As a memory refresher, most questionnaires use a "Problem/Action/Results" inquiry for every position held and with every employer for whom a client has worked.

The key (to quote from the questionnaire) is to "think of as many problems as you can that you both faced and were able to solve to some satisfaction. Briefly describe the problem; next, the action you took to solve or alleviate it; then, the results or consequences of that action. Specifically mention, for example, situations or conditions that improved, dollars saved or earned for the firm, ideas adopted by the firm, dollars in increased sales for the firm, etc." The form on page 13 will help you arrange your accomplishments in a Problem/Action/Results structure.

Completing such a form will give you a nucleus of data from which to frame a powerful, achievements-oriented Experience section. Concentrate on utilizing achievements consistent with your career direction, and spend as little space as possible on aspects of previous positions that have no bearing on the kind of job you're after now. Similarly, devote more attention to current or recent career-related positions than on those held earlier in your professional life. Don't appear to be dwelling on the past. If you attained similar goals early in your career as well as more recently, load them in your current experience and keep the past relatively spare.

Most Recent Position

Title _____

Overall Duties

1. _____

2. _____

3. _____

4. _____

5. _____

6. _____

Significant Achievement

Problem _____

_____

Action Taken _____

_____

_____

_____

Results (Quantify Where Applicable) _____

_____

_____

_____

Key Skills Demonstrated

_____

_____

_____

_____

(Repeat for prior positions)

The obvious exception to this advice is if you are in the process of a career change back to one held when you were younger. In this instance the wiser course is to list first those positions, responsibilities, and accomplishments from the career you want now under a heading immediately identifiable to the reader's need, such as RETAIL EXPERIENCE. Try to use the entire first page to chronicle this part of your professional background. You will then be following your stated Objective and Summary with experience that backs up your intentions. The only possible negative to this strategy is that the inclusive dates in the margin relative to employment may go back a decade or more. Defuse this by a parenthetical note or asterisked footnote after the dates, such as "See page 2 for current experience."

One of our clients had spent five years managing restaurants after a successful retail career and wanted to go back to the field he realized was his first love. We accomplished this by filling the entire first page with retail experience without ever referring to his more recent restaurant experience on page 2—except for a footnote. Page 1 of the résumé is shown on page 15.

Notice in this résumé the action verb that begins each entry under EXPERIENCE: *Supervised, Devised, Identified, Hired, Ordered,* and so on. These are all powerful action verbs. They are also both accurate and effective. Use the list of action verbs on page 278—as well as a good dictionary or thesaurus—to be sure each of your entries opens with the best possible, *honestly expressed* action verb.

Sequence is important not just for career changers, however, but for anyone interested in the most effective possible résumé. Think of your résumé as a script for both you and the interviewer. This is particularly true of the Experience section. Each entry is a cue to be picked up by the interviewer as he or she wishes and singled out for elaboration if it piques interest and as it relates to the position available.

The accomplishments should be broken up into bite-size entities for the interviewer to spot and absorb quickly. The interviewee, on the other hand, should view each entry as the basis for a leading question, about which he or she has rehearsed responses of anywhere from one to ten minutes, determined by interviewer interest.

This being so, it is extremely important not only to include those points of maximum appeal but to sequence them by degree of importance—almost the way you learned to write a topic outline in your first composition course. Where appropriate, buttress or quantify an accomplishment to further whet the reader's interest. Follow a main point with appropriate subpoints. Let's take an example from the résumé of another retail executive:

- Developed marketing programs to reposition corporation as necessary
    - —Created 120-store test to analyze customer buying patterns for purpose of maximizing inventory investment (later implemented in all 320 stores)
    - —Initiated and implemented merchandise line plan to fully develop previously nonformalized corporate policy

And later in the résumé:

# JACK M. MARCHESCHI

602 Walnut Street, St. Charles, IL 60144
Office: (708) 584-1930     Home: (708) 584-7993

---

***OBJECTIVE***     RETAIL SENIOR MANAGEMENT

***SUMMARY***     Eight years' retail managerial experience, including two years' ownership of upscale gift shop with annual revenues of $500,000+; strong sales promotion, inventory control, and purchasing skills. Multilingual.

***RETAIL EXPERIENCE***     J. W. MAYS DEPARTMENT STORE, Aurora, IL
*Senior Buyer*

*1990 to 1993\**
- Supervised ordering, pricing, display, and marketing of all giftware, crystal, glassware, silverware, china figurines, and imported merchandise
- Devised incentive plan responsible for sales increase of 15% on volume of $3.5 million annually
- Supervised 10 assistant buyers and sales personnel
- Identified and assigned new vendors to anticipate market trends

LINAS GIFT SHOP, Elmhurst, IL
*Owner*

*1988 to 1990*
- Overall bottom-line responsibility; established and maintained overhead; supervised bookkeeping
- Hired, trained, and managed 3 salespeople
- Attended regional and national gift shows to determine trends and generate merchandising and marketing ideas

MOHANS, LTD., New Canaan, CT
*Sales Manager*

*1985 to 1987*
- Ordered, displayed, priced, and advertised all women's and men's clothing
- Supervised 18 salespeople
- Increased sales by 30% in first year; responsible for 25% of volume of $2.5 million
- Achieved 13½% profit sharing, highest in company

\* For current experience, see page 2

- Assumed total responsibility for start-up and opening of individual store

    —Led and managed all areas (merchandising, operations, personnel, and intercommunity relations) to achieve sales volume and profit objectives

    —Trained, developed, and managed Assistant Managing Director, 6 Operational Department Managers, and 13 Merchandising Managers

    —Established environment of full employee input preparatory to store opening, keeping motivation and morale at optimum levels

The chief point to remember in writing and laying out this section is to make all key aspects of every entry as visible as possible so as to permit the reader to take in your strengths at a glance and to select for more careful reading those that relate closely to the target position. The layout, in fact, is as important as the writing. Don't underestimate it. Sound data presented in a sloppy or unclear manner are as ineffective as a badly written résumé. As you go through the sample résumés in this book, look as closely at the design as you do at the writing.

Speaking of design, one way to control the appearance of your printed materials is to select an appropriate typeface and type size. By "appropriate" we mean a visual effect that you are comfortable with but at the same time does not distract from the message you are trying to convey. Stay away from script faces, for example, or anything overly dramatic or cute. Several sample faces and fonts (meaning boldface, italic, or "regular") are exhibited on page 18. Most printers will either have these faces or be able to approximate them. Choose a matching letterhead for cover, networking, and application letters as well. If you are having difficulty getting your complete résumé onto two pages, perhaps coming down a point size (from 12 to 11, for example, for purposes of communicating with your printer) will be a better idea than cutting an essential entry. Use your printer or a friend with a good design sense to help you decide. (Those of you with a sophisticated computer setup will think we are referring to the printer in your home; the rest of you will think we're talking about the printer in your local copy shop. You are both right.)

Finally, each opening that comes your way gives you an opportunity to target your résumé—not only your Objective and Summary but the Experience section as well. Carefully review every entry with an eye toward its relevance for the job in question. It may be that a juxtaposition of one or two entries will position you more effectively against the requirements of a particular job—or that a skill or accomplishment you didn't include for one reason or another will be right on target this time. Keep on the lookout for ways to target your résumé and heighten your candidacy at every stage of your job search.

# Education

Start with your most advanced degree, and include the name and location of the institution, your major, year of graduation (if you're under 45), and all career-oriented scholarships and academic awards. Mention of any fraternity or sorority affiliations may hook you into the social-academic version of an Old Boy network; on the other hand, it may irritate a former Independent who considers all college social organizations snob factories. You might want to wait and work this into the interview if you think you're being interviewed by a Brother or Sister.

List any career-related extracurricular activities. Include all career-related courses or programs completed, whether company-sponsored or paid for by you. If you are not a college graduate, list institutions attended anyway, with inclusive dates but without additional comment; this may be perceived as defensive.

# Licenses and Certifications

Include only those licenses and certifications that are career-related, without elaboration.

# Additional Personal Data

Career-related hobbies—yes.

Marital status, height, weight, number and ages of children, state of health (it's always "excellent" anyway, at least on résumés we've seen), availability of references (when they want them, they'll ask)—no. Exception: Sales managers sometimes impute a greater sense of stability to married candidates than to single ones. Taking advantage, where applicable, of this bias may be enough reason for salespeople to trumpet their married status.

## Sample Typefaces Used in Letterheads

Garamond

**CLARK T. MAJORS**
6445 Cecil Avenue, Amarillo, TX 79110
Home: (808) 863-0439        Office: (808) 622-7070

Optima

BEVERLY NORDQUIST
3121 Snyder Aveune
Brooklyn, New York 11313
Home (718) 401-3195      Office: (718) 448-6192

Helvetica

**WILLIAM SNOW, JR.**

Ridge Farms Road
Monroe, LA 70114
(318) 838-7653

Univers

JOHN STUART GEISLER
400 EAST 58th STREET      NEW YORK, NY 10022
(212) 668-1932

Bauer Bodoni

**ROSE A. POLLENTIER**
**33 RUSSELL STREET**
**FRESNO, CA 93725**

**TELEPHONE (209) 614-3349**

Galliard

*Robert S. Tinnon*
7060 Shoup Ave., #183
Canoga Park, CA 91303
818/347-2183

New Baskerville

**JAMES S. COULOS**
6 Sandgate Place, Chattanooga, TN 37406
(516) 401-7732

Melior

GENE M. JAEGER
881 ST. CHARLES DRIVE
THOUSAND OAKS, CALIFORNIA 91360
805/495-2590

Times Roman

IRENE C. ERDAY
17 Marietta Road, Allentown, Pennsylvania 18105

Futura

**JAMES R. LARSON**
6371 Edgehurst Drive
Darien, CT 06820
(203) 655-4138

Palatino

**HARRY EPKE**    140 Benchley Place, Morristown, New Jersey 07960    (201) 338-5050

Bembo

*Mildred A. Wilson • 1736 Pinehurst Lane • Tucson, AZ 85706*

# Sample Résumés

The résumés reproduced in this chapter have been categorized among the following standard corporate functions and services:

Communications
Finance
Human Resources and Development
Information Systems
Legal
Marketing
Operations
Research and Development

This creates a few awkward catchalls, among them the inclusion of all educational and health care positions under Human Resources and Development and some engineering and science-oriented positions under Research and Development. Similarly, we have included under Communications—perhaps arbitrarily—most art and design, public relations, film, television, museum, music, editorial, and writing positions.

Check the back cover to see if the particular job you are after is included in the appropriate function or service area—or perhaps one or more close to it—and most likely you will be able to draw what you need from more than one example. Better yet, if you have the time, skim all of the samples in this chapter. It may well be that suggestions for several of your résumé entries will appear in career fields completely different from your own.

Several specific problem situations have been addressed in a number of these résumés. The more common among them are delineated below by category and page number. If you don't find your situation here, labeled as you diagnose it, read through all the résumés anyway. A crossover solution may occur to you for a problem you might never have identified as similar to your own.

Page 44: Career change from public to private sector
Page 46: Career change from public to private sector
Page 58: Career change from public to private sector
Page 62: Absence of postcollege experience
Page 68: Career change from public to private sector
Page 70: Slight career change within sphere of interest
Page 72: Slight career change to similar industry
Page 76: Resumption of career interrupted years earlier
Page 78: Slight career change within industry
Page 86: Highlighting exemplary accomplishment early in career
Page 90: Aggressive problem/solution explication of accomplishments
Page 94: Slight career change within industry
Page 96: Career change from public to private sector
Page 102: Career change from public to private sector
Page 112: Slight career change within industry
Page 116: Resumption of career interrupted years earlier

# COMMUNICATIONS

# KAREN ANN HASSELHOFF

1214 Tobiasson Road
Orem, Utah 84123
(801) 486-1497

## *SUMMARY*

An accomplished leader with 18 years' experience in the areas of special education, publishing, and educational software development. Exceptional strengths in team building, project planning, product design, third-party vendor relations. Specific accomplishments include consistent delivery of multitiered projects under budget and on schedule, successfully creating and supporting divergent project teams, and establishing industry standards for quality. A dedicated and creative motivator with excellent communication, problem-solving, and team-building skills.

## *PROFESSIONAL EXPERIENCE: SOFTWARE DEVELOPMENT*

### LUNA INTERACTIVE, INCORPORATED                    1994–present
Salt Lake City, Utah

*Executive Producer*

Manage the development process for all interactive multimedia and off-line products.

- Revised and finalized both business and product plans to facilitate successful funding by investors.
- Established software development process to ensure delivery of quality product.
- Developed production schedules to meet aggressive sales and marketing requirements.
- Revised prototype programs for presentation to investors.

### WASATCH LEARNING CORPORATION                      1985–1994
Provo, Utah

*Project Manager,* Curriculum Enhancement Operations (1994)

Coordinated and facilitated the product development process in multiple curriculum areas. Acted as a liaison between lead designers, Group Director, and other departments. Most significant contribution: The early completion of a critical sales piece has generated revenue 30% greater than its projected development costs (as of June 30, 1994).

- Wrote and implemented product plans.
- Developed and implemented procedures for the development process and established criteria for products in collaboration with curriculum team leaders.
- Developed documentation prototypes.
- Scheduled staff and projects for completion within a company-wide release schedule.
- Recruited, supervised, and evaluated staff of 12 consultants.
- Identified production problems and developed corrective action plans.
- Represented department on company-wide project teams to determine schedules, resolve pre- and postproduction issues, and facilitate developing group consensus.
- Provided prerelease training to Sales, Marketing, Education Services, and Training.

***Senior Instructional Designer,*** Home-School Connections Department (1991–1993)

Led teams of instructional designers, programmers, artists, writers and consultants in the development of product enhancements to support and complement existing products already in use in the field. Most significant contribution: All assigned enhancements met or exceeded revenue projections.

- Reviewed and approved third-party materials for use by company and coordinated contracts with vendors.
- Managed production of integrated activity guides, including developing initial content and format requirements, recruiting and supervising contract writers and reviewing and editing.
- Wrote and revised technical documentation and curriculum implementation manuals.
- Trained sales staff and education consultants in implementation of each enhancement.

***Instructional Designer,*** Elementary Reading Department (1987–1991)

Designed and wrote courseware, managed the design and production of accompanying tests, and wrote user documentation to support courseware.

- Developed prototype test format and implemented innovative design across all levels of reading/language arts curriculum.
- Created computer-delivered and off-line tutorial material for adult users and educators.
- Managed teams of up to 24 consultants in matching lesson content to objectives.
- Maintained and monitored the progress of existing courseware through the various production cycles

***Senior Quality Assurance Analyst,*** Quality Assurance Department (1985–1987)

Initiated standardized testing procedures, established curriculum standards based on state recommendation, and trained staff members. Reviewed and edited on-line courseware. Most significant contribution: the development and implementation of the company's first published guidelines for production, 95% of which are still in use 9 years later.

- Designed and implemented original curriculum quality assurance training program, which included guidelines for design, production and review of courseware.
- Reviewed and edited courseware for grades K–6.

**McGRAW-HILL/CTB**                                                    **1982–1985**
Monterey, California

**Assistant Editor,** PMI/MS Project

- Wrote and edited mathematics items and teacher resource materials for criterion-referenced tests.
- Read and critiqued unsolicited test proposals, recommending publication as indicated.

## *EDUCATION*

University of California, Berkeley: B.A., Psychology, 1980.

*Roberta O. Lencioni*　　　　5605 Fortiesciew Road • San Diego, CA 92108
(619) 299-4723

*BUSINESS DEVELOPMENT/PROJECT MANAGEMENT*

**QUALIFIED BY:** A successful background in division and corporate management with significant and creative contributions to corporate growth and development. Areas of experience:

- Division management
- Project management
- Advertising/promotions/special events
- Research and analysis
- Writing/editing
- Product development
- Training/seminars
- Strategic and market planning
- Budget planning and development

**EXPERIENCE:**

*Management:*
- Total management marketing product development, and bottom-line responsibility for Product Development Division, National Learning Corporation.
- Improved bottom-line plan in a recession environment with revenues off 25%.
- Reduced clerical and editorial time and burden by 25% with introduction of word processing.
- Wrote and negotiated product development contracts.
- Total management control of newly created National Learning Institute Division.
- Designed, developed, and managed a new course for SAT preparation.
- Designed and manufactured women's accessories.

*Training:*
- Trained National Learning Corporation and public school reading achievement center personnel.
- Designed, developed, and implemented a variety of training manuals and programs for company-owned and franchised centers.

*Marketing/ Communications:*
- Managed all aspects of marketing/sales activities for National Learning Corporation, Product Development Division.
- Assisted in marketing public school contracts.
- Designed and implemented a professional relations program for Reading Game centers in new market areas.
- Designed and wrote collateral and sales promotional pieces.
- Created, wrote, and supervised production of print and electronic advertising programs.
- Wrote and produced quarterly newsletter.
- Organized and conducted promotional seminars and presentations.
- Planned and coordinated with womenswear stores on wardrobes for career women.
- Created and established a successful marketing program to expand retail customer base.

*Product Development:*
- Member of special team conducting research on business opportunities in new educational technology.
- Assisted in the concept design of a strategic business plan for entry into educational technology markets.
- Designed and supervised production of more than 50 supplementary instructional programs for major publishers.
- Negotiated and supervised implementation of client contracts.
- Worked with technical team to design and develop computerized version of a reading management system that cut labor costs by 20%.
- Developed classroom reading management materials.
- Wrote original diagnostic/prescriptive tests.
- Designed a computer-assisted reading program.

**CHRONOLOGY:**
- Murray Consultants, Inc., Pasadena, CA  *1994–present*
  Educational/Curriculum Specialist

- National Learning Corporation, Santa Monica, CA,  *1980–1994*
  Vice-President, Educational Services
  Vice-President, General Manager, American Learning Institute
  Vice-President/General Manager, Reading Development
  Vice-President, Special Projects
  Director of Contract Services
  Director of Learning, the Reading Game

- Santa Barbara City Schools, Santa Barbara, CA  *1977–1980*
  Teacher and Reading Specialist

**COMMENTS:**

*"Superior ability to learn new technical skills and concepts...outstanding creative processes and sales ability...well organized, goal oriented...key skills: networking; market analysis; establishment of new products and business...an outstanding person."*

Dr. Barry Murray, President
Murray Consultants, Inc.
Gardena, CA

*"Demonstrates thorough knowledge of P&L...excellent problem solver...liked and respected...well organized...spots problems, resolves and takes initiative... excellent verbal skills; tough negotiator...not a 'yes' person. Very goal and results oriented."*

Lawrence Ackerman, President
Rund McNeeley Corp.
Chicago, IL

*"Creative ability is her most valuable attribute...one of the most knowledgeable specialists in reading instruction in the United States...technical abilities in all areas of training are outstanding...did an excellent team management job... very successful in sales and marketing...will tackle new opportunities and solve new problems...will be an asset to any employer; we are very sorry to lose her."*

Martin Dagliesh, President
National Learning Corp.
Santa Monica, CA

*"Exceptional ability with people...can manage efficiently with an eye to bottom-line results...particularly effective in marketing...a seasoned manager."*

Kenneth Costa, Consultant
Washington, D.C.

**EDUCATION:**
B.A., Education, and Credential, University of California at Santa Barbara, *1977*
M.A., in progress

**AWARDS AND HONORS:**
Kappa Delta Pi (an Education Honorary), Dean's List,
Scholarship Chair (Pi Beta Phi)

**ORGANIZATIONS:**
International Reading Association
Alumni Association, UCSB
Association of Media Producers (Board Member, President)

## *Elena M. Randall*

410 Kirk Road  •  Janesville, Wisconsin 58313  •  (414) 784-0391

### SUMMARY OF SKILLS

- Eight years' editorial experience with leading publishers, focusing on the children's educational technology market.
- Experienced in developing content for online publishing environment. Currently writing new publishing plan to expand the interactivity of the online environment and to develop for CD-ROM platforms.
- Award-winning writer. Winner of the 1994 Ed Press Award for Editorial Excellence.
- Keynote speaker, guest lecturer, and panel moderator for numerous national and international conferences, seminars, and courses (see attached list).
- Frequently quoted by national press (*USA Today, Parenting, Publisher's Weekly*) as a spokesperson on issues in technology, children's software, education, and publishing.
- Serve as judge for numerous software design awards programs, including Smithsonian/ComputerWorld Awards, Software Publishers Association Codie Awards, and the National Information Infrastructure Awards.

### EDUCATIONAL TECHNOLOGY EMPLOYMENT HISTORY

#### *Editor in Chief*

*Classroom Computer* magazine, published by Raintree Press, Milwaukee, Wisconsin
December 1991–present

- Direct the editorial of a 70- to 90-page, four-color, controlled-circulation, advertising-based magazine, published eight times during the school year. Manage a staff of three editors, two designers, and freelancers.
- Successfully redirected the editorial of the magazine to focus on technology in the context of school change, making the magazine a leading voice in the educational technology market.
- Instituted numerous innovative columns, including "Emerging Technologies" and "Home Learning Software," which recommends edutainment software for parents to buy.
- Directed the art redesign of the magazine, resulting in a magazine that is highly readable, well laid-out, and extremely user-friendly.
- Put the magazine on America Online. Currently writing new publishing plan to expand the interactivity of the online environment and to develop CD-ROM products.

#### *Software Review Editor*

*Classroom Computer* magazine, published by Raintree Press, Milwaukee, Wisconsin
August 1989–December 1991

- Selected and sent out for review software titles for each issue of the magazine. Edited reviews. Met regularly with software publishers to preview new titles.
- Redesigned the software review section to make it more reflective of the way readers buy software and easier to glean pertinent information.
- Wrote numerous cover stories and other articles for the magazine on technology in education, including the annual report on the software industry. Was the first among educational journalists (and many trade writers) to write about the impact of optical technologies on education publishing.

#### *Associate Editor*

*Teaching & Computers* magazine, published by Raintree Press, Milwaukee, Wisconsin
August 1989–June 1990

- Responsible for selecting and sending out for review software titles for each issue of the magazine. Edited reviews. Met regularly with software publishers to preview new titles.
- Wrote cover stories and other articles for the magazine on technology in the classroom, including the annual Teachers' Favorite Software roundup.

### Editor

Sunburst Communications, Pleasantville, New York
December 1986–August 1989

- Project Editor for hands-on science curriculum funded by the National Science Foundation and designed by Education Development Center, Newton, Massachusetts. Responsibilities included codesigning software components, editing and designing a teacher's guide, and reviewing and selecting video and other ancillary products for the curriculum.
- Software Editor, responsible for writing and editing teacher's guides to educational software games and programs.

### Freelance Writer

New York, New York
1989–1991

- Wrote freelance articles on educational technology for various publications, including *Business Week*, *Instructor*, and *America's Agenda*, as well as marketing writing for educational technology groups.
- Public Relations Writer, responsible for writing press releases, handling the press, and demonstrating software at trade shows to influential buyers.

## SUMMARY OF OTHER PROFESSIONAL EXPERIENCE

Boston University, Boston, Massachusetts
Department of English, September 1983–August 1986

*Assistant Director, Freshman-Sophomore English Program*
- Designed and managed class and teaching schedules and planned budget for largest department at BU; coordinated 75 faculty, 100 courses, and 2,500 students per term.

*Teaching Fellow; Supervisor, Teaching Fellows*
- Taught Expository Composition and Introduction to Creative Writing; supervised first-term Creative Writing teaching fellow; served on Admissions Committee.

## EDUCATION

Stanford University
Professional Publishing Course, July 1993

Master of Arts, Creative Writing
Boston University, 1985

B.A., Comparative Literature and Drama
University of Michigan, Ann Arbor, 1978

## SPEAKING ENGAGEMENTS (PARTIAL LISTING)

MECC/Ties Great Technology Get-Together, November 1994
State University of New York, Stonybrook, November 1994
National School Board Association, October 1994
Harvard University, Graduate School of Education, October 1994
New Jersey Association for Educational Technology, May 1994
National Association of School Textbook Administrators, February 1994
Apple Computer, January 1994
Association of American Publishers, January 1994
IBM, December 1993
National Association of Partners in Education, December 1993
Washington State School Board Association, November 1993
Association for Computers in Education, November 1993
Software Publishers Association, October 1993
EdNet, October 1993
International CD-ROM Conference, April 1993

# HARRY K. ELLIS

1901 Queen Avenue Street, Alexandria, VA 22314
*Home:* (703) 791-1951 · *Office:* (703) 899-4236

**OBJECTIVE**

Upper management position in book and multimedia publishing.

**SUMMARY OF QUALIFICATIONS**

Eighteen years of book publishing, microcomputer software development, and information services experience. Extensive background in new product development and project management. M.B.A. in Computer Applications and Information Systems.

**WORK EXPERIENCE**

*September 1990– present*

**EDUNET PUBLISHING COMPANY**
Arlington, Virginia

### Editorial Director, Computer Education

Create and implement publishing plan for new unit of leading educational publisher. Acquire, develop, and publish new book and multimedia products. Hire and train staff and assemble all resources required to achieve publishing objectives. Manage product and departmental expense budgets.

- Received Distinguished Achievement Award in Marketing for *Lester Riley's Introduction to Computers*, a college-level introductory computing program.
- Published Macintosh educational series by James B. Street, leading trade book author.
- Developed more than 60 new titles for the educational and training markets on Word, WordPerfect, Lotus 1-2-3, Excel, Paradox, Access, and other leading commercial software applications.
- Published multimedia middle school computer literacy program, *Understanding Computers Through Applications*, for Texas state adoption.
- Formed copublishing venture with Osborne to adapt trade computer books to the educational market.
- Signed agreements with major software vendors, including Microsoft, WordPerfect/Novell, Lotus, and Borland, to become an educational reseller and to obtain prerelease software.

**ISI (Institute for Scientific Information, Inc.)**
Philadelphia, Pennsylvania

*August 1988– August 1990*

### Director, New Products Division

Led new product development for world's largest commercial scientific database publisher. Managed technical and project management staff. Evaluated new product concepts, recommended new product ideas to management, and oversaw the planning, design, implementation, and commercial introduction of new database products in print, diskette, and CD-ROM formats.

- Guided the development of *Current Contents on Diskette* for IBM-compatible and Macintosh computers. (*Current Contents* is the world's most widely used weekly information service in the sciences.)
- Managed the development of CD-ROM database products, including the award-winning *Science* and *Social Sciences Citation Indexes*, the most comprehensive annual resources of scientific and social science research.

*August 1986–*
*August 1988*

### Director, ISI Software

Managed software division of major scientific database publisher. Oversaw sales, marketing, programming, documentation, and technical support staff in the development and distribution of text management and retrieval software and other scientific applications.

- Led the development of IBM-compatible and Macintosh database products.
- Achieved back-to-back record sales years, 1986–1987.
- Expanded product line through acquisitions and internal development.

**McGRAW-HILL BOOK COMPANY**
New York, New York

**Training Systems Division**

*January 1985–*
*July 1986*

### Editor, Data Processing and Information Center

Oversaw the publication of computer-based training (CBT) products. Worked with software developers and quality assurance companies to plan, design, implement, and test new training software products.

- Published *FastStart* PC tutorial software line that included CBT for DOS, Lotus1-2-3, dBase, and other application software packages.
- Supervised the creation and placement of national space advertising for a new CBT product line.

**Microcomputer Software Unit**

*January 1984–*
*December 1984*

### Project Manager

Managed the planning, design, implementation, and testing of computer-assisted instruction (CAI) products for the educational marketplace.

- Acquired and published Apple authoring system package.
- Developed project management guidelines and procedures for start-up software group.

**EDUCATION**

**NEW YORK UNIVERSITY**
New York, New York

***Leonard N. Stern School of Business***
*M.B.A., Computer Applications and Information Systems.* June 1985. Elective area focus: Marketing and Management.

**MONTEREY INSTITUTE OF INTERNATIONAL STUDIES**
Monterey, California

*M.A., International Studies.* Western Europe Area Studies. June 1976. Minors in International Economics and French.

**UNIVERSITY OF DENVER**
Denver, Colorado

*B.A., Political Science.* December 1973. Minors in History and French.

# JANE BERGQUIST

146 Billings Street
Sharon, MA 02149
Tel. (508) 563-3432     Fax (508) 738-9100
Office (617) 348-4187

## SUMMARY

Extensive publishing achievement and management experience with high-growth companies gained in the educational publishing industry:

| | |
|---|---|
| *STRATEGIC PLANNING* | Developing long-term strategic plans for accelerated and profitable growth |
| *EDITORIAL MANAGEMENT* | Designing and implementing innovative publishing and product development plans; manageing author creativity and multifunctional project teams |
| *LIST DEVELOPMENT* | Developing integrated marketing plans through "Pacesetter Model" |
| *TRAINING AND DEVELOPMENT* | Conducting nation-wide teacher training workshops, focus groups, and sales presentations, traveling extensivley in the United States |

## EXPERIENCE

1985–present     **FORDYCE PUBLISHERS, Boston, MA,** educational publishing division of International Webster

*Editorial Director, Secondary School Language Division,* 1987–present

Promoted to develop publishing strategy and direct acquisitions for secondary school foreign language list in Spanish, French, and German:

— Signed and developed one of the most innovative and prestigious foreign language lists in the industry, achieving consistent growth and sales increase of 500% over five years to $5 million
— Prepared and managed department budget with full P&L responsibility
— Supervised editorial staff and led Secondary School Publishing Team
— Designed market research strategy resulting in top-selling Spanish and French series
— Directed cross-language field testing of new materials in more than 100 school districts
— Presented foreign language programs for acceptance in major state adoptions
— Wrote board paper with analysis and recommendations for list acquisition
— Directed photo and video shoots in Europe and Latin America
— Served as chair of the Thomson Division Executive Committee Advisory Group, 1991–1993
— Received Editorial Award for Excellence and Leadership

*Senior Developmental Editor, Secondary School French,* 1986–1987

Promoted to research and publish for new markets:

— Successfully designed organization and scope of secondary school French program
— Conducted extensive customer focus groups across the United States
— Directed formal market research study resulting in integrated marketing plan

*Developmental Editor, College Spanish and French,* 1985–1986

Recruited to publish innovative educational materials:

— Published ten titles, including first discourse-based textbooks in the market
— Established Fordyce as an education partner with New England Teachers' Collaborative
— Coled training in innovation for new author teams

1983–1985  **D. C. HEATH & CO., Lexington, MA,** an educational publishing division of Raytheon Co.

*Associate Editor, Modern Languages, School Division*

Recruited to develop and produce major ancillary programs in Spanish and French:

— Developed workbooks and testing programs for market-leading textbook series
— Edited *Spanish* and *French for Mastery* newsletters, circulation 15,000+
— Selected to receive Raytheon Company Corporate Award for Outstanding Performance

1982–1983  **NEWBURY HOUSE PUBLISHERS, Rowley, MA**

*Assistant Editor, Foreign Languages, Linguistics, ESL*

Appointed to assist Managing Editor:

— Edited Spanish, French, and ESL manuscripts
— Coordinated photo research for EXPRESS ENGLISH, an international ESL program

## *EDUCATION*

B.A., Romance Languages and Literature, magna cum laude, Boston College, 1982
*Minor:* Secondary Education
Certificate with Highest Honors, *Instituto de Estudios Europeos,* Madrid, Spain, 1985
Teacher Certification, Spanish and French, 1987

## *MEMBERSHIPS*

Women in Publishing (Steering Committee)
American Council on the Teaching of Foreign Languages
American Association of Teachers of Spanish
American Association of Teachers of French
French Library, Boston
Boston Computer Society

## *LANGUAGES*

Spanish, French, Italian

## *PROFESSIONAL DEVELOPMENT*

Coursework in Practical Leadership, High Performance Teams, Financial Management, Business Strategy, Marketing Management, Managing Change, Intensive Italian

**PAUL TOWNSAND**     118 West 87th Street, New York, NY 10024     (212) 873-7721

**OBJECTIVE**     *PRODUCTION EDITOR*

**SUMMARY**     Editor with production expertise and the ability to schedule and manage the activity of art, editorial, and production staffs. Knowledgeable in all phases of production editing, including consultation with authors and work assignments for in-house and freelance staff members. Able to remain unruffled and maintain a steady, concentrated work flow despite tight scheduling and other pressures. Background in medical, scientific, and foreign language books and periodicals.

## EDITING EXPERIENCE

*1990–1995*     FREELANCE EDITOR, New York, NY

- In-house editorial production supervisor for Macmillan's Medical Books Division, Free Press, Schirmer and other publishers
  — Managed projects from design survey on concentrated manuscript, through all phases of proof, to final checks of blueprints and press sheets
  — Assigned work to freelancers and in-house copy editors
  — Corresponded and consulted with authors
  — Collaborated with manufacturing supervisors

- Copy editor of 12 to 15 titles per year for such clients as Jason Aronson, Inc.; Time, Inc.; and Arthur D. Little, Inc.
  — Copyedited manuscripts, jacket copy, and promotional material
  — Handled proofreading, slugging, and checks on repros, blueprints, and press sheets

- Guided and supervised editorial staff of 12 on four-volume *Encyclopedia of Bioethics* (a popular title at a $250 price tag)
  — Drew up 5-page style guide that was widely copied and circulated throughout parent company
  — Checked over all copy editing of 3,000-page manuscript

- Reviewed and corrected manuscripts copyedited by others whose work did not meet professional standards

*1985–1990*     PRAEGER PUBLISHERS, New York, NY

**Copy Editor**

- Production and copy editing for 15 to 18 projects annually
  — Copyedited manuscripts, jacket copy, and promotional material
  — Handled proofreading, slugging, and checks on repros, blueprints, and press sheets
  — Assigned work to freelancers and in-house copy editors
  — Corresponded and consulted with authors

- Responsible for two of Praeger's most popular titles: *The Life and Death of Adolf Hitler*, by Robert Payne, and *The Wall Street Gang*, by Richard Ney

*1979–1985*      CURRENT DIGEST of the SOVIET PRESS, New York, NY

**Managing Editor, *Current Digest*; Co-Editor, *Current Abstracts***

- As Managing Editor, *Current Digest of the Soviet Press*
  - Supervised staff of 12 translators, copy editors, and indexers
  - Selected and abridged material in Russian for translation
  - Wrote headlines and captions
- As Coeditor, *Current Abstracts of the Soviet Press*
  - Instrumental in the inauguration of new monthly magazine
  - Surveyed 24 Soviet periodicals for articles of compelling interest to academic, government, and media subscribers
  - Capsulized selected material and copyedited other articles
  - Selected graphic art for reproduction
  - Wrote headlines and captions

**EDUCATION**      COLUMBIA UNIVERSITY GRADUATE SCHOOL of JOURNALISM
1979—MS, Journalism

PRINCETON UNIVERSITY
1975—B.A., Art and Archaeology (graduated cum laude)

U.S. ARMY LANGUAGE SCHOOL, Monterey, CA

U.S. ARMY INTELLIGENCE SCHOOL, Fort Holobird, MD

**LANGUAGES**      Russian—Reading, writing, conversation, translation
French—Reading, conversation

# WILLIAM A. POST

20 Waterside Plaza, New York, NY 10010      (212) 889-1427 (home)    (212) 867-0530 (office)

**OBJECTIVE:**    EDITORIAL/MARKETING MANAGEMENT, EDUCATIONAL PUBLISHING

**SUMMARY:**    Comprehensive experience editing and publishing educational textbooks at elementary and secondary levels. Recruit, contract, and motivate authors; direct, motivate, and correlate work of editors and writers on multigrade projects running concurrently. Initiate conceptual programs and designs. Demonstrated ability to solve problems, meet challenging goals, and expedite production.

**EXPERIENCE:**

1989–present

**ACADEMIC PUBLISHING, INC.**
New York, New York

*Editorial Director*, Reading and Language Arts Departments, Text Division
           (1994–Present)

- Recruit and supervise senior authors for development of text programs in basal reading, spelling, grammar and composition.
- Directed 4 editors and 25 freelance writers in development and publication of industry-leading remedial reading system.
  - Comprises 150 published novels and 7 instructional kits for grades 4–10 (additional 25 novels in work).
  - First program to offer high-interest reading material to elementary school students reading at first-grade level.
- Conducted teacher focus groups and worked with outside consulting firm to prepare market research study reports for presentation to senior management.
- Explore and research programs produced by other publishers in the field.
- Represent company at state and regional curriculum and subject area meetings; conduct state and regional workshops in reading and language arts.
- Effectively discharge responsibility for implementing projects accounting for 50% of division revenue.

*Associate Editorial Director*, Reading Department, School Division (1993–1994)

- Supervised material for and publication of *Kicks*, elementary-level reading magazine.
- Initiated and developed *Speed*, a secondary-level magazine.
- Developed and published remedial math program for grades 4–6 (Academic has no math department).

*Supervising Editor* (1991–93)

- Directed staff of three division editors in Kicks Libraries, Kicks Reading Skills Program, and Academic Listening Skills program, from manuscript acquisition through publication.

*Editor, Kicks Libraries* (1989–1991)

- Acquired manuscripts, assessed readability level and edited material for publication.

1988–1989     **NEWTON COLLEGE OF THE SACRED HEART**
Newton, Massachusetts
- Assistant Professor of Education

1987–1989     **CLINTON JOB CORPS**
Clinton, Iowa
- Teacher, Basic Education

1986–1987     **J. B. YOUNG JUNIOR HIGH SCHOOL**
Davenport, Iowa
- Teacher, Eighth-Grade English

## EDUCATION:

1986     Harvard Graduate School of Education, M.A.T.,
English Education

1984     University of Nebraska, Lincoln, Nebraska
B.S., English Education

**AFFILIATIONS:** American Association of Publishers, Social Issues Committee
Chair of Education Committee and member of Publications Committee,
    St. Peter's Church

# HENRY EDMONDS

400 East 85th Street    New York, NY 10022
(212) 688-2251

**OBJECTIVE:**    *EDITORIAL MANAGEMENT*

**SUMMARY:**    Fifteen years' experience in production of texts, magazines, and multimedia instructional programs for leading publisher. Excellent understanding of components controlling manufacturing costs and generation of editorial revenues. Responsible for significant number of text publishing success stories.

**EDITORIAL EXPERIENCE:**

*1982–*
*present*

McGRAW-HILL, INC., New York, New York
*Project Editor, Text Division* (1988–present)

- Plan and budget multimedia instructional programs accounting for more than 10% of divisional revenue
- Achieve product goals through supervision of staff, varying from 14 to 25 on any given project area, including freelance writers and consultants
- Participate in sales campaigns aimed at securing text adoptions in key states
- Conduct workshops for secondary teachers; led two state-wide seminars and conducted five regional National Council of Social Studies workshops
- Member, Computer Technology Committee, charged with streamlining and scheduling of production
- Work closely with Rights and Permissions Department, both in drafting of authors' contracts and in obtaining permissions from other publishing houses
- Now developing on-level, basal text entry for high school U.S. history market, possibly the most competitive social studies market in precollege text publishing; program tested positively in 1989 field surveys
- Refashioned *American Adventures*, best-selling multimedia history program, into basal format (both soft- and hardcover) without sacrificing popular appeal
  — Extensive rewriting, reediting, and additions resulted in adoption by 15 states and most dramatic sales increase on a text program in company's history
  — Convinced upper management that regional variations were unnecessary, thus decreasing manufacturing costs by approximately 50%
- Produced a simplified world history multimedia program that is a steady seller and has a loyal following among teachers
  — Selected and guided 10 writers, 10 consultants, a designer, an illustrator, and several indexers and caption writers, all working against tight deadlines
- Coauthored *Tropical and Southern Africa* (currently in seventh printing), one of seven original volumes in World Cultures Program

*Concurrent Freelance Projects*

— Contributing editor for 250-page book on basic legal principles for lay public in association with American Bar Association and scheduled for publication by Elsevier/Dutton
— Author, *Junior Scholastic* articles on California history and government and on presidential qualifications
— Wrote and produced four-page adult discussion guide for NBC-TV News to accompany three-hour telecast on American foreign policy
— Editor for one unit of Webster McGraw-Hill world history, *Echoes of Time*
— Wrote numerous Scholastic teleguides on such subjects as Alistair Cooke's *America*, *David Copperfield*, and New York City circa 1880–1990
— Coauthored nine "map-paks" for W. H. Sadlier, Inc.; more than 370,000 copies of these skills-oriented study materials are still in print

*Senior Associate Editor, School Division–Magazines* (1982–1988)

■ Hired as Assistant Editor in 1982; in quick succession of promotions, became Associate Editor, Managing Editor, then Senior Associate Editor within five years

■ As Senior Associate Editor of *American Observer*, researched and wrote one or two articles weekly

■ As Managing Editor of *Junior Scholastic*, brought about circulation turnaround of one of company's two highest-circulation magazines
— Worked to give magazine a clear, lively style and brighter appearance; edited lead articles
— Supervised staff of 12, including writers, artists, and production personnel

| | |
|---|---|
| *1980–1982* | MEDICAL ECONOMICS, INC., Oradell, New Jersey<br>*Associate Editor* |
| *1979–1980* | TIME, INC., New York, New York<br>*Head Copy Boy*, *Time* magazine |
| **EDUCATION:**<br>*1978*<br>*1976* | STANFORD UNIVERSITY, Palo Alto, California<br>M.A., U.S. History (University Scholarship)<br>B.A., History |
| | COLUMBIA UNIVERSITY, New York, New York<br>Coursework in Accounting |
| **LANGUAGES:** | Some Spanish and very limited Japanese |
| **AFFILIATIONS:** | Sigma Delta Chi Professional Journalism Association |

*Willing to relocate*

# Roberta Lowrey

21 Fairfax Gardens, Hackettstown, NJ 07840
*Home:* (201) 852-6413
*Office:* (201) 852-4225, ext. 51

**OBJECTIVE**    NEWSPAPER EDITOR

**SUMMARY**    Astute interviewer and reporter capable of handling varied assignments. Experienced in editing and page makeup. Creative assessor of story ideas and material and able to visualize concepts for news value publicity. Knowledge of basic photography. Willing to accept and carry out travel assignments.

**EXPERIENCE**

2/92–
present

THE *FORUM* — Biweekly Newspaper
State Publishing Company
Hackettstown, NJ

*Copy Editor*

- Edit copy for four reporters, write headlines, size pictures, and help with page makeup
- Cover municipal beat

*Special Sections Writer*

- Charged with responsibility for three sections of the paper: Real Estate, Leisure, and Fashions
  — Covered and wrote stories, rewrote releases, and took photos
  — Made up sections

2/89–8/91    *ARGUS OBSERVER*—Daily Newspaper
Matheur Publishing Company
Ontario, OR

*Reporter*

- Covered county beat and improved coverage (and subsequent circulation) by introducing additional beats
  — Economic development
  — Health planning
  — Municipal
  — Extended zoning and planning
- Wrote feature stories and took own photos
- Filled in for wire editor and did other deskwork as needed
- Substituted for editor during a six-week absence

*Society Editor*

- Put together daily Family Page from the bottom up
  — Covered and wrote stories, edited releases, took photos
  — Handled correspondents' news
  — Made up page and wrote headlines

**EXPERIENCE (cont.)**

5/88–2/89    STATE OF OREGON, Disability Prevention Division
Portland, OR
- Typed psychology reports for therapy program

**EDUCATION**  Willamette University, Salem, OR
1983, BA, English
— Received Helen S. Pearce Award as outstanding senior woman English major
— Worked as reporter and composition manager for newspaper
— Worked as aide in public information office
— President, Alpha Phi Sorority
— Secretary, Mortar Board

Portland State University, Portland, OR
— Course in Reporting I

**MEMBER**  Ontario Press Club; served as secretary

**TRAVEL**  Backpacked through England, Ireland, Scotland, Germany, Italy, Spain, and Austria, 8/87–12/87

**TEARSHEETS SUBMITTED UPON REQUEST**

## MARTIN DUPRÉ

20 Oakwood Court
Rockville Centre, NY 11570

Home (516) 764-1520
Work (516) 536-7500

**OBJECTIVE:** *NEWSLETTER EDITOR*

**SUMMARY:** Writer and editor with ability to simplify the complex and solve publication and scheduling problems. Record of successful new publication introductions. Expertise in taxes, fringe benefits, pensions, personal finance, estate planning, insurance, trusts.

**EXPERIENCE:**

BARNSWORTH PUBLISHING, Rockville Centre, New York
*Director of Publishing*

1992–present

- Write and edit three highly successful monthly newsletters of steadily increasing circulation through better coverage of material.
- Positioned company in banking field by creating a pamphlet program, thus expanding market beyond insurance field.
- Placed company in lucrative pension and profit-sharing market via creation of sophisticated, syndicated pension trust letter.
- Revitalized previously lagging pamphlet program by editing on-shelf material.

*Freelance Writer* (concurrent with position at Barnsworth)

American Institute of Certified Public Accountants; Warren, Gorham & Lamont; Main, Hurdman & Cranstoun; *Estate Planner's Quarterly; Dental Management; Physician's Management.*

MATTHEW BENDER & COMPANY, New York, New York
*Chief Editor, Insurance & Pensions*

1985–1992

- Created and wrote four-page syndicated monthly insurance newsletter, accompanied by 50-page technical analysis, that became leading newsletter in field.
- Created and wrote pension trust syndicated monthly newsletter for banks—despite lack of in-house expertise—by thoroughly researching field and interviewing experts. Circulation grew to 50,000 (40 banks) within one year.
- Wrote classic, highly successful booklet for insurance industry after Tax Reform Act of 1984 by utilizing in-house material and special knowledge of insurance.
- Aided in writing bank (nonpension) trust letters.

DUNKIRK ASSOCIATES, Latham, New York
*Vice-President, Editor in Chief*

1980–1985

- Editor in Chief, directing staff of 15 editors; responsible for all aspects of 12 insurance publications, including writing, editing, production scheduling, and promotion.
- Raised quality and consistency of copy while maintaining tight production schedule.
- Increased productivity and accuracy of staff by assigning key writers to subject areas rather than publications.

COPLEY INTERNATIONAL, New York, New York
*Editor*

1978–1980
- Wrote weekly newsletter and brochures on topics of international business investment throughout world.

BUSINESS INTERNATIONAL, New York, New York
*European Editor*

1977–1978
- Wrote portion of weekly newsletter and brochures dealing with investments in Europe.

1973–1977
LEHMAN BROTHERS, New York, New York
*Economist* (1975–1977)
*Trainee Economist* (1973–1975)

NEW YORK STATE DEPARTMENT OF LABOR, New York, New York
*Labor Speechwriter*

1969–1971
- Wrote policy speeches for New York State Industrial Commissioner.

**INTERESTS**     Biking, walking, jazz, reading.

*Writing samples available on request.*

# Susan Jane Clemons

415 West 96th Street #3H, New York, NY 10027
*Home:* (212) 666-5216 · *Work:* (212) 694-0200

**OBJECTIVE**   TECHNICAL WRITING:   Position closely allied with research
department of pharmaceutical manufacturer

**SUMMARY**   Technical writer with sophisticated medical and chemical laboratory
experience. Talent for comprehensible and stimulating presentation of highly
complex technical data. Doctorate in Chemistry and postdoctoral research at
Columbia University College of Physicians & Surgeons. Coauthored four
articles in the field of bio-organic chemistry published by the *Journal of the
American Chemistry Society* and *Photochemical Photobiology*.

**PUBLICATIONS**   S. J. Clemons, V. Haughton, J. S. King, & K. Blevins, "A Nonbleachable
Rhodopsin Analogue Formed from 11,12-Dihydroretinal," *J. Am. Chem. Soc.,*
*89,* 6210 (1993).

K. Blevins, V. Haughton, S. J. Clemons, M. Cole, M. Lukens, & B. Randall,
"Double Point Charge Model for Visual Pigments: Evidence for
Dihydrorhodopsins," *Photochem. Photobiol., 39,* 875 (1993).

B. Randall, U. Goettl, K. Blevins, V. Haughton, S. J. Clemons, M. Cole, &
M. Lukens, "An External Point Charge Model for Wavelength Regulation in
Visual Pigments," *J. Am. Chem. Soc., 201,* 6684 (1994).

R. Linder, S. West, K. Blevins, S. J. Clemons, V. Haughton, "Incorporation of
11,12-Dihydroretinal into the Retinae of Vitamin A Deprived Rats,"
*Photochem. Photobiol., 43,* 91 (1995).

## RESEARCH AND TECHNICAL COMMUNICATIONS EXPERIENCE

*1991–present*   COLUMBIA UNIVERSITY COLLEGE OF PHYSICIANS & SURGEONS,
New York, New York

### *Postdoctoral Fellow, Arteriosclerosis Research Training Program*

- Summarize experimental work in one-hour semiannual presentations for
  medical doctors, biologists, and other researchers
  — Developed format which dramatically increased comprehension and
     interest in experiments by audience with little knowledge of or
     enthusiasm for synthetic chemistry
  — Wrote and distributed summaries that emphasized objectives, expected
     and observed results, and explanations of possible discrepancies in and
     interpretations of experiments
  — Supplemented written work with flow charts and tables
- Design and conduct independent experimental research on Vitamin A
  metabolism; evaluate results
  — Successfully isolate critical factors affecting experimental results through
     careful recording and analysis of procedures followed in sensitive process
     not easily duplicated

- Equipped unused biological/clinical laboratory with instruments to perform synthetic reactions and other chemical procedures
  — Negotiated for instruments specially designed and produced by Chemistry Department; acted as liaison between Director and Chemistry Department and set up account for payment

1987–1989   COLUMBIA UNIVERSITY, DEPARTMENT OF CHEMISTRY, New York, New York

*Teaching Assistant*
- Closely supervised 15 students in general chemistry lab, evaluating students' mastery of general laboratory techniques and giving help where needed
- Prepared sample time schedule and suggestions for saving time to encourage timely, neat and organized completion of student work

1988–1993   *Writing and Research Experience* gained in conjunction with work for doctorate, Columbia University, New York, NY
- Presented paper at 1990 meeting of American Chemical Society in Chicago under title of "A Nonbleachable Rhodopsin Analogue Formed from 11,12-Dihydroretinal"
- Prepared and referred manuscripts for publication in technical journals
- Presented two departmental seminars
- Prepared 190-page doctoral thesis on "Bio-Organic Studies in Visual Pigments; Formation of 11,12-Dihydrorhodopsin from 11,12-Dihydroretinal"
  — Thesis included background of project, literature review, description of original research and results, and detailed experimental section

EDUCATION   COLUMBIA UNIVERSITY, New York, New York

| | |
|---|---|
| 1991–present | Postdoctoral Research Fellow, College of Physicians & Surgeons |
| 1992 | Ph.D., Chemistry |
| 1989 | M.S., Chemistry |

DOUGLASS COLLEGE OF RUTGERS UNIVERSITY, New Brunswick, New Jersey

| | |
|---|---|
| 1987 | B.A., Chemistry |
| | Graduated with High Honors |
| | Elizabeth Laudenslager Clark Scholarship |
| | President, Rutgers Chapter, Iota Sigma Pi Chemistry Society |

WATERS ASSOCIATES, New York, New York

| | |
|---|---|
| 1992 | Course in use of high-pressure liquid chromatograph |

LANGUAGES   Working knowledge of French and German

# MICHAEL HERRICK

214 47th Street, Lindenhurst, NY 11757
Res: (516) 226-1829     Bus: (212) 374-3254

*OBJECTIVE:*   To transfer my expertise and experience as a FORENSIC COMMUNICATIONS SPECIALIST to the private sector

*SUMMARY:*   Highly skilled in administration and operation of audio laboratory, with special emphasis on techniques of voice identification and tape enhancement. Intimate knowledge of uses of adaptation of technical equipment to investigations. Practiced and effective lecturer. Creative designer of strategic training programs. Thorough researcher. Capable organizer and implementer of innovative systems and procedures.

*CAREER HIGHLIGHTS:*

1970–present     NEW YORK POLICE DEPARTMENT, New York, NY
Commanding Officer, Tape and Records Unit     (1988–present)

**Administration**

- Proposed, researched, established, and currently supervise Forensic Audio Laboratory of the Communications Division
  — Provide NYPD with speaker identification and tape enhancement capability
  — Provide prosecutors with admissible evidence
  — Procedures have resulted in cost saving of more than $250,000 over past three years; more effective utilization of investigator hours in major criminal investigations and terrorist activities
  — Supervise 15 tape and audio technicians and voice print examiners
- Responsible for 911 Tape Logging System (largest in world—200 channels)
  — Organized, refined, and maintain system that supplies more than 5,000 tape recordings per year, in cooperation with investigators and officers of the court
- Proposed, established, and supervise correlated records unit enabling efficient and timely pinpoint recovery of specific crime information (from 911 master reels and computer printouts reduced to microfiche)
- Maintain efficiency and integrity of specialized electronics equipment valued at more than $300,000; initiated, implemented, and maintain security procedures

**Training/Lectures/Presentations**

- Coach attorneys in effective introduction of sound recordings to ensure their admissibility as evidence; instruct employees in use and application to investigative and prosecutorial process
  — Conducted ongoing 911 seminar program for district attorneys resulting in more effective use of 911 tapes and records in New York criminal court proceedings
- Lecturer, forensic communications courses: biennial Homicide Investigations Course attended by FBI and state police personnel from all over country; biennial Criminal Investigators' Course structured for local law enforcement agencies
- Guest lecturer at 1987 NY State District Attorneys' Association workshop
- Coauthored status report on development of audio laboratory for presentation at 1987 convention of American Academy of Forensic Sciences in New Orleans

**Investigation and Consultation**

- Act as departmental consultant on forensic and 911 communications with all departments and with officers of the court
- Act as consultant in liaison with state and federal agencies
- Continue research in legal and scientific considerations through consultation with private sector and academic researchers to maintain state-of-the-art technological proficiency
- Conducting investigation into technique of using sound spectrograph to determine if subject is actually under hypnosis
- Conducting investigation on the effects of aging in speaker identification

**Career Progression, NYPD**

| | |
|---|---|
| 1970 | Joined department; assigned to routine patrol duties |
| 1977 | Assigned to Emergency Service Division; rescue and sniper work |
| 1980 | Assigned to Detective Division; served in Bureau of Identification as fingerprint technician |
| 1985 | Promoted to sergeant-supervisor of tactical patrol force unit of 30 officers, charged with riot control and special weapons tactics |
| 1986 | Transferred to Communications Division, with supervision and training of 911 operators and dispatchers |

**EDUCATION:** **Specialized Training and Certification**

| | |
|---|---|
| 1991 | Advanced Voice Identification course, Michigan State Police |
| 1988–91 | Annual International Association of Voice Identification Seminar (different location each year) |
| 1990 | Magnetic Tape Analysis course, FBI Laboratory, Washington, DC |
| 1990 | Security Management course, New York Police Academy |
| 1984–1985 | Specialized Spectrum Analysis, Queens College |
| 1983–1985 | Annual Carnahan Crime Countermeasures Conference University of Kentucky |
| 1984 | Spectrum Analysis Techniques, FBI course, New York City |
| 1983 | Voice Identification Techniques, Voice Identification, Inc., Laboratory, Somerville, New Jersey |
| 1980 | Management Techniques and Principles, New York Police Academy |
| 1979 | American Management Association course, New York Police Academy |
| 1972 | Basic and Advanced Fingerprint Identification, NYPD Criminal Justice Courses, John Jay College |

**MILITARY:** 1965–66 and 1969–1970—U.S. Army, Sergeant First Class
NCO Academy, Munich, Germany—six-week Leadership course
Communications Section Leader

**MEMBER:** International Association of Voice Identification
Acoustical Society of America

**QUALIFIED:** Certified Voiceprint Examiner

# JACK L. GRIMES

670 MANNAKEE STREET     ROCKVILLE, MD 20850
HOME: (301) 340-4801     OFFICE: (202) 389-1602

**OBJECTIVE**

**MANAGER, DEPARTMENT of PUBLIC AFFAIRS
or GOVERNMENT RELATIONS**
**Scientific or other technologically oriented corporation**

**SUMMARY**

Extensive experience working directly with heads of Fortune 500 corporations, federal agencies and Congress. Skilled in assessing importance of specific issues and designing successful issues-oriented actions

## PROFESSIONAL HISTORY

**1986–present**

NATIONAL ASSOCIATION of SCIENCES/NATIONAL RESEARCH COUNCIL, Washington, D.C.

**Executive Director, Board on Minorities in Engineering & Sciences**

- Direct planning, organization, and administration to implement science personnel policy utilizing $4 million annually
  — Coordinate efforts of 65 corporations, 15 federal agencies, and 112 universities participating in program
  — Establish national priorities and initiatives, guide development and allocation of resources, and monitor achievement of goals

- Influence federal policy and action through communications, negotiation, and the creative utilization of human resources
  — Work with Cabinet and agency heads and members of Congress in formulating and implementing appropriate laws and regulations
  — Provide significant linkages between academic research facilities, the National Science Foundation, and federal departments

- Increased corporate contributions to university minority engineering projects to $11 million, effecting a 400% expansion in corporate participation within six years
  — Facilitated participation of AT&T, DuPont, Exxon, and General Electric as corporate pacesetters

- Established national initiatives that increased minority undergraduate engineering enrollment, from 4.5% to 7% of the total undergraduate engineering population, within six years

- Organized national symposium with 800 prominent leaders from government, industry, academic institutions, and civic organizations; coordinated semiannual meetings for 35 corporate leaders to address national workplace problems
  — Produced national reports used as guides by corporations and funding agencies in establishing funding priorities

- Prepare budgets and plan and staff all functions

**Part-time Consultant**

- Assisted in key management at AT&T, Ford Motor Company. Olin Corporation, General Electric Company. RCA Corporation, Rockwell International, and Xerox Corporation
  — Advised corporate leadership on recruitment of employees to expand technical base, distribution of funds in minority-related areas, regional development activity and corporate-academic linkages
  — Organized corporate-financed regional and professional engineering societies

**1981–1986**   NEW YORK INSTITUTE OF TECHNOLOGY, Albany, New York

**Director, Engineering Opportunity Program**

- Conceived and developed first successful university recruitment and educational program in engineering for women and minority students; created model written up by Departments of Labor and Education for use as national referent
- Placed minority enrollment at NYIT within country's top ten institutions by implementing 75% increase in successful minority matriculation
- Expanded services while maintaining quality through development of first external fund-raising activity for university minority programs
  — Obtained $15,000 from Alfred P. Sloan Foundation and other corporations
  — Established financial aid office and received federal grants for needy students; obtained grant from New York Department of Higher Education

**1977–1981**   EXPERIMENTAL EDUCATION PROJECT, Paterson, New Jersey

**Director** (Part-time)

**1972–1981**   EASTSIDE HIGH SCHOOL, Paterson, New Jersey and C. A. JOHNSON HIGH SCHOOL, Columbia, South Carolina

**Chairman of Mathematics Department, Science Instructor, Guidance Counselor**

**EDUCATION**   SYRACUSE UNIVERSITY, Syracuse, New York
1980: M.S., Chemistry—National Science Foundation Fellowship
ALLEN UNIVERSITY, Columbia, South Carolina
1972: B.S., Chemistry

**Management Training**
General Electric Management Development Institute: Management of Time, Manpower, and Money, 1986
University of California at San Diego: Institute for Management Training (sponsored by Department of Defense), 1985

**PUBLICATIONS**   "Parity for Minorities in Engineering: Myth or Reality," *Engineering Issues*, April, 1992
"The Image and Relevance of Engineering in the Black and Puerto Rican Community," *New Jersey Science Teachers Journal*, 1983
"Engineering Opportunity Program: A Special Program for Disadvantaged Students," April 1985 issue of *Engineering Education*

**PROFESSIONAL AFFILIATIONS**
Arthur S. Flemming Awards Committee
American Society for Engineering Education
American Association for the Advancement of Science
National Society of Black Chemists and Engineers

## ELIZABETH R. LINTON

302 North Chestnut Avenue, Livingston, NJ 07039
(201) 992-9726

**OBJECTIVE:** *PUBLIC RELATIONS/CORPORATE COMMUNICATIONS*

To apply publicity/public relations expertise in the editorial, music, and arts field to a position in community affairs.

**SUMMARY:** More than 15 years' experience in writing, publicity, public relations and media placement. Ten years with publishing houses. Creative designer of promotional concepts. Excellent coordinator of diverse groups working toward single goal. Discerning interviewer and organizer of material and campaigns.

### CAREER HIGHLIGHTS:

*1991–present* CLOVER PUBLICATIONS, INC., New York, NY
*Director of Publicity*

- Conceive and follow through on promotional campaigns for major books
- Place publicity in national publications; set author interviews on radio and TV; negotiate store tie-ins
  — First full-length Clover review in *The New York Times*; national recognition of Clover
  — Special in-store displays at F.A.O. Schwarz and Lord & Taylor
  — Constantly develop reviewer lists
- Work closely with editorial and sales

*1988–1991* AMERICAN FEDERATION OF TELEVISION AND RADIO ARTISTS, New York, NY
*Committees Coordinator*

- Established committees of varied segments of membership; successfully attained positive communication
  — Maintained liaison between local members and executive staff and between AFTRA and "outside" influences
- Worked with highly confidential information

*1987–1988* DISTRICT COUNCIL 37, EDUCATION DEPARTMENT, New York, NY
*Writer/Administrative Assistant*

- Publicized courses offered by council to its members; coordinated with educational institutions relative to scheduling and registration
- Wrote and published course handbook (became standard literature for department)

*1986–1987* SIMON & SCHUSTER, New York, NY
*Associate Director of Publicity*

- Wrote and designed all publicity and sales promotional material; selected and placed visuals
  — Increased press coverage and sales through copy frequently acclaimed by reviewers and authors
- Booked authors on network and local television and radio shows
- Promoted from Assistant Director in 1985

*1983–1986*     SCHRIMER BOOKS, New York, NY
*Freelance Editor*
- Handled all editorial production functions for this division of Macmillan Company, from manuscript through blues

*1981–1983*     MERCURY PHILLIPS RECORDS, New York, NY
*Director of Publicity, Classical Division*
- Brought relatively unknown label to attention of national music media — First complete recording of Berlioz's *Les Troyens* named Recording of the Year for 1982
- Set up interviews with newspapers and magazines and appearances on radio and TV for recording artists; promoted open recording sessions and parties
- Maintained still existing liaison with press agents, reviewers, radio stations, and press agents

*1979–1981*     WASHINGTON NATIONAL SYMPHONY, Washington, D.C.
*Editor, Program Book*
- Wrote 95% of program notes for concert repertoire and laid out weekly program book published for concert audiences
- Maintained liaison between printer and concert office

*1978–1979*     THE *CHRISTIAN HERALD*, New York, NY
*Assistant Editor*
- Read manuscripts for publishing potential; read books and manuscripts for Book Club potential
- Edited articles: copyreading, proofreading, rewriting, cutting

*1976–1978*     AVON BOOKS, New York, New York
*Editorial Assistant*
- Read hardcovers and manuscripts for potential paperback publication
- Wrote cover copy
- Put together two anthologies: opera and vampire literature

**EDUCATION:**     Columbia University, New York, NY
1976—M.A., Music/English

Hofstra University, Hempstead, NY
1971—B.A.

**SCHOOL ACTIVITIES:**     Represented Music Department at Long Island Contemporary Arts Festival
Worked on college newspaper and literary magazine
Participated in symphony orchestra and chorus

**LANGUAGES:**     Read, speak, and translate German

**MEMBER:**     Publishers Publicity Association

# KIT LOUX

33 West 95th Street, New York, NY 10024
(212) 580-6620

**OBJECTIVE**  *RECORDING INDUSTRY—PUBLIC RELATIONS/PROMOTION*

To utilize my recent experience and training in the music business in an entry-level position as promotions assistant, with growth potential in the promotion area.

**SUMMARY**  Knowledgeable in area of artist promotion. Trained in music and stagecraft, including writing of lyrics for special occasions. Relate well with people. Competent director of employees and contract talent. Eager to learn music business "from the ground up." Free to travel.

## RELEVANT EXPERIENCE

1990–present  MUSICBOX, INC.
London, England

**Managing Director, U.K. Branch**

- Introduced firm to United Kingdom and managed entire operation, consisting of personal delivery of singing telegrams for special occasions.
- Auditioned, hired, and directed singer-artists.
- Arranged for and secured radio and television appearances/interviews as publicity and procured and placed all advertising.
- Sold service to prestigious clients, many of whom were in the recording business in London.
- Selected clients: Polydor Records, Pink Floyd Music, the Who, Island Records, CBS Records, EMI Screen Gems Music, BBC Radio & Television, Chrysalis Records.
- Wrote successfully received lyrics for songs used in telegrams.
- Handled all office procedures and finances and secured and trained replacement director.

1989–1990  MUSICBOX, INC.
New York, New York

**Courier/Lyrics Writer**

- Initiated and promulgated innovative singing telegram service for company and delivered first in-person message in costume.
- Appeared on TV and in press interviews in recognition of service's news value.
- Sold orders over phone and wrote lyrics for customers.

1989
Part-time  AMERICAN MANAGEMENT ASSOCIATION
New York, New York

**Market Research**

- Secured information for sales department.

| | |
|---|---|
| 1984<br>Summer | VOCATIONAL FOUNDATION, INC.<br>New York, New York |

**Job Developer**
- Phone communication with top management of business firms to secure jobs for unemployed youth. (Successfully placed about 100 youths during summer.)

| | |
|---|---|
| 1976–1979<br>While in school | CHILDRENS HOSPITAL<br>Washington, D.C. |

**Volunteer**—4- to 10-year-olds
- Worked well with debilitated children, getting them to eat and keeping them entertained and happy.

U.S. CONGRESS
Washington, D.C.

**Office Assistant**
- Attended Senate and House meetings with Congressman Jack Lee (Arkansas). Worked office machines under supervision of his secretary.

FAIRFAX COUNTY PUBLIC SCHOOLS
Fairfax, Virginia

**Teacher's Aide**
- Supervised children and gave them extra scholastic aid.

## EDUCATION

Chatham College, Pittsburgh, Pennsylvania
Drama major; Music and French minor
Royal Academy of Dramatic Art, London, England
Graduated, 1987

## CAREER-RELATED COURSES AND ACTIVITIES

Theater Productions—performing and stage managing
Choir Touring—performing and managing
Photography—Pittsburgh Film Institute
Acting/Scene Study—Lee Strasberg Theatre, New York
Acting/Scene Study—HB Studio, New York
French—read, write, speak
Extensive travel

## MEMBER

Actors' Equity

# CHARLES A. SLABAUGH

**930 Third Avenue, New York, NY 10022**
**(212) 758-9929**

*OBJECTIVE*_____

**MEDIA PLACEMENT SPECIALIST/ACCOUNT SUPERVISOR**

*SUMMARY*_____

Six years' public relations experience in both private and public sectors. Excellent broadcast and print media placement record. Good writer and researcher, with strong orientation to deadline and detail. Farmiliar with state-of-the-art technology in film, video, and multimedia. Particularly skilled in organizing and managing special events. Maintain consistent reputation for integrity with producers and editors.

*EXPERIENCE*_____

1991–
present

**CHARLES SLABAUGH ASSOCIATES, INC., New York, New York**
**President**

- **National Marine Manufacturers Association**—Initiate radio, television, and print promotion for eight industry-owned and -operated boat shows nation-wide
  — Supervised National Boat Show broadcast media coverage for four consecutive years, culminating in 16 placements in 1993 (local, network, and syndicated, including CBS Morning News, INN, *PM Magazine*, *Entertainment Tonight*, Satellite News Channel, Cable News Network; and ABC, NBC, and Mutual radio networks)
  — Generate economic/business stories and publicity for boat shows in Norwalk (Connecticut), Chicago, Philadelphia, Baltimore, and Minneapolis/St. Paul, including the *Today Show* and *Good Morning America*
  — Created ticket giveaway programs to increase market penetration of regional boat shows; developed Boating Radio Network, providing audio material on boating industry

- **Worrell 1000**—Handle prerace publicity and press operation of 1,000-mile sailboat race from Fort Lauderdale to Virginia Beach, with extensive print and broadcast coverage in Florida, North Carolina, South Carolina, Georgia, and Virginia; supervise television crews and print media traveling with race, including CBS Sports, *Sports Illustrated*, *60 Minutes*, AP, UPI, *Miami Herald*, and various boating publications

- **Rath Organization**—Total responsibility for two monthly newsletters (writing, editing, design, and production; photography supervision; article solicitation); created seminar program for Pitney Bowes

- **Direct national publicity tours**—for variety of clients:
  — Gerry Spiess (*Yankee Girl*, smallest boat to cross Atlantic and Pacific)
  — Curtis and Kathleen Saville (hold transatlantic rowing record)
  — David Ganz, *World of Coins and Coin Collecting* (Scribners)
  — Jim Hendricks, owner of *African Queen*
  — Joe Franklin, Memory Lane Nostalgia Convention

*EXPERIENCE (cont.)* _____

**1989–**   **SLABAUGH'S RARE COINS, New York, New York**
**1991**    **Manager,** Sales Promotion

- Bought, sold, and cataloged rare coins to wholesale and retail clientele

- Trained in auction sale promotion, including advertising, releases, catalog preparation, and coin photography

**1987–**   **GERALD A. ROGOVIN PUBLIC RELATIONS, INC., Boston, Massachusetts**
**1989**    **Writer/Researcher**

**AGNEW ASSOCIATES, INC., Boston, Massachusetts**
**Account Coordinator**

**REPRESENTATIVE PETER HARRINGTON (Massachusetts)**
**Legislative Aide**

**GOVERNOR MICHAEL MERRIWETHER (Massachusetts)**
**Student Intern**

*EDUCATION* _____

**UNIVERSITY OF PENNSYLVANIA, Philadelphia, Pennsylvania**
- Wharton School of Business, Executive Education Program, 1991

**SYRACUSE UNIVERSITY, Syracuse, New York**
- Master's candidate in Public Relations Administration

**BOSTON UNIVERSITY, Boston, Massachusetts**
- B.S., Public Relations (cum laude), 1986

**NEW YORK UNIVERSITY, New York, New York**
- Film Production Workshop (200-hour intensive program)

**NEW YORK INSTITUTE OF TECHNOLOGY, New York, New York**
- Television Production Workshop (200-hour intensive program)

*AFFILIATIONS* _____

Public Relations Society of America
Publicity Club of New York (recipient of Distinguished Service Award)
International Association of Business Communicators

# ANDREW GARVERICK

*900 West End Avenue, 8E • New York, NY 10025 • (212) 865-6690*

**OBJECTIVE**

PRODUCER/MEDIA PROGRAMMING

**SUMMARY**

Experienced media producer with high degree of artistic and technical expertise. Trained in total approach to use of media. Fully informed on state-of-the-art advances in media production, including the latest video editing techniques. Excellent interpersonal skills. Experienced writer, producer and supervisor of creative and technical personnel.

**EXPERIENCE**
1990–present

MERCER McDONALD (Public Relations), New York, New York

*Manager, Audiovisual Department* (1991–present)

- Organized and developed Audiovisual Department of one of the nation's premier PR firms
- Direct day-to-day operations of department, including preparation of budgets, purchase of new equipment, and supervision of both creative and administrative personnel
- Produce, direct, and script media programs, including videotapes, multiprojector slide shows, and computerized graphics
  — Clients include Sun Company, Inc.; Honeywell; Children's Television Workshop; U.S. Department of Energy (Solar Energy Project); Merle Norman Cosmetics; Emery Air Freight
  — Awarded John Starr Writing Award, 1992
- Work intensively with clients to develop programs to fulfill publicity objectives within scheduling and budgeting requirements
  — Present array of concept proposals from which clients can choose most suitable program
  — Develop production budgets and schedules, including services of photographers, graphic artists, video editors, and other media vendors
  — Rated consistently high by clients for expertise, on-schedule performance, and follow-up
- Instrumental in generating substantial new business by working closely with both internal account staff and clients
- Select, supervise, and coordinate efforts of vendors in film and video; work with top-quality editors, utilizing state-of-the-art facilities

*Technician* (1990–91)

- Wrote proposal outlining methods for improving Audiovisual Department's profitability and capabilities based on analysis of client needs; resulted in promotion to Manager

**1987–present**

FREELANCE MEDIA PRODUCER, New York, New York

- Client list includes CBS Publications Group, *Interface Age* magazine, Park Avenue Mall Association, and Chacma, Inc.
- Produced radio commercial campaigns for nationally distributed computer magazine
  — Scripted edited, and coordinated all aspects of production
- Directed and wrote sales and motivational slide presentations
  — Scripted and edited and coordinated talent, recording, photography, production of special-effect slides, sound mixing, and cueing
- Produced promotional videotape for management consulting firm
  — Cowrote script and coordinated all aspects of production

**1988–1990**

PACE UNIVERSITY, Pleasantville, New York

*Media Coordinator*

- Coordinated production-oriented program to develop nursing media curriculum, developed and wrote scripts, designed program and supervised television production

**1987–1988**

UNIVERSITY OF WISCONSIN MEDIA CENTER, Madison, Wisconsin

*Assistant Coordinator, Multimedia Laboratory*

- Produced media programs, including color videotapes and multi-image slide programs; acted as cameraman in color studio and coproduced several productions
- Supervised use of sound studio and four-room presentation facility
- Proposed ideas for new work and methods for improving programming

**EDUCATION**

Columbia University, New York, New York
1990—M.S., Public Media

University of Wisconsin, Madison, Wisconsin
1987—Graduate courses in film production

University of Wisconsin, Madison, Wisconsin
1985—B.A., Philosophy/Psychology

**PROFESSIONAL AFFILIATIONS**

National Academy of Television Arts and Sciences

# JOE GUARINO

150 Great Pine Lane
Pleasantville, NY 10570

OFFICE: [212] 765-2967
HOME: [914] 769-3296

| | |
|---|---|
| **OBJECTIVE** | **PROGRAMMING/MANAGEMENT—TELECOMMUNICATIONS INDUSTRY** |
| **SUMMARY** | Ten years' experience developing and managing international artists for live performances and television programming. Skilled administrator and supervisor of creative and technical personnel. Excellent track record creating and expanding domestic and international markets. Thorough knowledge of media advertising and publicity. M.B.A. in International Marketing. |

## MANAGEMENT EXPERIENCE

**1985–present**

JOE GUARINO ENTERPRISES, LTD. (entertainment management),
New York, New York

**President**

- Management and Marketing Development—promotion, publicity, touring and production—for more than 20 contemporary recording artists
- Budget, plan and organize record productions and concert tours; negotiate recording and publishing contracts, personal appearances, advertising endorsements, and TV appearances
- Supervise staff of 8, including 5 account executives; initiated successful system for providing full service to clients while reducing overhead
- Executive producer for precedent-setting engagement of major comedian on Broadway
- Created separate TV division for additional client exposure
  - Produced, packaged or created concept for more than two dozen international and domestic television programs or series, sponsored by BBC, CBC, French Television, German Television, Japanese Television, Australian Television, and Los Angeles Cable Television
  - Booked various artists for more than 30 television appearances, including *Geraldo Live, Charles Grodin Show, Dick Cavett Show, Mike Douglas Show, Don Kirschner's Rock Concert* (NBC), *Midnight Special* (ABC), and *Dick Clark's New Year's Rock & Eve* (ABC)

**1983–present**

GREAT SOUNDS, LTD.
New York, New York

**President**
**Director, Business Affairs**

- Chief Administrator of 20-person staff, responsible for organization and planning of concert tours, personal appearances, record production, publicity, and marketing campaign
- Determine annual budgets and both short- and long-range cost projections to sustain profit levels

GREAT SOUNDS, LTD. (cont.)

- Instrumental in expansion of gross revenues to peak of $4 million
  — Developed video productions and advertising endorsements, creating $250,000 in new income; obtained world video rights for distribution to national independent TV stations
  — Generated $450,000 in guaranteed annual income after analyzing audience demographics of major rock group
  — Executive Producer for rock group's appearance at New York Metropolitan Opera
  — Developed international markets, coordinating personal appearances with record exports and publicity campaigns and increasing revenues by $500,000 annually
  — Arranged three-week tour of Eastern Europe, sponsored by Department of State

**1985–present**

ATV MUSIC (publishing)
New York, New York

**Management Consultant**

- Supervise and guide 10 songwriters and arrangers through creative and production problems
- Develop and implement marketing strategies
  — Arranged for writers to cowrite songs with artists who have recording contracts
  — Increased ad agency awareness of coterie of songwriters available for creation of original jingles
  — Brought about 50% increase in advanced income by negotiating international publishing agreements

**EDUCATION**

NEW YORK UNIVERSITY GRADUATE SCHOOL OF BUSINESS,
New York, New York
1983—M.B.A., International Marketing

ADELPHI UNIVERSITY, Garden City, New York
1981—B.B.A., Business & Finance
Dean's List, 1980–1981
President, School of Business Student Council
Vice-President, Marketing and Advertising Club

# ALICE BRANDEL

225 East 86th Street, #8B • New York, NY 10022
Home (212) 755-0434 • Work (518) 474-1029

## OBJECTIVE

*TV WRITING/PRODUCING/DIRECTING*—Commercial, cable, public, or industrial television

## SUMMARY

Award-winning writer/producer/director of televised programs, public service announcements and closed-circuit programs employing nationally known talent. Skilled at developing production budgets and hiring and directing creative staffs. Adept at designing program packages and software to fulfill specific client requirements.

## TELEVISION EXPERIENCE

**1986–**
**Present**    CENTER FOR LEARNING TECHNOLOGIES,
NEW YORK STATE EDUCATION DEPARTMENT, Albany, New York

- ◆ Write, produce, and direct television and closed-circuit training programs for adults and children, combining studio and electronic field production
  — Administer budgets of $3,000 to $100,000
  — Hire and direct production and creative staffs
- ◆ Created, produced, and directed award-winning, three-part media package to promote good nutrition
  — Package included 15 radio and 15 TV announcements, 30-minute public TV program, and 20-minute closed-circuit TV program
  — Received medal of excellence, International Film and TV Festival of New York
- ◆ Designed, produced, and implemented interactive, 40-hour children's TV series
  — Broadened and modernized curriculum through use of entertainment
  — Positive response by students evidenced in significant learning results
- ◆ Developed and produced ongoing state-wide teleconferences
  — Programs are "live" and broadcast by all New York State public television stations
  — Toll-free call-in provides direct answers to viewers' questions
- ◆ Consulted with diverse school districts, providing in-service training and recommending software and hardware specifications to achieve instructional objectives
- ◆ Created the "video memo" format as a way to disseminate information to staff at 756 locations

**1978–**
**1985**   ROCHESTER CITY SCHOOL DISTRICT, Rochester, New York
*TV Instructor* (1984–1985)
*Business Education Instructor* (1978–1984)

- Conceived, wrote, and served as on-camera host for 42-lesson, self-instructional TV series in business education used by 100 districts state-wide
  — Wrote three manuals to accompany the series
  — Series was telecast by public and cable TV stations and is used by the State Education Department's Employee Training Center
  — Established reputation of Rochester Televised Instruction Center and resulted in further awards of contracts for videotape production
  — Series resulted in effective replacement of classroom instruction with 79% pass rate and reduction of instructional costs by almost 50%
- Assistant Producer for 5 videotapes featuring the Rochester Philharmonic

## EDUCATION

Syracuse University, Syracuse, New York
1971—M.S., Business Education

Russell Sage College, Troy, New York
1968—B.S., Business Education
Graduated *cum laude* with High Honors in Business

University of Hawaii, Honolulu, Hawaii
1974—Six credits in Television Production

Indiana University, Bloomington, Indiana
1973—Nine credits in Television Production
Awarded H. Wilson Scholarship

New School for Social Research, New York, New York
1983—Developing Programming for Children's Television

## AWARDS

Ohio State Broadcasting Award for *Visual Learning*, with Gene Shalit and Walter Cronkite

International Film and Television Festival of New York Medal for *The Breakfast Connection*, with Lendon Smith, M.D., and Marilyn Michaels

*Partial list of productions available upon request*

# WILLIAM MONROE

417 EAST 58TH STREET, APT. 18D, NEW YORK, NY 10022 • (212) 935-1725

**OBJECTIVE**     *COMMERCIAL INTERIOR DESIGN*

**SUMMARY**     Interior designer with ten years of commercial and residential design experience. Thorough knowledge of trade sources. Understanding of city codes and Building Department routine and bureaucracy. Comprehensive knowledge of commercial planning systems and office landscaping.

## DESIGN EXPERIENCE

*1984–present*     DANIEL STERLING, INC., New York, New York

*Head Designer* (1985–present)

*Assistant Designer* (1984–85)

- Design commercial and residential spaces and direct all facets leading to completion of projects. Supervise assistants, ensuring on-schedule production of quality work. Negotiate with architects, vendors, and tradespeople, scheduling and coordinating their activities.

- Achievements
  Discotheque Parfait, New York City
  Executive business offices, Exemplar International Insurance Co., Fort Lee, New Jersey
  Rare Form contemporary restaurant, New York City
  Solarium for president of Perrier Water Co. (featured in *Town & Country* magazine)
  Private residences for leading social figures in New York City
  Solarium for Richard Todd of the New York Jets, New York City

*1986–present*     FREELANCE PROJECTS

- Packaging concept for Alan Fortunoff (owner of Fortunoff's), New York City

- Textile design collection for Schumacher Decorators Walk, Riverdale Fabrics, New York City

- Kent Bragaline, New York City

- Album cover logo and publicity T-shirts for Darryl Hall and John Oates, Arista Records, New York City

- Skating Club set and costume design—Utica Figure Skating Club, Clinton Figure Skating Club, Hamilton Figure Skating Club, Ice Club of Syracuse

*1983–1984*    TABER INTERIORS, New York, New York

*Assistant Designer*

- Developed designs, conceptualizations and renderings of floor plans, elevations and layouts under tutelage of Head Designer. Co-ordinated design elements and became acquainted with trends in design field.

*1982–1983*    BLOOMINGDALE'S, New York, New York

*Designer*

- Created residential interiors, utilizing existing retail product lines

*1980–1982*    SELF-EMPLOYED DESIGNER
(Concurrent with pursuit of M.F.A.)

- Conceptualized and designed various boutiques, shopping plazas and restaurants

*1977–1979*    CARRIER CORPORATION, Syracuse, New York

*Assistant Designer, Corporate Planning*

- Drawing, drafting, and rendering

**EDUCATION**    COLUMBIA UNIVERSITY, New York, New York
1988—M.F.A. (GPA: 3.8/4.0)

SYRACUSE UNIVERSITY, Syracuse, New York
1977—B.F.A., Interior Design (GPA: 4.0/4.0)
Dean's List, eight semesters

**CERTIFICATION**    Permanent Certified Design Instructor, New York State Board of Regents

# Sally Marcus

340 EAST 57th STREET
New York, NY 10022
(212) 730-2196

**OBJECTIVE** *Architectural design* in the area of planning and designing private residences and public spaces.

**SUMMARY** Creative spatial planner with ability to combine function and aesthetics in a variety of environments. Broad background in architectural history and theory, human factors and urban studies. Studied under prestigious experts in fields of city planning; contract, residential and lighting design; and landscape architecture. Knowledgeable and skilled practitioner of computer-assisted design.

**EDUCATION** Parsons School of Design, New York, New York
1995—B.F.A. Program, Environmental Design

Columbia University, New York, New York
1992–1993—Urban Studies

**DESIGN
EXPERIENCE
1991–1995**
• Spatial planning for bazaar: the Burke Institute fund-raising
• Interior design consultant to Mrs. Rebecca Noonan, New York
• Design consultant and spatial planner for Deanne, Bellow & Roth, Inc.
• Apprentice to Rita Blass, AIA, South Salem, New York

**DESIGN
ASSIGNMENTS
1993–1995**
PINE ISLE RESORT HOTEL, Gainesville, Georgia
Design of winter/summer resort

MIDTOWN POCKET PARK, Newark, New Jersey
Design of two-level public plaza in center of business
district

SEAMEN'S RESTAURANT, New York, New York
Renovation of three-story residence, Upper East Side

SOLAR ENERGY-EFFICIENT HOUSE, Jacksonville, Florida
Typical two-family brownstone home adapted for energy
efficiency

**OTHER
EXPERIENCE
1986–1991**
Stony Brook Day Camp, Dover, New Jersey
Camp Counselor (four summers)

YW/MHA, West Orange, New Jersey
Hotline Phone Counselor

St. Louis, Missouri, Public Schools
Tutor

Extensive travel throughout Europe and the United States

# Yvonne C. Miller

207 Hudson Street, Apt. 5N, New York, NY (212) 226-5525

### GRAPHIC ARTIST AND ILLUSTRATOR

### *OBJECTIVE*

Illustrator in a growth position leading to design responsibility

### *SUMMARY*

Experienced in a broad spectrum of commercial art,
including technical and advertising graphics.
Utilize Illustrator, Quark 3.1, and Photoshop.

### *EXPERIENCE*

1994–1996    *Technical Illustrator*, VOLT INFORMATION SCIENCES, INC.,
Syosset, New York
- Coordinated in-house and farmed-out steps in production process,
  including assigning artists, camera, and proofing
- Illustrated viewgraphs, flow charts, and forms; adapted photos as
  graphic illustrations; drew and lettered cartoons, flipcharts, and posters
- Did layout, page makeup, and pasteup for manuals and graphs; did
  pasteups for trade magazine and telephone company publication ads
- Charged with responsibility for complete production of company
  display, from rough layout to finished art

1994–present    SELECTED FREELANCE ASSIGNMENTS
*Graphs*, CBS Radio Sales Research Department, New York, New York
*Brochure and consumer ad illustration*, Jasper Industries, Oyster Bay,
   New York
*Ink illustrations, Xerox and color photo adaptation*, New Community
   Theatre, Huntington, New York
*Murals*, Gent's World, Madison, Wisconsin
*Posters and murals*, Concourse Hotel, Madison, Wisconsin
*Display ads and billboards*, Sel Metals Corporation, Holbrook, New York
*Textbook illustrations*, McGraw-Hill Book Company, Inc., New York,
   New York

### *EDUCATION*

University of Wisconsin, Madison, Wisconsin
   1992–1994, Fine Arts

Technical College, Old Westbury, New York
   1992, Course in Photography

State University of New York, Farmingdale, New York
   1990–1991, Art Advertising

# FRANK LOYKOVICH

| | |
|---|---|
| 3275 Santa Monica Boulevard<br>Los Angeles, CA 92301 | *Home:* (310) 946-6695<br>*Office:* (310) 889-2875, Ext. 246 |

*OBJECTIVE*  **ART DIRECTOR/CORPORATE COMMUNICATIONS**

Seeking corporate position where my expertise in editorial design will be employed in communications media for both external and internal circulation.

*SUMMARY*  Experience in graphic design for production of magazines, brochures, annual reports, conference displays, newsletters, book jackets, house organs, and other collateral units. Capable production strategist in selecting freelance talent, interfacing with vendors and editorial and public affairs departments, and overseeing production budgets. Knowledgeable about broadcast media advertising and public relations requirements. Discerning in adapting research to specific markets.

## *CAREER HIGHLIGHTS*

1990–present  **EARL E. GRAVES LTD. & SUBSIDIARIES**
Santa Monica, California

*Associate Art Director*

- Assist Art Director in producing visuals for total packaging of 260,000-circulation magazine
- Select freelance talent, negotiate fees, oversee average $15,000 monthly budget, and supervise five-member staff
- Expedite workload traffic flow to meet camera-ready processing deadline
- Conceive and design print ads and collateral for company-owned radio stations
- Conceive and design brochures and other collateral material for station Public Affairs Director for exhibitions and presentations
- Conceive and design material for Publisher's public policy presentations
- Research demographics and create chart material in marketing to the community

1987–1990  FREELANCE GRAPHIC DESIGNER
Los Angeles, California

- Sold own talents successfully to clients for design of corporate stationery, promotional brochures, book jackets, inside book design, conference displays, newsletters, house organs, trade ads, and general advertising
- Maintained customer relations with advertising agencies, publishers, and corporate art directors

1986–1987    LIVING TOGETHER PUBLICATIONS, INC.
New York, New York

*Media Representative*

- Advertising account executive for 200,000-circulation magazine supplement in top 20 markets newspapers
- Established new major accounts for personal care and cosmetic products (including Clairol) as new entries into ethnic market

1985–1986    VIZMO PRODUCTION, INC.
New York, New York

*Staff Designer*

- Created and designed graphic presentation for NBC-TV, including national and local newscasts and the *Today Show*
- Created and designed weather maps, slide titles, and promotional material for Media Sales Department

1984–1985    PERFECTION PHOTO, INC.
New York, New York

*Associate Designer*

- Designed typography for packaging, print ads, direct mail, brochures, and magazines

1981–1983    McGRAW-HILL, INC.
New York, New York

*Staff Designer, Corporate Art Department*

- Correlated book jacket and sales collateral with editorial, advertising, and marketing departments
- Designed annual reports and slide presentations

*OTHER ACTIVITIES*

— Worked with editor in refocusing editorial content of NAACP's *The Crisis*; redesigned and restructured features and departments of the publication
— Consulting Art Director and Lecturer, New York University: editorial design; production of magazine as term project

*EDUCATION*    1981—New York City Community College, Brooklyn, New York
Advertising and Design Theory
1980—School of Visual Arts, New York, New York

*MEMBER*    Graphic Artists Guild
Society of Publications Designers
New York Type Directors Club

*AWARDS*    New York Art Directors Club, 1993 Merit Award

# HOWARD D. PAPPAS

*10 Hall Avenue • Freehold, NJ 07728*
*(201) 780-1576*

*OBJECTIVE*  <u>CHORAL DIRECTOR, COLLEGE OR UNIVERSITY</u>

*SUMMARY*  Ten years' experience as choral director in schools at elementary, secondary and college levels, including three years as church minister of music. Creative teacher with ability to motivate students in appreciation of and participation in all phases of music. Skillful conductor in training and performances. Active and artistic performer.

*RELEVANT EXPERIENCE*

*1988–present*  MARLBORO TOWNSHIP PUBLIC SCHOOLS, Marlboro, New Jersey
*Teacher of Music*
- Train and direct school chorus and prepare students for assembly and public performances
  — Also teach classes for trainable special needs children
  — Assist classroom teachers in program preparation
- Initiated change in curriculum to include related arts approach to teaching music as prescribed by the Orff-Schulwerk method
  — Coordinate the study of singing, dance, speech, playing musical instruments, and ear and sensitivity training
- Compose and arrange songs (both words and music) for children
- Introduced conceptual approach to general music program, giving students a more defined insight into music
- Served as curriculum consultant to school district in Orff techniques; served on Related Arts Committee to develop multidiscipline, multimedia experiences

*Concurrent*  FAIRLEIGH DICKINSON UNIVERSITY, New Jersey
*1991–1992*
- Directed university chorus (25 students for credit courses) on part-time basis; conducted two public concerts

*1987–1988*  MOORESTOWN FRIENDS SCHOOL, Moorestown, New Jersey
*Teacher of Music*
- Directed high school and junior high school chorus; taught music as elective to high school students and general music in grade school
- Created a course in eighth-grade general music based on rock-and-roll history, through both styles and performers

*1988–1989*  PLACERVILLE PRESBYTERIAN CHURCH, Placerville, New Jersey
*Minister of Music*
- Trained and directed adult choir, developed outstanding repertoire of sacred music, and trained and directed junior choir
- Conducted choir for Sunday services, presented two cantatas at Christmas, and presented Bach motet at Spring Concert

1984–1986        JUILLIARD SCHOOL, New York, New York
                 *Teaching Fellow*
                 • Assisted choral director in all aspects of managing department (served in his stead during several four- to six-week absences)
                 • Charged with responsibility for concert arrangements, library, attendance, grades, and interoffice communications
                 • Conducted and rehearsed Juilliard Chorus while director was on tour for professional engagements
                 • Prepared Juilliard Chorus for historic production of opera *Macbeth*, by Ernest Bloch
                 • Instructed classes in choral conducting
                 • Only candidate accepted for enrollment in 1984
                   — Recipient of Frank Damrosch Prize

1983–1986        NEW JERSEY CHORALE, Rutherford, New Jersey
                 (while attending school)
                 *Conductor*
                 • Developed chorale into a prestigious company with a repertoire that attracted sponsors for more lucrative contracts
                 • Conducted chorale's first concert featuring a full-length classical work with orchestra
                 • Substantially improved chorale's financial condition through removal of deficit by increased bookings

OTHER WORK       • Professional freelance soloist and choral singer
                 • Recordings of educational records for
                   — Victor Kayfetz Productions, 1984
                   — American Book Company, 1986
                 • Solo recital for Monmouth Symphony League, March 1991
                   — Eight sound filmstrips for DHHS-funded elementary music program
                 • Private instruction in voice, piano, and theory

EDUCATION        Juilliard School, New York, New York
                 1986—M.M., Choral Conducting

                 Trenton State College, Trenton, NJ
                 1981—B.A., Music Education (Vocal)
                 1981—Conducting Fellowship, Aspen Music Festival; Singer, Aspen Choir

                 Westminster Choir College, Princeton, New Jersey—
                 Orff-Schulwerk Courses

*MEMBER*

College Music Society                       American Orff-Schulwerk Association
Music Educators National Conference         Central New Jersey Orff-Schulwerk Association
New Jersey Music Educators Association       New Jersey Education Association
National Education Association

*CERTIFICATE*   New Jersey Permanent Teaching Certificate

**RICHARD SPOSITO** ■ 200 East 33rd Street, Apt. 6A ■ New York, NY 10016 ■ (212) 532-4455

*OBJECTIVE*    Editor in or technical consultant to a publishing house

*SUMMARY*    More than 15 years' experience in all phases of music: Composer, Arranger, Conductor, Performer, Instructor and Business Manager. Compositions have been performed in Carnegie Hall. More than 10 students have become stars; hundreds have become professional musicians and singers. Play piano and flute; familiar with all instruments.

### PROFESSIONAL HIGHLIGHTS

1985–present    NEW YORK SCHOOL OF MUSIC, New York, New York

*Chairman of Music Theory Department/Instructor*

- Instruct both graduate and undergraduate students in music theory
  — Organized courses of study
  — Originated new courses in Advanced Ear Training
- Oversee auditions for prospective applicants
- Recommend instructors and substitutes for hire
- Train new instructors
- Hundreds of former students have gone on to play or sing professionally
- Currently in joint authorship of a music theory workbook for beginning high school students in the Preparatory Division of Manhattan School of Music (September 1996 projected publication date)

Concurrent    *Leader of Jazz Combo*
1989–present
- Write and arrange compositions, direct appearances, and perform on the piano and flute
- Book appearances in New York metropolitan area for weddings, bar and bat mitzvahs, cocktail parties, and holiday events
- Manage all financial affairs and arrangements for group, including billing and collection

Concurrent    BROOKLYN COLLEGE, Brooklyn, New York
1986–1993    *Adjunct Lecturer*

- Taught assigned Music Theory and Music Appreciation courses to music and non-music majors

1978–1992    SEAMAN'S METHODIST CHURCH, Brooklyn, New York
*Music Director*

1983–1985    NEW YORK CITY COMMUNITY COLLEGE, Brooklyn, New York
*Adjunct Lecturer*

- Taught assigned Music Appreciation courses to nonmusic majors

| | |
|---|---|
| 1975–1982 | **NEW YORK CITY BOARD OF EDUCATION**, Brooklyn, New York |

*Teacher of Orchestral Music* (1979–1982)
- Trained students on all orchestral instruments
- Instituted home use of instruments to increase interest in orchestra
- Developed orchestra from 10 poorly trained players into well-disciplined musical group of 60 instrumentalists

*General Music Teacher* (1975–1979)
- Taught Music Appreciation courses to general classes
- Trained and rehearsed school Glee Club

*EDUCATION*
Manhattan School of Music, New York, New York
1985—M.M., Music Theory/Piano
Thesis: "Ear Training Program for College Freshmen"

New York University, New York, New York
1980—M.A., Master of Music Education

Howard University, Washington, D.C.
1972—B.A., Music Education (cum laude)

*HONORS*
— Inducted into Pi Kappa Lamda, Howard University
— Elected President of Student Council
— Received Lucy E. Moten Fellowship for European study and travel, 1973
— Achieved highest score on Regular Teacher Examination (orchestral music), Board of Education of New York, 1979

*ORIGINAL COMPOSITIONS*

"Serenity for Solo Flute"
"Theme and Variations for Piano and Bassoon"
"Piano Sonata in One Movement"
"Woodwind Quintet No. 1"
"Woodwind Quintet No. 2" (performed at Carnegie Hall)
"Theme and Variations for Woodwind Quintet"

*MEMBER*
American Music Center
Music Theory Teachers of New York State

*CERTIFIED*
Music Teacher for New York State

**SEYMOUR GOLDMAN** • 1500 York Avenue, Apt. 5B • New York, NY 10021
(212) 249-6625     (212) 249-1523

**_OBJECTIVE_**     **ORCHESTRAL CONDUCTOR/CHORAL DIRECTOR**
To devote broad experience and expertise to conducting an established orchestra, or to developing and conducting a concert orchestra and/or chorale that may be only at the conceptual stage

**_SUMMARY_**     More than 15 years as musical director and conductor for prestigious organizations, including symphony orchestras, opera companies, and university and church chorales. Frequently toured Europe and South America for concert engagements. Possess full repertoire of classical and semiclassical scores.

## _EXPERIENCE_

**CONDUCTOR**

*Current*     WHITTENBURG CHOIR COLLEGE, Princeton, New Jersey
**Music Director**
• Conduct University Symphony Orchestra
• Member, piano faculty

NATIONAL COUNCIL OF THE ARTS, New York, New York
• Commissioned to organize Latin American Symphonic Choir

*1990–1994*     MONTAUK ORCHESTRA, Long Island, New York
• Music Director and Conductor

FIRST METHODIST CHURCH, Setauket, New York
• Choral Director with 10–15 concerts per year

*1991–1993*     HOPE OPERA COMPANY, Long Island, New York
• Orchestral and Choir Director
• Directed and conducted operatic performances, including *I Pagliacci, Tosca, Magic Flute,* and *Cavalleria Rusticana*

*1988–1990*     STATE UNIVERSITY OF NEW YORK AT STONY BROOK, New York
• Served as Assistant Conductor for four semesters

*1980–1993*     BUENOS AIRES CONSERVATORY, Buenos Aires, Argentina
• Conductor for orchestra and chorale; Piano Instructor

**TOURING CONDUCTOR**

*1985–present*     • Guest Conductor in South America and Europe (Italy, France, Poland)
— Conducted 15 concerts in South America (July/August, 1986) with engagements in Chile, Argentina, Uruguay, Paraguay, and Bolivia

**INSTRUCTOR**

*1984–present*     PRIVATE INSTRUCTOR, New York, New York
• Instruct in piano and conducting; coach voice
— Currently coaching 15 professionals; have coached 60–65 professionals
— Have instructed more than 120 nonprofessionals

*1985–1988*    NEW YORK INSTITUTE FOR THE EDUCATION OF THE BLIND,
New York, New York
- Member of the piano faculty

*1983–1994*    PRIVATE INSTRUCTOR, St. Louis, Missouri
- Taught piano and solfege

*1979–1983*    PRIVATE INSTRUCTOR, Buenos Aires, Argentina
- Taught piano, solfege, ear training, and harmony

**JUDGE**    NEW YORK STATE SYMPHONIC MUSIC ASSOCIATION
- Annual Spring Festival for entries in piano, chorus, and orchestra

NEW YORK STATE MUSICAL EVALUATION CENTER
- First National Competition, 1988–1989

## *EDUCATION*

**DEGREE PROGRAMS**    STATE UNIVERSITY OF NEW YORK AT STONY BROOK, New York
    (Full Scholarship)
1985—M.M., Orchestral Conducting/Choral Conducting
GENERAL URQUIZA NATIONAL CONSERVATORY OF MUSIC
  Buenos Aires, Argentina (Full Scholarship)
1983—Ph.D., Conducting
1982—M.M., Music; Orchestral and Choral Conducting
1979—B.M., Piano/Analysis

**ADDITIONAL TRAINING**

STATE UNIVERSITY OF NEW YORK, Oneonta, New York
1987—Seminar in Choral Conducting and Analysis
MARIANO SIJANEK, Buenos Aires, Argentina
1985 — Opera seminar (6 weeks)
PRIVATE INSTRUCTION, St. Louis, Missouri
1982–1988 — Orchestral and Choral under professional directors

## *PROFESSIONAL AFFILIATIONS*

American Symphony Orchestra League
Musical Educators National Conference
Musicians Club
Piano Teachers of New York

*LANGUAGES*    Fluent in Spanish, Italian, and French; working knowledge of Portuguese
and German

*CITED*    *Reader's Digest*, October 1987 (also published in all 15 foreign language
editions)
*People* magazine, June 5, 1988
Various magazine and newspaper articles, United States and abroad

**Raymond W. Clancy** · 6518 Grant Place · West New York, NJ 07093 · (201) 867-7777

**OBJECTIVE**  *MUSEUM DEVELOPMENT/PROGRAM ADMINISTRATOR*

A position employing experience in educational program development and knowledge of anthropology, classical antiquity, and presentation and promotion.

**SUMMARY**  M.A., Anthropology. Experienced in program development in anthropology, American history, language and humanities, and enrichment programs for gifted and talented students. Adept at negotiation, persuasion, and promotion. Knowledge of fund-raising, budget development, organization and production.

**HIGHLIGHTS**
- Magazine Production—coordinated all aspects including design, layout, editing, and printing
- Film and Theatrical Production—from conception to production, including scripting, casting, lighting and direction
- Fund-Raising and Special Promotions—conceived and directed money-raising events through use of film, sales, and theater

**TECHNICAL SKILLS**
- Audiovisual equipment (super-8 film and 1/2-inch video cameras, projectors, voice recorders, copy stands, Repronar, slides and filmstrips)
- Darkroom facility: 35 mm color and black-and-white (develop and print)
- Holography

**PROGRAM DEVELOPMENT EXPERIENCE**

1982–present  DUPONT BOARD OF EDUCATION, Dupont, New Jersey
*Instructor*
- Anthropology, Latin, American History, Humanities
- Developed and implemented six new curricula in Anthropology, Latin, and Political Science
- Conceived, developed, and initiated first school-wide anthropology course
- Achieved full enrollments in elective courses through intense promotional campaigns; maintained enrollment by combining humor and drama with solid exposure to subject matter
- Assisted with development of humanities program

DUPONT SCHOOL DISTRICT
- Participated in setting district- and school-wide goals to ensure enhanced education and special programs for gifted and talented children
  — Developed specialized curricula in science, art, and communications
  — Conducted intensive research into existing programs for gifted and talented students

*(continued)*

DUPONT SCHOOL DISTRICT (cont.)
- Adviser to school literary and art magazine
  - Directed unique fund-raising ventures
  - Prepared budget and selected vendors within budgetary outlines
  - Supervised staff of 20
  - Coordinated production, including design, layout, editing, and printing
- Active in school organization
  - Elected Chairman of 8-member Faculty Council
  - Member of committee on development of educational goals for entire district
  - Member of Committee for Faculty Evaluation
  - Advise and oversee budget distributions of student language, science, theater, athletic, newspaper, and chefs' clubs
  - Secured favorable increases and benefits in negotiations with district Board of Education
  - Convinced Board of Education to publish official policy book to clarify personnel policies
- Produced three 15-minute films and directed two full-scale theatrical productions for fund-raising and promotion

## RESEARCH AND WRITING EXPERIENCE

1981      STATEN ISLAND INSTITUTE, New York, New York
*Foundation Researcher*

1980      WNYC RADIO, New York, New York
*Freelance Writer/Researcher*
- Researched and wrote programs on consumer frauds and exposés on home service industries and food pricing

**EDUCATION**    Montclair State College, Montclair, New Jersey
1989—M.A. in Anthropology

St. Peters College, Jersey City, New Jersey
1982—B.A. in American History
Multiple minors in English, Latin, Philosophy, and Education

**LICENSES**    Licensed to teach American History, English, Latin, and Anthropology by the state of New Jersey

**LANGUAGE**    Latin—reading and translation

**INTERESTS**    Photography, classical music, jazz

# ELEANOR GOLDMAN

250 West 89th Street   ·   New York, NY 10025   ·   (212) 580-6692

## OBJECTIVE

*MANAGEMENT—OFFICE/PERSONNEL*

## SUMMARY

More than ten years' experience in supervision of office procedures and personnel recruitment and management. Creative designer of work-flow systems to eliminate duplication of effort and increase proficiency and productivity of staff. Administer confidential projects with dispatch and discretion. Astute negotiator with vendors of supplies, equipment and services.

## BUSINESS HIGHLIGHTS

1986–present    INTEGRATED RESOURCES, INC.
New York, New York
Office Manager and Personnel Manager

*Office Manager*

- Supervise staff of 152 secretarial and clerical personnel
  - Serve as liaison for middle management with executive suite
  - Train clerical personnel in procedures and office equipment
  - Administer vacation policies and schedule vacations
- Purchase office supplies, equipment, furniture, and services
  - Supervise maintenance crew for two floors and suites on four other floors of 41-story building
  - Maintain liaison with NYNEX relevant to equipment and service for this office and 14 subsidiaries of company
  - Supervise all communications invoices
- Have complete responsibility for special projects
  - In process of moving offices: supervising decor, purchasing furnishings, consulting on phone installation, allocating office assignments, arranging of files and equipment, selecting and supervising of movers, and expediting printing of new stationery
  - Administer maintenance of corporate apartment for visiting VIP's

*Personnel Manager*
- Recruit, interview, and hire clerical personnel (in last six months, interviewed 300, hired 50, and trained 15)
- Negotiate contracts with staffing vendors
- Maintain confidential records, supervise benefits, process insurance claims
- Prepare payroll, biweekly input sheets, quarterly reports, and unemployment insurance and W-2's
- Designed and implemented smoothly operating personnel system
- Wrote personnel manual and developed records systems

1981–1986    **RESTAURANT ASSOCIATES INDUSTRIES, INC.**
New York, New York

*Central Files Supervisor*
- Set up central files system and supervised clerical personnel
- Maintained confidential employment and labor contracts

Summer 1981    **BOARD OF EDUCATION, CITY OF NEW YORK**
Brooklyn, New York

*Teacher's Aide*
- Supervised school students on day-camp trips; assisted in classroom work

1980–1981    **UNITED STATES TESTING COMPANY**
Hoboken, New Jersey

*Consumer Tester*
- Administered consumer testing program for food items
- Persuaded casual shoppers to participate by responding to test and filling out questionnaire

1978–1979    **WILBUR ROGERS DEPARTMENT STORE**
Port Authority Bus Terminal, New York, New York

*Cashier/Salesclerk*
- Assisted customers with purchases
- Handled cash and ran register check at close of business

### SKILLS

Word Perfect, Excel, Powerpoint

### EDUCATION

Allen University
Katherine Gibbs School of Business
W&J Sloan School of Interior Decorating
American Management Association: Getting Ahead in Personnel

### INTERESTS

Fashion, interior decorating, dancing, sports, and travel

# KATHERINE SINORADZKI

River Bend Road, New Canaan, CT 06840
(203) 966-0318

**OBJECTIVE**    *CRUISE DIRECTOR*

**SUMMARY**

Six years' experience as cruise director and passenger on voyages of from 18 to 90 days in Caribbean, Mediterranean, South Seas, Transpacific, and the Greek Islands. Strong background planning, budgeting, and supervising daily on-board activities. Assist passengers in familiarization of ship's facilities and activities, as well as ports of call. Particular facility for "people matching" to see that greatest number of passengers meet those of similar interests and tastes, thus ensuring enthusiastic repeat passengers and referrals. Widely traveled in Europe, Near and Far East, South America, Australia, New Zealand, and South Sea Islands. Nine-year resident of Japan. Fluent in Spanish; read and interpret Japanese.

**RELEVANT
EXPERIENCE**

*1980–1986*

FINNISH AMERICAN LINE, New York, New York
Cruise Director, SS *Kungsholm*

Planned, budgeted and supervised eight to ten recreational and social activities daily for approximately 500 passengers of widely varying interests and energy levels.

— Scheduled and oversaw ship-wide tournaments (cribbage, deck tennis, shuffleboard, scrabble, and so forth).
— Dropped or added activities in midcruise as necessary to accommodate unique passenger interests.
— Provided activity information and other "ship's news" to passengers through cabin-delivered daily programs, posters, and public address announcements.

Developed ability to introduce passengers of like interests to one another, thus encouraging friendships that led to numerous repeat passengers and referrals.

— Organized "captain's sit-down cocktail parties," so arranged as to permit optimum passenger introductions.
— Conducted "special interest" parties bringing together "Repeaters," "Singles," "Masons," and so on, to permit meeting of people of like interests.

Acted as "liaison officer" between passengers and ship's staff, conveying questions, complaints, comments and suggestions; worked closely with purser, and dining room staff.

Also worked closely with entertainment staff, special activities staff, and land tour staff in disseminating information to passengers about their various functions.

NEW YORK STOCK EXCHANGE, New York, New York
Gallery Director, Public Relations Department

*1980–1986*     Served frequently as Exchange spokeswoman in contacts with media; worked with print and broadcast media representatives to keep Exchange functions and brokerage office procedures in public eye.

— Worked with newsmen and feature writers on articles about Exchange.
— Wrote and delivered daily radio broadcast on WNYC concerning various aspects of Exchange and financial operations; gave daily price quotations on selected list of stocks.
— Made guest TV and radio appearances on behalf of Exchange (e.g., the *Today Show*).

Designed, organized, and supervised Stock Exchange exhibit in U.S. Pavilion at Exposition International in Brussels.

Supervised 13 tour guides in overseeing operations of Visitors' Gallery, including conducting tours for up to 2,000 visitors daily.

— Escorted special individual and group visitors on in-depth tours of Exchange and financial area; entertained individuals and groups during visits to New York (as escort to shops, theaters, and restaurants).
— Arranged luncheons for guests of the Exchange, working with chefs on menus and occasionally working as hostess.

**CURRENT EXPERIENCE**     SELF-EMPLOYED, New Canaan, Connecticut
Landscape Designer

Design, execute, and supervise construction of gardens and garden structures (principally Japanese), such as rock gardens, pool houses, tea houses, bridges, waterfalls, decks, dams, and swimming pools, for clients nationwide.

**EDUCATION**     PARSON'S SCHOOL OF DESIGN, New York, New York
NEW YORK INSTITUTE OF FINANCE, New York, New York
MISS PORTER'S SCHOOL, Farmington, Connecticut

**LICENSES AND CERTIFICATES**     Registered Representative and Security Analyst, New York Stock Exchange
Private Pilot's License
Radio Operator's License

**LANGUAGES**     Fluent in Spanish; speak and read Japanese.

# Margaret York

78-20 AUSTIN STREET
KEW GARDENS, NY 11415
(212) 847-6721

**OBJECTIVE**

Long-term commitment to reputable consumer magazine as an associate or contributing editor.

**SUMMARY**

Skilled in all aspects of handling manuscripts: rewriting, copy editing and proofreading. Experienced in judging manuscripts and dealing with authors. Expert speller and grammarian.

## RELEVANT EXPERIENCE

*November 1991– present*

**Assistant Editor**, MACFADDEN WOMEN'S GROUP
• Evaluate, rewrite, and edit new manuscripts
• Proofread galleys; check page proofs and final pages
• Maintain close liaison with Home Service, Art, and Production Departments

*June 1991– November 1991*

**Production Editor**, JOHN WILEY AND SONS
• Edited and proofread copy for four technical magazines
• Checked final pages and incorporated authors' corrections onto proofs
• Logged manuscripts; used Greek symbols and type specifications

*April 1987– June 1990*

**Production Editor**, AMERICAN SOCIETY OF MECHANICAL ENGINEERS
• Solely responsible for journal
— Copy editing, proofreading, transferral of authors' corrections onto final pages
— Page layout, sizing of figures and photographs, pagination, check of final pages

*January 1986– June 1986*

**Traffic Editor**, SIMPLICITY PATTERN COMPANY
• Controlled flow of pages to and from printer
• Informed Art and Design Departments about changes in page sequence

*April 1985– October 1985*

**Assistant Copy Editor**, AMERICAN INSTITUTE OF AERONAUTICS AND ASTRONAUTICS
(Duties similar to those at John Wiley)

**EDUCATION**

Molloy College, B.A. in English, 1985

**LANGUAGES**

French and Latin

# FINANCE

# COLLEEN McDONALD

4021 Snyder Avenue
Brooklyn, NY 11203
Home: (212) 856-7321     Office: (212) 489-6300

## SUMMARY

Fifteen-year banking career: eight years of branch operations management capping seven years in varied ground-floor services. Adept at control of cash losses and forgeries and able to structure work assignments for maximum efficiency and customer service. Fully knowledgeable of NOW accounts, money market accounts, and safe deposit procedures.

## BANKING AND FINANCE EXPERIENCE

**1981–present**    UNITED MUTUAL SAVINGS BANK, Brooklyn, New York

*Branch Manager and Officer* (1992–present)

- Structure and supervise functions of 20 branch employees to ensure maximum efficiency and security
  — Charged with direction of daily work assignments of nine tellers, new accounts and safe deposit personnel; and clerical, maintenance, and security staffs
  — Restructure work flow depending on daily requirements
  — Conduct salary reviews
- Decreased annual overtime costs by nearly $10,000 and increased efficiency by revamping Teller Department
  — Trained tellers in all facets of unit; wrote training outline for execution by Head Teller
- Eliminated cash losses and forgeries over past five years through vigorous implementation of security measures
- Conduct bimonthly meetings to ensure good security practices among tellers
- Maintain minimum total cash- and working-drawer levels
- Execute frequent internal audits of cash, traveler's checks, and bonds
- Able to take on expanded responsibilities and troubleshoot during emergencies
- Assume Assistant Vice-President's functions during periodic absences of up to three weeks' duration
- Substitute for managers in other branches on emergency basis
- Troubleshoot computer malfunctions and improper data entries
- Performed above responsibilities since 1986, beginning as Banking Operations Assistant; promoted to Assistant Manager in 1989 and Manager in 1992

*Head Teller* (1983–1986)

- Supervised 11-member Teller Department, completely restructuring Department to increase efficiency and customer service
- Organized work flow and staggered hours based on analysis of customer traffic patterns
- Centralized equipment and supply locations for increased utility

*New Accounts Clerk* (1981–1983)

- Opened regular savings and society accounts, sold traveler's checks and bonds, and stopped payments on checks and money orders
- Administered estate and guardian accounts, securing and completing necessary tax waivers, letters of administration, and court orders
- Issued personal savings and demand loans; proved daily balances for all loans

*Teller* (1981)

- Performed full range of teller services: Conducted deposit and withdrawal transactions, issued money orders and tellers' checks, cashed checks and traveler's checks, accepted loan payments
- Maintained bank security through close scrutiny of all transactions

1979–1981    MERRILL, LYNCH, PIERCE, FENNER & SMITH, New York, New York

*Cashier*

- Accepted payment for stock margin accounts, acted as liaison with salespeople, operated teletype and PBX switchboard, responded to telephone and mail inquiries from customers

1977–1979    MANUFACTURERS HANOVER TRUST COMPANY, New York, New York

*Operator, Check Sorting Machine*

## EDUCATION

*Professional Seminars* (study sponsored by United Mutual Savings Bank)

Financial Institute of Studies, Fairfield, Connecticut
1988—Intensive one-week seminars on Branch Management, Women in Management

AIB, New York, New York
Six-week course in Life Insurance

## CERTIFICATIONS

Certified by state of New York as Notary Public and Life Insurance Agent

## AFFILIATIONS

Savings Bank Women

**ANDREW K. MELON** · 1600 Hitchcock Road · Wantagh, NY 11793 · (516) 781-7321

**OBJECTIVE** **_VICE-PRESIDENT, COMMERCIAL/INDUSTRIAL LENDING_**
(commercial bank, commercial finance company, or leasing company)

**SUMMARY** Fourteen years' industrial lending management experience, including ten as vice-president with three major commercial banking institutions. Thoroughly experienced in all aspects of credit, administration, development, collection and legal. Particular expertise in equipment financing and leasing. Managed $74 million portfolio that increased 250% over five-year period.

**EXPERIENCE**

*1988–present* LONG ISLAND TRUST COMPANY, Garden City, New York

*Vice-President, Commercial/Industrial Credit*

- Develop, originate, and administer direct and indirect loans; successfully increased portfolio from $30 million (1988) to $74 million (1993)
- Develop major customers and new business in coordination with branches
- Serve as member of Credit Committee, acting on commercial and industrial loan requests and line-of-credit renewals
- Administer all activities of department, prepare and monitor budget, oversee collections, conduct direct solicitation of new business
- Direct personnel administration; supervise staff of five
- Conceived and implemented simplified procedures and improved communications with resulting increased work flow and departmental capability

*1988* JANLIN LEASING CORPORATION, Melville, New York

*Vice-President, Credit/Marketing*

- Initiated credit investigations and established documentation procedures for processing lease and finance paper
  — Arranged for discounting paper

*1984–1988* SECURITY NATIONAL BANK, Melville, New York

*Vice-President, Monthly Payment Business Loan and Equipment Finance Departments*

- Originated, coordinated and processed direct branch loans and indirect loans through equipment dealers and leasing companies (lending authority: $250,000)
- Increased loan portfolio from $14 million to $33 million; achieved balanced mix of industries
- Prepared and periodically analyzed budget
- Reviewed recommendations on loans that exceeded staff authority limits
- Coordinated legal, accounting, and personnel functions within department; supervised staff of nine

(cont.)

SECURITY NATIONAL BANK (cont.)

- Directly negotiated loans with other bank officers, bank customers, attorneys, and accountants
- Evaluated computer reports; implemented new forms, reporting procedures and follow-up systems; created departmental operating manual

*1980–1984*    FRANKLIN NATIONAL BANK, New York, New York

*Assistant Vice-President, Metropolitan Division of Industrial Credit*

- Managed loan portfolio of $25 million, increasing loan volume by 25%
- Solicited new industrial loan customers; introduced new loan customers to other bank services including payroll accounts, trust services, letters of credit, accounts receivable financing and real estate financing
- Supervised staff of six

*1974–1980*    FEDERATION BANK AND TRUST COMPANY, New York, New York

*Assistant to Vice-President, Industrial Credit Department*

- Beginning as credit investigator and documentation clerk, was promoted to assistant cashier with medium five-figure line of credit; then to assistant vice-president with low six-figure line of credit
- Responsibilities included budget preparation, development of branch loans, overall management, and personnel direction

**EDUCATION**    New York Institute of Credit, New York, New York
1976—Business and Banking courses

Moberly Junior College, Moberly, Missouri
1972–1974—Business Administration

New York Institute of Technology, New York, New York
Business courses (continuing professional education)

# JOHN TUMINO

25 NORTHRIDGE ROAD, OLD GREENWICH, CT 06870
Home: (203) 637-6653     Office: (212) 980-8573

**OBJECTIVE**   **SENIOR MANAGEMENT, BANKING**

**SUMMARY**   Highly motivated and creative international banker with distinguished service and profitability record in New York, London, Paris and Amsterdam.

**CAREER HIGHLIGHTS**

**1983–present**   CITICORP INTERNATIONAL
New York, New York

**Vice-President for Europe, Mideast and Africa**
New York, New York (December 1986–present)
- Direct all Edge Act marketing and account service for EMEA–New York
- Control demand balances in excess of $75 million and 90% of 40,000-plus monthly transaction volume
- As senior credit officer for both parent bank and Edge Act subsidiary, govern EMEA–New York exposure
- Contributed substantially to design of deposit-based earnings credit system for Islamic clients, offsetting cost of future credit services
- Principal force in redesign of accounting and profitability models

**Vice-President and Representative** (December 1985–December 1986)
**Assistant Vice-President** (January 1984–December 1985)
Amsterdam, The Netherlands
- Managed corporate and correspondent relationships throughout 23-nation area, coordinating efforts with U.S. associates
- Directed compilation and analysis of data relative to the economics of developing nations; wrote acceptable business plans accordingly
- Met with senior ministers and heads of state throughout Africa and developed strategies for establishment of credit limits with French West Africa
- Designed and implemented special correspondent agreements with compatible European banks, in effect creating a branch network overseas for Citicorp
- Consistently surpassed annual goals set for deposit gatherings, loan volume, profitability, and staffing

**Assistant Vice-President, Corporate Finance**
London, England (February 1983–January 1984)
- Responsible, as part of team effort, for origination and implementation of new merchant and corporate capabilities for Citicorp in Europe

| | |
|---|---|
| **June 1982–**<br>**January 1983** | BANK OF AMERICA INTERNATIONAL, LTD.<br>London, England |

**Manager**
- Set up and managed umbrella administration for credit, loan services, and syndication areas

| | |
|---|---|
| **January 1980–**<br>**June 1982** | BANK OF AMERICA INTERNATIONAL S.A. (LUXEMBOURG)<br>Paris, France |

**Assistant Vice-President and Loan Officer**
Banque Ameribas
- Member of original team that formed aggressive new merchant bank. Assembled portfolio in excess of $250 million, over three-year period, on nominal capital

| | |
|---|---|
| **September 1977–**<br>**January 1980** | IRVING TRUST COMPANY<br>New York, New York |

**Assistant Manager**
- Coordinated, with treasurers and finance vice-presidents, bridge loans and stock option financing programs for major corporate relationships

| | |
|---|---|
| **October 1976–**<br>**September 1977** | TRADE BANK AND TRUST COMPANY<br>New York, New York |

**Assistant Credit Manager**

| | |
|---|---|
| **February 1975–**<br>**September 1976** | BANKERS TRUST COMPANY<br>New York, New York |

**Retail Platform Associate; Branch Operations Supervisor; Collection Clerk; Teller**

**EDUCATION**
Columbia University, B.A., Economics, 1979
University of Geneva (Switzerland), 1970, Certificate in French Language and Civilization
Joint Studies Program, Stanford University/Crocker National Bank: Advanced Techniques of Credit and Financial Analysis
New York Institute of Credit: Accounting Survey Lecture Series; Credit and the Uniform Commercial Code Lecture Series
National Credit Office: Applied Course in Credit and Financial Analysis

**LANGUAGES**
Bilingual French-English; read Dutch and Spanish

**CITATION**
*Who's Who in the World*

**MEMBERSHIPS**
New York Institute of Credit (former)
New York Credit and Financial Management Institute
U.S. Chamber of Commerce (NL) (present)

## FRED BUXTON

212 West 79th Street
New York, NY 10024
(212) 873-5123

### CONTROLLER/FINANCIAL MANAGER

**OBJECTIVE**  To fully utilize experience in management, planning and financial control

**SUMMARY**  Fourteen years' experience in financial and business planning, marketing and controller functions for a manufacturer, an airline, and a brokerage firm

**HIGHLIGHTS**
- Conceived and implemented TWA "Getaway," now the most popular of all airline credit card systems
- Assisted in negotiating the transfer of TWA control away from the Hughes organization
- As media liaison, used marketing and advertising to make general public aware of the negotiability of industrial diamonds
- Developed capacity for improving relations between factory and office workers to increase production and cut costs
- As a general manager, tightened financial controls and directed short- and long-term business planning

**EXPERIENCE**

1991–1996  **Controller** reporting to the President
SCOMILL MANUFACTURING COMPANY,
Brooklyn, New York
— Responsible for entire financial structure in a manufacturing environment
— Managed $22.3 million budget for both manufacturing and administration
— Implemented ADP data processing system for payroll and for A/P-A/R: system reduced time interval between shipment and receipt of payment

1983–1990  **General Manager**, reporting to President and
Executive Vice-President
GEMCO EQUITIES, INC., New York, New York
— Developed and managed $4.6 million budget
— Guided long-range planning as well as day-to-day operations, reporting to the President and the Executive Vice-President

**EXPERIENCE (cont.)**

— Directed new product development and product introduction strategies
— Established liaison between the industry and the public through effective marketing and advertising

1977–1983    **Director of Corporate Planning**, reporting to Operations Vice-President
TRANS WORLD AIRLINES, New York, New York
— Analyzed business trends and profits on short- and long-term basis
— Designed and implemented profit plans and control systems
— Developed and implemented TWA "Getaway" credit card

**EDUCATION**    Columbia University, New York, New York
M.B.A. in Business Finance (1977)

Georgetown University, Washington, DC
B.B.A. Magna cum laude in Business Finance (1975)
—President of Student Body

LaSalle Extension University
Dale Carnegie Course

**MILITARY**
**SERVICE**    1967–1971   U.S. Navy
Rank: Lieutenant (JG)

**SPECIAL**
**SKILLS**    Licensed pilot (Multiengine instrument rated)

# SUSAN FISHER

1400 Ocean Avenue · Brooklyn, NY 11230 · (212) 258-6575

Financial officer and operating executive with expertise in institutional administration and financial development. Functional experience in human resources management and computer accountancy.

## PROFESSIONAL EXPERIENCE

1994–1996    BENNINGTON COLLEGE, Bennington, Vermont
*Director of Business and Financial Operation*

CFO reporting directly to the President. Administer all nonacademic financial services, including personnel, budget, data processing, plant administration, auditing, purchasing, investments, real estate, and insurance administration.

— Effected savings of $250,000 annually in plant maintenance by adopting subcontracting system

— Instituted energy conservation program that reduced use of oil by 50% (300,000 barrels annually—a current cost avoidance of approximately $200,000 per annum)

— Elected Treasurer of Board of Trustees (first time in school history a nontrustee named to this position)

— Renegotiated food service contract, resulting in $120,000 annual savings, a 25% cost reduction

— Revised health and pension package to provide improved coverage at reduced cost

— Member or Chair of 14 operational, planning, and advisory committees

— Served as ERISA coordinator and Affirmative Action Officer

1984–1994    QUEENS COLLEGE, Flushing, New York
*Business Manager (1989–1994)*

Bursar, with full responsibility for accounting functions, purchasing, budget, payroll, personnel, benefits administration, auxiliary enterprises, and warehouse operations.

— Chief operations manager during period of operational budget growth from $16 million to $60 million in five years

— Personally supervised office staff of 180 people, including 4 Assistant Business Managers and 10 other professionals

— Planned and implemented Queens College's first computerized budget; negotiated unionization of food service staff

— As part of three-person team, negotiated HUD contract for $15 million

— Member or Chair of 21 operational, planning, and advisory committees

— Established principles for joint faculty-student action and supervised revision of college legislative structure as administrative member of the Ad Hoc Faculty Student Committee of campus governance; prepared final draft of college restructuring plan

QUEENS COLLEGE (cont.)
*Assistant Business Manager (1985–1989)*
*Assistant to Business Manager (1984–1985)*
(Budget Officer)

— Completely revised budget system, purchasing procedures, and accounting methods to comply with newly passed CUNY Construction Fund Law; overhaul required close collaboration with all university departments

1983–1984    WOODMERE ACADEMY, Woodmere, New York
*Assistant to Headmaster (Business Manager)*

— Administered all fiscal affairs

— Responsible for budget, payroll, purchasing, food service, plant maintenance, student transport, and general accounts

— Administrative member of Parents' Board, requiring empathy with nonacademic viewpoint

1976–1982    ADELPHI ACADEMY, Brooklyn, New York
*Assistant to Headmaster*

— Appointed Acting Chair of English Department (1978). Within a year, was made Director of Development and Fund-raising

— Conceived and directed program for tracing lost alumni: boosted funds raised by 1000%; revived contact with more than 1,000 potential donors

— Supervised financial affairs and physical plant

## OTHER EXPERIENCE

1982–1983    BROWN UNIVERSITY CLUB

— Elected to Board of Governors as full-time volunteer

— Organized three fund-raising performances—raised more than $25,000

— Chair of Brown University Bicentennial Program in New York

## EDUCATION

Columbia University: Graduate Study in School Administration
University of Michigan Graduate School of Business: Institute in Program Budgeting
Brown University: A.B., English and American Literature

## PROFESSIONAL MEMBERSHIPS

National Association of College and University Business Officers
Eastern Association of College and University Business Officers
Practicing Law Institute
American Association of Higher Education

# PETER SEATON

60 East 10th Street • New York, NY 10003
(212) 673–7321

| | |
|---|---|
| **OBJECTIVE** | FINANCIAL ANALYST |
| **SUMMARY** | Three years with active and diverse private trust. Emphasis on investment and management of assets. Evaluate investment potential of venture capital situations and going concerns, monitor holdings, troubleshoot assignments. Exposure to financial analysis in many industries and business situations. |

**EXPERIENCE**

**1991–present**  ATC COMPANY, New York, New York
Asset and Investment Analyst

*VENTURE CAPITAL PROJECTS*

Evaluate opportunities for equity participation in new ventures, conduct comprehensive project analyses, analyze long-run growth and profit potential, and recommend action.

*Example*  Recommended financing cosmetics company with innovative product concept

*Result*  Company now making an operating profit on annual sales of more than $1 million; employs 600 sales personnel in 13 states. (Subsequently appointed to Board of Directors, with full participation in financial planning and policy decisions.)

*Example*  Advised creation of a company to utilize patented Biophonics technology in greenhouse food production.

*Result*  Twenty-five production units now in operation; cost-efficient technology gives company international franchise potential.

*REAL ESTATE ASSIGNMENTS*

Cash flow and ROI analysis, purchase and sale evaluations, pro forma and operating statement preparation, determination of real estate development potential, and troubleshooting.

*Example*  On-site in Anchorage, Alaska, developed turnaround plan for 19-building apartment complex with 55% vacancy rate.

*Result*  Improved financial procedures, negotiated financing, repositioned property for the market. Vacancy rate reduced to 40% after only three months; purchase offer under consideration is $1.5 million higher than offer received prior to turnaround plan. (Definitive market survey now used by Anchorage banks.)

*Example*  Evaluated offer for one of the trust's shopping centers in Pennsylvania.

*Result*  Analysis utilized in negotiating 29% increase in offer; resulted in sale of the property.

| | |
|---|---|
| *INVESTMENT MANAGEMENT* | Charged with monitoring the performance and security of current holdings and analyzing other investment opportunities. |

> *Example*  Evaluated acceptability of common stock offered in lieu of note repayment by manufacturer of pay-TV hardware.
>
> *Result*  Identified financial weaknesses caused by confused management and marketing efforts; recommended holding the note to secure priority claim on promising technology in case of default or bankruptcy.
>
> *Example*  Analyzed opportunity to invest in regional operations of national fast food chain.
>
> *Result*  Showed profit-margin projections of investor group to be greatly overstated. Prevented potential $700,000 loss.

*OTHER ASSIGNMENTS*

Acquisition analysis of company engaged in air and ground transport for the entertainment industry

Monitor and manage securities portfolio

Negotiate distribution of assets in order to dissolve a corporation

Evaluate proposal to develop Florida Cable-TV station

**PRIOR EXPERIENCE**

Court Liaison for New York County, Court Referral Project, New York, New York
Supervised staff of 14 (1986–1989)

Supervisor, Legal Department, Samaritan Halfway Society, Inc., New York, New York
Supervised staff of 8 (1983–1986)

High School Graduate Trainee Program, Citibank, New York, New York
Trusts and Securities Operations (1981–1983)

**EDUCATION**

New York University, New York, New York (1/89–2/93)

January 1988 — B.A., Economics/Philosophy
Recipient, Arts and Sciences Scholarship
Earned 100% living expenses; worked 30 hours per week

January 1994 — Candidate for January admission to M.B.A. program at NYU

# Donald Chu

100 Hidden Lake Drive, Apt. 18L · North Brunswick, NJ 08902
*Home:* (201) 297–4340 · *Business:* (215) 293–5261

**OBJECTIVE**     *MANAGER OF FINANCIAL/ECONOMIC PLANNING*

**SUMMARY**      Directed and trained an economic and financial planning group whose members function as internal consultants to senior management. Demonstrated expertise in

— financial analysis and management reporting
— systems design and development
— short-range budgeting, expense control, and forecasting
— productivity analysis and long-range asset and resource utilization
— operations consolidation and divestiture
— oral and written communications to senior management

Group activities have resulted in significant regional productivity improvements and direct expense saving exceeding $500,000 in the past six months alone.

## EXPERIENCE HIGHLIGHTS

1990–present                                              MOBIL OIL CORPORATION
*Supervisor, Systems and Financial Analysis*     Valley Forge, Pennsylvania (1992–present)

Manage, train, and develop group of eight M.B.A. analysts responsible for systems development and financial planning to optimize return on investment. Review long-range resource requirements; coordinate management sciences activities.

- Successfully implemented politically sensitive departmental reorganization that consolidated all economic planning within controller's portfolio.
- Initiated proposal to optimize manufacturing facility that, when implemented, will pay back in 18 months and realize saving of $400,000 annually.
- Achieved 200% productivity gain within planning unit by computerization of delivery fleet statistical reporting.
- Proposed centralization of internal and external computer activities with anticipated saving of $40,000 annually.

*Senior Financial Analyst*                                      Scarsdale, New York (1992)

- Developed computer model to analyze profitability of existing business
  — Application resulted in a service station divestment program and district consolidation.
  — Annual saving of $300,000 in overhead and salaries.
- Designed and implemented a control system to ensure efficient utilization of outside time-sharing vendors and internal operations; saving of $5,000 annually.
- Restructured supervisory span of control within Credit Department to improve internal communications. As a result firm priorities were established, and past-due balances were sharply reduced.
- Established credit appraisal system for evaluating financial risk ultimately implemented by regional controller.

MOBIL OIL CORPORATION (cont.)
(1991)

*Staff Analyst*

• Increased unit productivity by more than 100% through computerization of routine management reports.
• Monitored regional service station operations budget and introduced computerized reporting system that pinpointed variances and trends.
 — Provided sales management with improved tools for sensitivity analysis.
• Significantly improved sales forecasting techniques.

*Controller Trainee* (1990)

• Prepared budget forecast of $11 million depreciation expense, 18 months in advance; actual 1978 expense was under projection, with variance of 0.2%.
• Developed for new engineering maintenance centers control and monitoring procedures that reduced administrative workload and paper flow and established financial controls.

9/87–5/94 KENDALL, BOWERS & COMPANY, INC.
*Consultant* Stamford, Connecticut (Part-time)

Performed statistical analysis for management consulting firm specializing in employee relations counseling.

9/85–8/87 MOBIL PIPELINE CORPORATION
*Pipeliner* Rochester, New York

Supervised 5 to 10 contracted hourly employees and was responsible for planning, organizing, directing, and controlling a 5-month pipeline maintenance project. Surpassed management objectives.

**EDUCATION**     New York University, New York, New York
1991—M.B.A., Corporate Finance–Quantitative Analysis
Thesis:   "An Analysis of the Impact of Vertical Divestiture on the Financial Environment of a Fully Integrated Petroleum Organization"

New York University, New York, New York
1989—B.S., Operations Management/Behavioral Science

University of Miami, Miami, Florida
1983–1985—Statistics/Psychology

**HONORS**     Founders' Day Award, New York University
Dean's Honor Roll, New York University

**PROFESSIONAL ASSOCIATIONS**     Beta Gamma Sigma Honorary Business Society
Alpha Kappa Psi Professional Business Fraternity

# John Hawkins, C.P.A.
*250 Main Street, Apt. 3G • Millburn, NJ 07041*
*Home (201) 379-4761 • Office (212) 790-5206*

**OBJECTIVE**

A senior financial management position with a publicly owned company or a large privately owned company.

**EXPERIENCE SUMMARY**

Twelve years' experience with Deloitte Haskins & Sells, an international public accounting firm. For the past two years, assigned to Executive Office in New York, where responsibilities include publication writing and departmental administration. The previous ten years, assigned to the Audit Department of the Memphis office, with client responsibilities, teaching assignments, and office administration.

**EXPERIENCE**

**Executive Office of Deloitte Haskins & Sells**    **1995–1996**
New York, New York

- Wrote the firm's booklet *Audit Committees: A Director's Guide,* describing the activities of an audit committee and presenting the firm's view toward its evolution.

- Assisted international and domestic offices in such activities as writing proposals, making contacts, and furnishing information on other firms.

- Edited practice development publications about the firm, its services, and topics of current interest to the profession and clients.

- Participated in the development of the Deloitte Haskins & Sells advertising campaign, including research in connection with the benchmark study.

- Prepared practice development programs for presentation at all national and regional firm meetings.

- Assisted in the supervision of the department, including assignments of personnel, budget preparation, and coordination of departmental activities with other departments.

**Deloitte Haskins & Sells**    **1985–1995**
Memphis, Tennessee

- Supervised audit engagements of publicly and privately owned companies. Client industries included manufacturing, insurance companies and agencies, real estate development, leasing, and agricultural, retail, and professional athletic organizations.

- Prepared constructive service letters and internal control comments for presentation to officers and directors.

- Supervised engagements for registration statements on Form S-1 and for annual reports on Form 10-K.

- Performed a special investigation for a brokerage client into the use of bond proceeds by a public utility district.

**John Hawkins, C.P.A.**/*page 2*

**Deloitte Haskins & Sells (cont.)**

- Taught at six of the firm's national and regional seminars. Topics included technical accounting, auditing, and management training.
- Designed uniform accounting system and ticket sales system for each franchise of a professional athletic league. Wrote audit programs and supervised engagement to audit gate receipts for each game played.
- Handled various administrative responsibilities for the office including manager in charge of recruiting, assignment director, and staff counselor.

**EDUCATION**

B.S., with major in Accounting, Mississippi State University, 1985.
Member, Beta Alpha Psi and Beta Gamma Sigma honor societies.

**ORGANIZATIONS**

American Institute of Certified Public Accountants and Memphis Chapter of Tennessee Society of C.P.A.'s.

Junior Achievement of Memphis; former member of Jaycees, Kiwanis, and Planning Executives Institute; Vice-President and Treasurer of a private school.

# MARY OLSON
2660 SEDGWICK AVENUE
BRONX, NY 10468

———————

HOME: (212) 298-7725

**OBJECTIVE**    Responsible position with an organization specializing in taxation and/or accounting

**SUMMARY**    More than 20 years' experience in tax accounting, preparation, and consultation, with full knowledge of federal, state, and local compliance statutes. Proven ability to interact with company presidents and controllers in effecting compliance with regulations. Expert investigator and interviewer. Capable motivator of personnel, with definitive training experience. Additional experience as insurance field representative and assistant sales manager.

## PROFESSIONAL HIGHLIGHTS

*1978–present*    NEW YORK STATE TAX DEPARTMENT, White Plains, New York
*Tax Agent*

One of 18 agents to service five-county area of Westchester, Rockland, Putnam, Sullivan, and Orange Counties

- Investigate and interview taxpayers, taxpayers' representatives and corporate executives regarding problems in compliance with tax laws
  — Secure and verify financial statements, analyze statements for accuracy, investigate claims of indebtedness
  — Interview relevant parties (bank officers, attorneys, county clerks and landlords) to determine validity of statements
  — Handle caseload of more than 1,000 annually (majority are business clients)

- Upon completion of investigation, write reports with recommendations (accepted 95% of time)
  — Payment arrangement: lay out all terms for payment
  — Seizure procedures: notify taxpayer, complete warrant, participate in confiscation actions, reverse seizure order when payment plan with sufficient control has been instituted

- Complete returns for taxpayers without accounting help
  — Ensures compliance and helps them avoid prosecution

- Assist in training new agents in enforcement proceedings

(Continuing involvement in tax return preparation and record keeping for family and friends on gratis basis)

*1979–1988*     TAX CONSULTANT (self-employed), Bronx, New York

Kept business records and prepared tax returns for clients throughout New York metropolitan area and in various other states

- Consulted with clients on all types of taxes; completed returns
  — Forms included federal, state, and local returns for taxes on payroll, sales, withholding, real estate, and personal property
- Developed clientele of more than 50 clients concurrent with Prudential employment

*1967–1988*     PRUDENTIAL INSURANCE COMPANY, Bronx, New York
*Assistant Manager* (1977–1979)

- Motivated staff to stimulate sales
  — To 50 agents in office, gave descriptive and motivational speeches dealing with aspects of successful sales techniques
- Recruited and trained new agents
- Served as mediator of complaints against agents
- Directly supervised 6 representatives

*Field Sales Representative* (1967–1977; 1979–1988)

Sold policies for life and health insurance and pension plans

- One of youngest agents ever hired by company
- Wrote more than $100,000/week four times; received numerous awards for superior salesmanship
  — Invited to annual business meeting and convention (restricted to top 20% of representatives) every year, 1967–1988
- Became No. 1 sales rep in New York in 1 year; remained in top category all 20 years of employment

**EDUCATION**     Westchester Community College, Valhalla, New York
1975–1977: Two years of Accounting

**PROFESSIONAL CERTIFICATIONS**
New York State Life Insurance License
New York State Insurance Broker's License

**MILITARY**     U.S. Marine Corps

# MORGAN JONES

250 Central Park West, New York, NY. 10010

**OBJECTIVE**    *INVESTMENT/MONEY MARKET PORTFOLIO MANAGEMENT*

**SUMMARY**    Money market economist with background in commercial/investment banking; areas of expertise include financial futures markets, cash markets, foreign exchange; interrelationships among domestic and foreign markets, and development of quantitative techniques as aids to trading

**EXPERIENCE**

1988–present    PETERS-JONES, INC., New York, New York
*Vice-President, Director of Research*

PRODUCT DEVELOPMENT
- Yield value of 1/32nd for GNMAs of different coupons and paydown rates, product useful for cash/futures positioning
- Futures parity table for various deliverable T-bonds for futures contracts
- Hedge ratio table for cash/cash arbitrage, taking into account yield and maturity effects
- Developed *new* formula for hedge ratio for T-bond spread vs. T-bill futures trades
- Developed innovative weekly chart package for firm's trade/sales personnel, permitting "ahead of the pack" Fed's policy monitoring
- Developed Implied Repo Rate Table for deliverable T-bonds, taking into account accrued interest
- Analyst and strategist on use of multiple hedging simultaneously of Eurodollar time deposit, T-bill, CD, T-bond futures

RELATED PROFESSIONAL ACTIVITIES
- Lecturer to financial professionals under the auspices of the American Management Association and the Financial Executives Institute
- Designed and implemented course on money markets for firm's trainees
- Conducted weekly information sessions for firm's trade/sales personnel on Fed's monetary policy and economic developments and their impact on financial markets
- Authored articles on short-term money market investments, use of financial futures, and SDRs for *Money Manager, Pension and Investment Age, Cash Flow Magazine,* and Lombard-Wall's in-house financial markets newsletter

1974–1988    MORGAN GUARANTY TRUST COMPANY, New York, New York
*Vice-President, International Money Management Group (1978–1980)*
- Conducted international cash management studies
- Introduced innovative procedures
  — Quantitative technique useful to exposure management function
  — A new approach to evaluation of a firm's cash management phase (resulting in indicated potential saving to client of up to $125,000 annually)
- Performed risk analyses of hedging decisions that utilized forward foreign exchange markets

MORGAN GUARANTY TRUST COMPANY (cont.)
*Vice-President/Monev Market Economist,*
*Treasurer's Division, Portfolio Investment Research Group* (1981–1986)
- Performed trade-off analysis of borrowing/lending decisions for bank's international treasury management
- Developed interest rate tracking models and forecasting techniques applicable to foreign exchange and foreign money markets as aids to traders
- Organized seminar on fundamentals of portfolio management, including spread and risk analysis and interest rate forecasting, resulting in increased effectiveness of sales staff

*Senior Operations Research Officer/Consultant to Treasurer's Division,*
*Operations Research Department* (1974–1981)
- Supervised and motivated staff of analysts charged with research into aspects of portfolio management
- Developed simulation models
  — for U.S. government bond market, used by Portfolio Manager for optimum bidding
  — for federal funds market, as aid to managing bank's daily money position
- Advised Pension Trust Department on portfolio performance evaluation techniques

| | |
|---|---|
| 1971–1974 | GRUMMAN AIRCRAFT ENGINEERING CORP., Bethpage, New York<br>*Research Mathematician* |
| 1969–1971 | UNITED AIRCRAFT RESEARCH LABORATORIES,<br>East Hartford, Connecticut<br>*Senior Mathematician* |
| 1966–1969 | STEVENS INSTITUTE OF TECHNOLOGY, Hoboken, New Jersey<br>*Research Engineer/Lecturer* |
| **EDUCATION** | 1975—M.B.A., Economics, New York University<br>1966—M.S., Applied Mathematics, Stevens Institute<br>1964—B.S., Mechanical Engineering, Stevens Institute<br>Additional studies include 1966–1969, PhD studies in Applied Mathematics, NYU; 1969, Credit and Financial Analysis Course, Dun & Bradstreet |
| **LANGUAGES** | Fluent in Russian and German<br>Familiar with French and Serbian |
| **MEMBERSHIPS** | New York Association of Business Economists |

# Lucy Ostrahand

250 Oak Drive
Philadelphia, PA 19012
(215) 547-1234

**OBJECTIVE**  SECURITIES MANAGEMENT

To employ expertise in stock research and trading portfolio investment and estate management in the Trust Department of a major bank.

**SUMMARY**
— Ten years' experience in marketing and sale of industrial and bank stocks as member
— Exhaustive researcher of growth potential ofparticular stocks in complete customer relations service
— In-depth knowledge of and marketing expertise with industrial and bank issues.
— Ninety-five percent successful selling stocks considered unmarketable

## BUSINESS HIGHLIGHTS

*1988–present*  MANN SECURITIES, Philadelphia, Pennsylvania

*Bank Stock Trader*  (1991–present)
• Initiated and instituted bank stock trading company in 1991, in addition to industrial stock trading
• Developed list of prospective customers; responsible for start-up and management of department
• Locate markets for inactive regional bank issues
• Trade stocks of 3,500 banks throughout country
• Maintain liaison with Commerce Clearing House in keeping bank quotes current and customer service timely
• Advise bank Trust Departments on buy/sell feasibility of illiquid issues
• Research and evaluate stocks for growth potential
• Responsible for increase in departmental profit from $15,000 in 1981 to more than $150,000 in 1986, with negligible additional expense to company and minimum increase in capital

*Industrial Stock Trader*  (1988–1991)
• Traded inactive industrials for clients
• Researched companies for appreciation in growth, seeking out undervalued issues and marketing to investment buyers with in-depth studies of company operation and production
• Located and traded expired tender offers

*1983–1988*  OTIS MARSHALL, INC. New York, New York
*Over-the-Counter Trading Department*

**EDUCATION**  Wagner College, Staten Island, New York
1983—B.A., Marketing/Accounting

Pace College, New York, New York
Advanced study in Industrial Psychology and Marketing

**MEMBERSHIPS** National Association of Security Dealers

# PAUL CHANG

625 WEST 10TH STREET
APT. 10E
PHILADELPHIA, PA 16411

TEL. NUMBERS:
(215) 866-2513
(215) 483-9875

**OBJECTIVE**   *PORTFOLIO MANAGER/FINANCIAL MANAGEMENT*

**SUMMARY**
— Three years' experience as an aggressive, sales-oriented brokerage house account executive
— Creative securities manager in developing options trading strategies in profitable customer service activity
— Thorough and definitive researcher into viability of market as a whole and of individual stocks
— Bilingual: English-Chinese

## BUSINESS HIGHLIGHTS

1986–present   MOORE & SCHLEY, CAMERON & CO., New York, New York

*Account Executive*

- Initiate research and development of options trading strategy for list of 50 clients; advise on covered writing
- Develop special portfolio strategies for individual customers
- Inaugurated advertising campaign in Chinese media; doubled market in Chinese community from 100 to 200 clients ($60,000 in earnings)
- Successfully developed strong leads from general advertising, with 20% conversion to sales
- Redesigned brokers' desks for maximum utility at minimum cost

1985–1986   MERRILL, LYNCH, PIERCE, FENNER & SMITH, New York, New York

*Account Executive*

- Promoted to Account Executive after short training period and charged with developing options trading strategy for account executive group
  — Completed training program in least time of any trainee

**EDUCATION**   Columbia University, Graduate School of Business
1985—M.B.A., Finance/Accounting

Columbia University, Graduate School of Arts and Sciences
1983—graduate study, Mathematical Sociology
President, Columbia Pine Society

National Taiwan University
1977—B.A., Sociology/Economics

## OTHER EXPERIENCE (in Taiwan)

1978–1980   CHINA AIRLINE—Supervisor, Traffic Department
1975–1977   ACADEMIA SINICA—Quantitative analysis of population survey of Taiwan
1973–1975   *CHINA DAILY NEWS*—Frequent analysis of foreign press articles

# STEPHEN BOGS

1410 Allison Road ▪ Providence, RI 03410
(401) 441-6620

**OBJECTIVE**  *INVESTIGATOR—CLAIMS/COLLECTIONS*

To apply in-depth experience with highly sophisticated collection and investigation procedures on behalf of corporate financial institution

**SUMMARY**  More than seven years with Internal Revenue Service as an officer in charge of investigation and resolution of business and personal tax problems. In-depth understanding of businesses, including collection, investigation, interviewing, and bookkeeping procedures. Knowledge of computer programming. Capable administrator and supervisor of personnel. Skills transferable to corporate application.

## HIGHLIGHTS OF EXPERIENCE

*1985–present*  INTERNAL REVENUE SERVICE
Providence, RI

*Revenue Officer*

Charged with independent responsibility for investigation and determination of tax claims against large accounts ($50,000 or more), with full authority to resolve problems

- Perform complex credit analyses in connection with tax liens, collateral agreements, and uncollectable accounts
- Conduct intensive investigations of large corporations and prominent high-income individuals to uncover hidden assets, analyze financial condition, and determine valuation of properties
- Maintain comprehensive and practical knowledge of current collection techniques, including
  — laws on rights of creditors
  — forced assessment and collection
  — lien priorities and bankruptcies
  — summons procedures
  — interpretation of public records
  — application of such laws and procedures in extremely complex and often delicate situations
- Originated new techniques and creative approaches in application of general tax and collection guidelines
- Developed keen ability to influence, motivate, interview, and educate persons who are generally fearful and uncooperative, through use of sophisticated interpersonal skills
- Assist taxpayers in understanding of regulations; negotiate payment schedules to fulfill obligations
- Serve as technical expert in matters before the tax court
- Serve as classroom instructor in training of IRS personnel; evaluate courses and recommend changes
- Received steady promotions to highest level in job category

*3/84–7/84*     DEPARTMENT OF SOCIAL SERVICES
*and*          Pawtucket, RI
*8/81–3/82*     *Caseworker*

- Investigated and assisted people on welfare
  — Determined need for assistance and made recommendations
- Worked independently in the field

**MILITARY**     U.S. Army, West Germany
4/82–1/84—Personnel and Administrative Specialist (Spec/5)

**EDUCATION**    St. John's University, Jamaica, New York
1981—B.A., Social Sciences
1984—Graduate School (courses in Accounting, Statistics, and Business Management)

Control Data Institute, New York, New York
1984–1985—Courses in Computer Programming (FORTRAN, COBOL)

# HUMAN RESOURCES
# & DEVELOPMENT

# LARRY M. HEINEMANN

481 SAMPSON STREET
ESCANABA, MI 49474
(616) 473-8613

**OBJECTIVE:    HUMAN RESOURCES MANAGEMENT**

**FANCHON FINANCIAL INFORMATION GROUP**, Escanaba, Michigan          1995–present
**Office of the President**

*Quick America:* Developed organization plans, formulated recruiting strategy, and coordinated all technical and managerial hiring for this real-time market data vendor's Installation, Marketing, Network, Sales, and Systems Departments, minimizing third-party recruiting cost.

*Quick Fanchon News:* Recruited the start-up team for this on-line financial news bureau, which recently attained 10,000 inquiries a week.

*Quick America and ONN:* Wrote human resource policy and advised regarding compensation, benefit, and related business issues.

**HEINEMANN ASSOCIATES**, Marquette, Michigan          1990–present

*Customer Service and Leadership Training:* Identify areas for development and conduct programs: American Express, Champion International, Kodak, New York Stock Exchange, Northern Telecom, Pfizer International, and Weyerhauser Forest Products. Volunteer Project: Institute of East/West Studies.

*Outplacement:* Assist with organizational upgrades and conduct group and individual career transition programs: American BankShares, Home Insurance, GE Consulting Services, Signet Bank, and Textron Lycoming.

**MILWAUKEE TIMES COMPANY**, Milwaukee, Wisconsin          1989–1990

*Corporate Director, Employee Relations:* Assessed, developed, and implemented programs and policies regarding employee climate in 53 subsidiaries. Recommendations spanned all areas affecting organizational performance, including productivity, union-free environment, management techniques, job enrichment, and physical plant.

Left the *Times* to develop personnel consulting business as part of Moran, Stahl & Boyer, premier relocation consultants, until core businesses were sold in 1990. Heinemann Associates founded at that time.

**THE DUN & BRADSTREET CORPORATION**, New York, New York          1980–1989

*Director of Human Resources*
*Reuben H. Donnelly Corporation* (1986–1989)

Reported to President. Member of Senior Management Committee. Responsible for organizational development and management education for 4,000 employees. Managed corporate staff of 15 professionals and three regional staffs of about the same size.

As a result of the breakup of AT&T, D&B Corporate subdivided this $1 billion yellow page sales division into three decentralized units. I retained human resources control of three fourths of the original organization, but was recruited by the *New York Times* for increased responsibilities.

## THE DUN & BRADSTREET CORPORATION (cont.)

*Corporate Manager of Management Development* (1983–1986)

Advised 200 D&B subsidiary General Managers in the development and implementation of management recruitment, staffing, and developmental activities. Designed and implemented an interactive database containing skills and work history of top 2,000 managers world-wide.

*Manager of Corporate Office Personnel and Assistant to Vice-President* (1980–1983)

Staff consultant to 50 subsidiary Personnel Managers in all phases of human resources policy and practice. Responsible for all personnel programs associated with recruiting and compensating of D&B headquarters staff. Coordinated implementation of first corporate-wide payroll, benefit, and personnel system.

## ROBERT H. SCHAFFER & ASSOCIATES  (1975–1980)

*Consultant:* Advised clientele in the private and public sectors regarding organizational effectiveness in the areas of productivity, product quality, customer service, and working environment. Clients included Canadian National Railway, Union Carbide Corp., Uniroyal, and the New York State Department of Education.

## OTHER EXPERIENCE

| | |
|---|---|
| 1994 | Coauthored two books released by John Wiley & Sons. A complete guide to job search: *Conquer Resume Objections*, and *Conquer Interview Objections*. Nominated as Book of the Year. |
| 1991 | Seminar Leader<br>Columbia University Business School |
| 1980–1990 | Adjunct Lecturer<br>New School for Social Research |
| M.B.A.—1975 | Columbia University Business School<br>Marketing and Corporate Relations |
| 1972–1975 | First Lieutenant, U.S. Army<br>Instructional Methods Division<br>Corps of Engineers, Headquarters |
| B.A.—1972 | St. John Fisher College<br>Rochester, New York |

## JUDITH AARONSON    84 Apple Road, Jamaica, NY. 11432 · (212) 523-3082

**OBJECTIVE**     **Pension Specialist or Administrator**

To fully utilize my experience in the field of pension benefits in a challenging position as a pension consultant or administrator.

**EXPERIENCE**     HARRY ALLAN CONSULTANTS, INC., New York, New York
**Research Assistant**

*1988–present*     Conduct pension and actuarial research as it relates to company's actuaries, consultants, and clients

— Review, digest, and abstract from newspaper and magazine articles pertaining to pension law
— Read and review from wide variety of industry and government publications articles dealing with health, life insurance, and actuarial studies
— Conduct telephone and written surveys based on client needs

METROPOLITAN LIFE INSURANCE COMPANY, New York, New York
**Issue Technician** (January 1988–July 1988)

*June 1987–*
*June 1988*     Issued Deposit Administration and Immediate Participating Guarantee contracts for roster of corporate clients

Drafted specimen plans, summary plan descriptions, and plan amendments to comply with client request for IRS final regulations

Prepared IRS Forms 5300, 5301, and 5302

Heavy ERISA research and analysis, utilizing experts in the field and drawing on government regulations

**Valuation Technician** (June 1987–January 1988)

Prepared actuarial valuation reports, summary annual reports, employee benefit statements, and employee census reports

Worked with Entry Age Normal and Frozen Initial Liability methods

Prepared IRS Schedules A, B, and 5500-C

NEW ENGLAND LIFE INSURANCE COMPANY, New York, New York
**Pension Benefit Analyst**

*1984–1987*     Analyzed pension benefit plans and contracts

Calculated benefits for quotations and retirements

Worked with deferred annuities and deposit administration cases

Trained new employees in calculation formulas and benefits purchase

**EDUCATION**     LONG ISLAND UNIVERSITY, M.A., Political Science, 1985

JOHN JAY COLLEGE, B.A., American Government/Constitutional Law, 1984

*Helen Scofield*

25 Hill Street
Boston, MA 02105
(617) 266-2575

**OBJECTIVE**   FOOD SERVICE MANAGEMENT

**SUMMARY**   Three years' experience in institutional food service and dietary consultation. Strong skills in supervision, menu planning, food preparation, forecasts and cost control. Ability to plan nutritious meals, including dietetic and vegetarian dishes, within budget.

**PROFESSIONAL HIGHLIGHTS**

August 1988–
present

HARVARD UNIVERSITY DINING SERVICES
Cambridge, Massachusetts

*Dining Services Supervisor*

- Supervise 35 persons in operation of college residence dining hall
- Write monthly marketing newsletter directed to dining service consumers
- Prepare data in order forecasting, menu planning, and inventory control for computer system
- Upgraded nutritional value of meals for 500 college students
- Developed menu cycle, lowering food cost and boosting profits for unit
- Established sanitation schedule

September 1987–
August 1988

BUREAU OF SCHOOL FOOD SERVICES OF BOARD OF EDUCATION
White Plains, New York

*School Lunch Manager*

- Supervised food service staff in four public schools
- Redesigned forms for evaluating employee performance
- Responsible for menu planning, food preparation service, scheduling, purchasing, inventory, payroll, and sanitation
- Designed food preference questionnaire (adopted and used by 19 schools)
- Set up Nutrition Committee to promote nutrition education and to obtain feedback from students, faculty, and parents

**EDUCATION**   Hunter College, New York, New York
1986—B.S., Foods and Nutrition
Additional Courses:
   Vegetarian Cookery, Yoga Institute, New York, New York
   Educational Writing, Pace University, White Plains, New York

**AFFILIATIONS**

   American Home Economics Association
   American Dietetic Association

# DORA MARTINEZ

80-12 180th Avenue
Howard Beach, NY 11414
(212) 845-6695

**OBJECTIVE**     DIRECTOR OF HUMAN RESOURCES

Personnel Manager with nine years' experience in human resources administration. Demonstrated ability to work effectively and congenially with employees at diverse levels. Comprehensive knowledge of recruitment, screening, and interviewing; policy implementation; benefits administration; and staff supervision. Adept at labor negotiations. Innovator with ability to increase employee morale and improve communications. Experience includes management, staffing and establishment of personnel procedures for two new facilities of a major corporation.

## PERSONNEL EXPERIENCE

1985–present     PERMITRON ULTRASONICS, DIVISION OF PERMITRON CORPORATION
Long Island City, New York
> Major manufacturer of biomedical, dental, and surgical equipment and industrial applications of ultrasonic technology (union shop with 160 employees)

*Personnel Manager*

- Responsible for recruitment, screening and interviewing of exempt, nonexempt, and hourly personnel for diversified employment areas
  — Maintain staffing of technical, electronics, research, medical, production instrument assembly, plant management, and general clerical functions
- Also responsible for staffing of New Jersey acquisition and new Connecticut facility while handling full personnel management functions in Long Island City office
- Extensively involved in labor relations, including participation in contract negotiations, administration, and interpretation of union contract and close interface with union
- Interpret and oversee implementation of all personnel policies; control administration of comprehensive employee benefit programs
- Introduced measures to improve communications and establish employment incentives
  — Created and issued first policy manual
  — Established ten-year service award club to promote better relationship between labor and management
  — Initiated company newspaper
- Establish and maintain EEO guidelines; ensure compliance with federal and state regulations

(cont.)

PERMITRON ULTRASONICS (cont.)

- Conduct wage and salary analyses to ensure competitive compensation position in industry
- Regularly achieve 30% under budget allocation for placement advertising and employment agency commissions
- Supervise 3-person department; delegate work flow to 15-person clerical staff

1984–1985    SINGER COMPANY, New York, New York

*Assistant, Compensation and Benefits Department*

- Assisted Director of Compensation and Benefits with office administration; processing of benefit action forms and payroll action forms on terminations, transfers, salary increases, and new employees; and all related correspondence
- Oriented employees relocating overseas regarding cultural, social, and psychological adjustments

1978    EQUITABLE LIFE ASSURANCE COMPANY, New York, NY

*Administrative Assistant*

- Assisted Director of Group Insurance Department
- Tour guide, responsible for orientation tours for new employees and visitors

*EDUCATION*    Queens College, Queens, New York
Business Major
1985–present—Numerous seminars on personnel and management, sponsored by AMA and other institutions

*PROFESSIONAL AFFILIATIONS*

International Association of Personnel Women
Queens Personnel Management Association

# MAY NELSON

10 Maple Avenue
Bedford Hills, NY 10507
Home: (914) 241-3420     Office: (212) 719-9233

## OBJECTIVE

*CORPORATE PERSONNEL*—Position in recruitment coordination with excellent potential for growth into personnel management

## SUMMARY

B.A. in Psychology/Business and continuing record of successful personnel experience. Adept at interpersonal and interdepartmental communications. Fully knowledgeable of laws governing recruitment procedures. Exceptional recruitment and counseling abilities. Strong organizational skills.

## PERSONNEL EXPERIENCE

*1990–present*   CAREER BLAZERS PERSONNEL SERVICES, New York, New York

*Branch Manager, Career Blazers Learning Center* (1994–present)

- Recruit full-time and temporary support staff, such as administrative assistants, secretaries, and other clerical personnel, for client corporations
  — Screen and interview applicants to match client specifications
  — Achieve exceptionally high level of client satisfaction through astute recruitment and perceptive counseling of personnel

- Enhance marketability and curriculum of Learning Center by counseling graduates regarding business etiquette and procedures
  — Increase confidence levels of graduates through placement in low-risk temporary employment slots in client companies
  — Coach graduates in telephone etiquette, proper dress and grooming, and behavioral expectations

- Call on clients and assist in coordinating evening seminars to establish awareness of Learning Center, create climate of acceptance, and increase utilization of available facilities
  — Reactivated approximately 25 resigned accounts as direct result of calls

*Assignment Manager, Career Blazers Temporary Services* (10/93–2/94)

- Recruited temporary applicants for client firms in areas of finance, marketing, advertising, and manufacturing

- Coordinated long-term project for R. J. Reynolds Tobacco Company requiring 50 to 60 models weekly for large-scale public relations project

*1989–1990*   UNION MUTUAL INSURANCE COMPANY, Elmsford, New York

*Disability Benefit Specialist*

- Interviewed approximately 40 prospective employees through company's College Recruitment Program and hired 15 for entry-level positions in sales and disability benefits
- Conducted full field investigations to determine validity of questionable claims
  — Worked closely with physicians, lawyers and other professionals to determine eligibility of claims
- Upgraded communications between Sales and Benefits Departments, bringing about substantial improvements in client services
  — Set up monthly meetings between Sales and Benefits Departments at 12 district offices and clearly defined long-term goals and short-term objectives
  — Gave lecture and participated in sales seminar for 200 employees
- Simplified insurance policy terminology for benefit of policy holders and claimants
- After only one year with company, invited to apply for supervisory position normally requiring a minimum of three years

## EDUCATION

State University of New York at Oneonta
1989—B.A., Psychology/Business and Economics

*Willing to relocate*

**LISA HOHMANN** • 73 Bleecker Street, #4B • New York, NY 10012 • (212) 260–8950

**OBJECTIVE**    *TRAINING COORDINATOR*

**SUMMARY**    Ten years' experience as trainer, manager, and occupational therapist designing rehabilitation and training programs for individuals and corporations. Knowledge of affirmative action legislation as it applies to both private and public sectors.

**BACKGROUND**    NEW YORK UNIVERSITY, New York, New York, Current

*Coordinator, National Interpreter Training Consortium*
$300,000 grant program for training development throughout the United States

- Responsible for collection, evaluation, and dissemination of information
  — Provide resource information
    • On national level, conceived on-site internship program for Executive Director of National Registry of Interpreters for Deaf
    • On local level, conducted training workshops throughout Northeast area
    • Preparation of quarterly and annual reports to DHHS

- Designed policy guidelines for disabled students and interpreter services involving all the schools' adjunct services of New York University

- Supervise staff of 20

- Production of training videotapes (produced by Ted Estabrook) available commercially throughout the United States to state and civic service organizations and private business sector
    • Wrote script for 35-minute tape
    • Cast tape, using more than 20 people

GOODWILL INDUSTRIES, New York, NY, 1994–1995

*Program Development/Deafness Specialist*

- Served as liaison between Office of Vocational Rehabilitation and Goodwill Industries
    • Responsible for counseling 60 clients regarding employment, training, medical, and other support services
    • Supervised internship program for graduate students
- Developed program for disabled clients and employees
    • Secured cooperation from business sector in providing individualized job orientation
    • Secured interpreters for clients and arranged for special tutors at no cost to Goodwill through effective use of available human resources
    • Developed human resource orientation program for corporations

FEDERATION EMPLOYMENT & GUIDANCE SERVICE, New York, New York, 1993–1994

*Rehabilitation Counselor*

- Managed programs of New York State rehabilitation clients
  — Provided evaluation and counseling services to adults with all disabilities
  — Developed all services for deaf clients
  — Administered in-service training for staff

CROTCHED MOUNTAIN CENTER, Greenfield, New Hampshire, 1988–1993

*Occupational Therapist*

- Evaluated clients' physical and emotional needs; devised individualized programs for all ages, all disabilities
  — Supervised all therapy aides, assistants, and students
  — Was instrumental in establishing departmental staff meetings between school and rehabilitation center
  — Served as Acting Director of department in 1992
  — Developed pioneer therapeutic horseback riding program for 40 students
  — As Secretary-General for Northeast Wheelchair Games, was responsible for housing, meals, and qualifying events for more than 120 participants

**OTHER EMPLOYMENT**

NEW YORK UNIVERSITY

*Adjunct Instructor*
Sign language for graduate students in School of Education and adults from School of Continuing Education (1993–1996)

*Sign Language Interpreter*
Deaf graduate students (1993–1994)

**EDUCATION**

New York University
M.A.—1994, Deafness Rehabilitation
Awarded full fellowship

Utica College of Syracuse University
B.S.—1988, Occupational Therapy

**PROFESSIONAL CERTIFICATIONS**

Rehabilitation Counselor, Certified Rehabilitation Counselor
National Registry of Interpreters for the Deaf, Sign Language Interpreter, C.S.C.

**AFFILIATIONS**

American Deafness and Rehabilitation Association (Chairperson, 1995–1996)
American Society for Training and Development

# JOSHUA HARRIS

220-01 124th Road · Laurelton, NY 11413

Business: (212) 978-4515                                    Home: (212) 580-9950

---

**OBJECTIVE**   *SECURITY MANAGEMENT*

**SUMMARY**   Ten years' experience as an officer with award-winning record in crime prevention and apprehension of perpetrators in New York City subways. Worked in both Uniform and Plainclothes Divisions. High conviction record. Established community relations, effectively reducing neighborhood crimes. Business experience includes training and motivating personnel.

### HIGHLIGHTS OF POLICE WORK
*(See page 2 for business experience)*

1981–1991   NEW YORK CITY TRANSIT POLICE DEPARTMENT, New York, New York

*Plainclothes Patrol*                                        (1987–1991)

- Initiated and conducted for employees of New York Telephone Company training programs in self-protection from robbery and assault in Grand Concourse Station
  — Approximately 100 employees attended each of three seminars in Telephone Company offices
  — Resulted in demonstrably appreciable rate of reduction of platform crimes, especially on paydays

- Investigated numerous robbery and assault complaints
  — Resulted in 25 to 30 arrests
  — Supplied District Attorney's office and grand jury with hard evidence, resulting in conviction of perpetrators
  — Testified successfully in court

- Worked closely with community organizations to decrease neighborhood crime
  — Strategy of coordinating patrol patterns with self-protective measures created dramatic drop in robbery and assault offenses

*Uniform Patrol*                                        (1981–1987)

- Responsible for revenue protection in mid-town Manhattan (protection of coin booths)
- Rode subway patrol; was responsible for apprehension of approximately 75 robbery suspects over period of service
- Practiced crime prevention on one-to-one basis by warning individuals of incorrect self-protective measures on subway platforms and on trains
- Was awarded decorations for distinguished police duty
  — Received 3 Meritorious Service Awards
  2 Distinguished Service Awards
  2 Honorable Mentions
  2 Letters of Merit

## BUSINESS EXPERIENCE

1991–present  **O-M OFFICE SERVICES/SUPPLIES COMPANY**
New York, New York

*Senior Buyer*
- Purchase all office supplies and equipment at wholesale for resale at retail
  — Maintain correspondence by mail and telephone with manufacturers
  — Administer bid procedure for quantity and large-ticket items
- Supervise staff of four employees

1978–1981  **CBS TELEVISION**
New York, New York

*Purchasing Expeditor*
- Responsible for accurate processing of all purchase orders and timely delivery of equipment and supplies
- Communicated with vendors; maintained liaison between vendors and departmental purchasing authorities
- Followed through on all purchase orders; handled problems smoothly
- Trained three additional expediters

## EDUCATION

Modesto Junior College, Modesto, California
1978—Associate in Accounting

## MILITARY

U.S. Air Force; honorable discharge with rank of Airman 2/c
1974–1978

# THELMA L. CUMMINGS

175 West 73rd Street, #8G
New York, NY. 10025

WORK (212) 960-2137
HOME (212) 496-4142

**OBJECTIVE**  *HOSPITAL ADMINISTRATOR*

Managerial/administrative position at the departmental level or in core administration

**SUMMARY**  M.P.A. degree and four years' experience in health care administration. Prepare and review budgets up to $500,000. Adept at troubleshooting and formulating systems to solve operational problems. Extensive personnel experience, including ability to supervise, motivate and counsel employees.

## HEALTH CARE ADMINISTRATION EXPERIENCE

1986–present  ST. JOSEPH'S HOSPITAL CENTER, New York, N.Y.
*Administrative Manager*, Emergency Services Department (1979–present)

Administer all aspects of Emergency Department, including line supervision of clerical staff of 21. Prepare budget and review expenditures, formulate and interpret departmental policies for all personnel; purchase and maintain equipment, oversee M.D. staffing of Screening Clinic

- Reduced projected overtime requirements by 40% annually through institution of relief position with staggered hours; cut overtime costs and improved staff morale
- Department came within budget in 1987 for first time in three years, owing to careful budget preparation based on actual spending adjusted for projected growth and inflation, monthly review of expenditures, and investigation of unusual expenses
- Upgraded levels of supervisory personnel in order to clarify lines of authority and improve accountability for clerical performance
- Conceived and implemented weekly multidisciplinary conference for review of problems and recommendation of appropriate actions, significantly improving both communication and staff cooperation

1985–1986  MONTESSORI HOSPITAL AND MEDICAL CENTER OF BROOKLYN, Brooklyn, N.Y.
*Manager, Personnel Grants*

Organized and administered operations of CETA on-the-job training program for 34 employees, including orientation, counseling, and partial supervision; ensured conformity to governmental regulations and effective liaison with outside agencies; initiated and maintained all data systems

- Hospital grossed more than $65,000 in nine months, owing to careful program implementation and monitoring
- Compiled and wrote CETA manual, clarified and systematized hospital's responsibilities for participation and reimbursement, and provided continuity for program administration
- Participated in personnel employment and wage/salary activities—for instance, communicated with union hiring hall, screened applicants, conducted salary surveys, and wrote job descriptions

1985     NEW YORK HOSPITAL, New York, New York
*Administrative Resident*

Rotated through hospital departments, line responsibility as Administrator-on-Call, completed special projects as assigned

- Successfully coordinated and collected Medicaid and Blue Cross surveys required for reimbursement in one-twelfth normal time; resulted in recommendation for employment at MHMCB
- Proposed systematization of photocopying operations and equipment for projected savings of 30%; data generated from this study was used to help equip new hospital under construction

## BUSINESS AND PUBLIC SERVICE EXPERIENCE

1985     DAVID DONLAN FOR COUNTY EXECUTIVE (political campaign), Garden City, New York
*Office Manager/Bookkeeper*

Set up systems for cash flow and fiscal operations, prepared financial statements for submission to Board of Elections, and arranged meetings with community and political leaders

1983     PILOT FABRICS CORPORATION, New York, New York
*Assistant Convertor/Shipping Supervisor*

Assisted in directing conversion of raw goods to finished textiles; served as liaison and troubleshooter to ensure on-schedule activity of mills, dyers, and truckers; and maintained effective communications with customers

1980-1981     UNITED WAY OF GREATER NEW YORK, New York, New York
*Fund-Raiser*

Organized and assisted campaign committees and groups; arranged promotional, educational, and fund-raising events

**EDUCATION**     NEW YORK UNIVERSITY, GRADUATE SCHOOL OF PUBLIC ADMINISTRATION, New York, New York
1985—M.P.A., Health Policy, Planning and Administration (4.0 cumulative average)

NEW YORK UNIVERSITY, WASHINGTON SQUARE COLLEGE, New York, New York.
1979—B.A., Religion (Founders' Day Honors Certificate; 3.9 cumulative average)

VASSAR COLLEGE, Poughkeepsie, New York
1974–1976—64 credits toward B.S., Religion and Biology (Dean's List)

Additional Professional Study:
1986—Grants Writing Seminar, North Group of Falls Church, Virginia
1982—Group Dynamics in Human Relations, New School for Social Research

**AFFILIATIONS**     American Public Health Association
American Hospital Association

# VILMA COVINAS

25 Locust Street
New York, New York 10040
(212) 304-6090

## OBJECTIVE

**EXECUTIVE POSITION AS NURSING ADMINISTRATOR OR DIRECTOR OF OPERATING ROOM/RECOVERY ROOM SERVICES**

## SUMMARY

Eighteen years' progressive leadership and administrative experience in a large, technologically advanced operating and recovery room complex. Strong background in planning, organizing, coordinating, directing, and evaluating patient care programs, management and operational systems, and orientation and staff development programs, as well as facilities expansion and renovation. Experienced in developing and analyzing patient scheduling, staffing and management information systems. Skilled in budgetary and fiscal management, with responsibility for administering $10 million budget. Expert in labor relations and contract administration. Well versed in interdisciplinary project management, problem solving, and communications. Knowledgeable about regulatory standards, medicolegal considerations, quality assurance, and cost reimbursement processes.

## EXPERIENCE

**FLOWER FIFTH AVENUE HOSPITAL,** New York, New York

*1981–present*  **Assistant Director of Nursing, OR/RR Division** (1991–present)

Manage delivery of safe and effective patient care in 35 operating rooms and 28-bed recovery rooms, requiring supervision of 225 professional and auxiliary nursing personnel and coordination with appropriate medical and hospital services

- Responsible for strategic planning, implementation, coordination, and evaluation of patient care programs and network of management and operational systems
  - Instituted nine new clinical programs in 1990 alone
  - Organized ambulatory surgery program
  - Devised synchronized system for OR scheduling and bed reservation
  - Planned and operationalized OR/RR transport system
  - Designed and implemented OR-CSS case cart exchange system, including standardization and cataloging of all instrument sets
  - Instituted system to expedite blood reservation and delivery for OR

- Establish and maintain effective staffing patterns, recruitment, retention, staff development and labor relations programs.
  - Devised formula for determining staffing requirements, with target of professional nursing staff providing intra- and postoperative care

**FLOWER FIFTH AVENUE HOSPITAL**

**Assistant Director of Nursing, OR/RR Division** (cont.)

— Developed and implemented orientation programs for nursing staff, residents, and medical and nursing students

— Initiated clinical preceptor and specialty rotation programs

— Reduced staff turnover rate from 10% to 1% by providing for expeditious fulfillment of vacancies and establishing atmosphere conducive to high morale and retention

— Coconducted Philippine recruitment, resulting in hiring of 100 nurses

• Develop and implement policies and procedures; monitor compliance

— Wrote and compiled specialty procedure/policy manuals for OR, RR, Cystoscopy, Endoscopy, Hyperbaric Chamber, and Ambulatory Surgery

— Wrote job description for all categories of divisional personnel

— Initiated and maintained surgeons' preference card system

— Developed and implemented risk management/quality assurance programs

— Directed activities relative to three successful JCAH inspections

• Project, prepare, and monitor capital and operating budget ($10 million) for ten cost centers; established OR/RR charging system

— Administer materials handling and cost containment program

— Negotiated contracts for procurement of high-usage/expenditure items

— Initiated standardization and development of perpetual suture inventory system, with consolidation of backup and ordering through CSS

— Initiated inventory system for grafts, implants, and orthopedic prostheses

— Initiated program for preventive maintenance and repair of specialized equipment

—Formalized mechanism for processing new program/product requests with budgetary impact

• Develop effective system for maintaining clinical and administrative records and reports

— Designed and implemented patient operative records

— Devised statistical system for reporting caseload and utilization

— Participated in development of computerized management information system, in conjunction with systems analysts, computer consultants, and programmers

VILMA COVINAS/page 3

**FLOWER FIFTH AVENUE HOSPITAL**

**Assistant Director of Nursing, OR/RR Division** (cont.)

- Plan, organize, and coordinate facilities expansion and renovation
  - Participated in planning, functional programming and establishment of current OR/RR facility, including selection/installation of equipment, as well as reorganization and expansion of staffing system
  - Coordinated renovation of ambulatory surgery and endoscopy suites
  - Planned for expansion of current RR facility
  - Participated on hospital advisory committee and ambulatory and surgical working groups in planning new hospital, including nation-wide on-site survey of major tertiary care hospitals

- Represent the nursing department in hospital and community activities
  - Participated on Medical Board Committees on Surgery, Medical Standards, Infection Control, and Disaster Planning, as well as various hospital project management teams and task forces
  - Represented the hospital on the New York City Health and Hospital Corporation–Emergency Medical Services Hyperbaric Advisory Council

**Nurse Coordinator, Operating Room/Recovery Room Division** (1990–1991)
35 operating rooms and 28-bed recovery rooms

**Clinical Supervisor, Gaisman Surgical Suite** (1988–1990) 13 rooms

1980–1981    ENGLEWOOD HOSPITAL, Englewood, New Jersey
**Staff Nurse, Operating and Recovery Room**

1978–1980    MARGARET HAGUE MATERNITY HOSPITAL, Jersey City, New Jersey
**Exchange Visitor, Labor and Delivery/Operating Room Units**

1977–1978    UNIVERSITY OF THE EAST MEDICAL CENTER, Manila, Philippines
**Staff Nurse, Surgical Unit**

EDUCATION    **COLUMBIA UNIVERSITY, TEACHERS COLLEGE,** New York, New York
1988—Master of Arts in Nursing Service Administration

**UNIVERSITY OF THE PHILIPPINES COLLEGE OF NURSING,** Manila, Philippines
1977—B.S., Nursing (College Scholar, two semesters; Entrance Scholar)

Completed numerous career-oriented continuing education courses sponsored by AORN, American College of Surgeons, American Society of Anesthesiologists, American Management Associations, Ethicon, AMSCO, and others.

## LICENSURE

Professional nurse licensure in New York and New Jersey

## CERTIFICATION

Professional Achievement in OR Nursing Practice, 1987–1990 (AORN)

## AFFILIATIONS

American Nurses Association and New York State Nurses Association

Association of Operating Room Nurses, Inc.: Various offices held in New York City Chapter, including President, Vice-President, Secretary, and Board Member; chair of various committees: Chapter Delegate to AORN Congress 13 years (Delegate Chair two years): Test Pool Item Writer, AORN Certification Examination; Chapter Liaison to National AORN Research Committee, 1989–present

Advisory Council of National AORN Committee for Collaboration with Industry

Medical-Surgical Industry Product Development/Evaluation Panels

Philippine Nurses Association of New York, Inc., President, 1990–1991

## PRESENTATIONS

"Documentation of Patient Care in the OR," AORN Conference, New York, New York, 1982

"O.R. Scheduling," AORN Conference, New York, New York, 1989

"Surgery, Then What? Patterns of Disfigurement," AORN Regional Workshop, New York, New York, 1989

"Developing the Operating Room Module for a Hospital Disaster Plan," 25th National AORN Congress, New Orleans, Louisiana, 1986

"Ethical, Moral, and Legal Aspects of Organ Homotransplantation," American Association of Critical Care Nurses Seminar, New York, New York, 1980

"Hazards of Ethylene Oxide Sterilizations," AORN-NCE Regional Institute, New York, New York, 1983

"Developing, Implementing, and Evaluating Nursing Care Plans for Patients in Surgery," AORN, New York City Chapter Workshop, 1981

# PENNY MORGAN

| | |
|---|---|
| 210-20 Village Road, Apt. 80A | Home: (212) 591-9791 |
| Parkway Village | or (212) 723-7244 |
| Jamaica, NY 11435 | Business: (212) 592-4180 |

**OBJECTIVE**  *SENIOR CHILD CARE COUNSELOR*

**SUMMARY**  Highly experienced in counseling/consultation with adolescents in institutional setting designed on campus plan or in a group home setting. Firm though sympathetic toward personal problems. Expert in motivating youngsters to complete education and aspire to vocational independence. Capable administrator, achieving satisfactory results within limited budget.

## HIGHLIGHTS OF PROFESSIONAL EXPERIENCE

1984–present  ST. JOSEPH'S CHILDREN'S SERVICES, Brooklyn, New York
*Senior Child Care Worker*
- Manage household, administer budget, supervise staff
- Care for physical, emotional, and spiritual needs of adolescent residents, ages 14 to 18; give support and affection
  - Consult on goal orientation, emphasize religion as a positive force in their lives, and help them see parents as positive role models, establish idea of organized and productive living (budgeting time and money for short- and long-range planning), and see how to help their younger siblings
  - Motivated at least 12 residents to return to school full-time
  - Motivated at least 3 to overcome alcohol problems
- Provide alternative activities—take them to plays, involve them in drama classes
- Motivate residents to learn vocational trades, and become self-reliant and self-supporting rather than rely on welfare for support
  - One recent resident completed course in pattern making and is now lucratively employed
- Interact with community as agency representative; interpret policies and principles of agency

1978–1983  LEAKE & WATTS CHILDREN'S HOME, Yonkers, New York
*Senior Child Care Worker*
- Duties similar to those at St. Joseph's

**EDUCATION**  Oxford and Cambridge Senior School Certificate

## LICENSES/CERTIFICATES

University of North Carolina
- 1987–1988, Group Child Care Consultant, School of Social Work
- General Certificate, Child Care Work

Swedish Institute, Stockholm, Sweden
- General Practices, Emotionally Disturbed and Handicapped Children

RESUMES•RESUMES•RESUMES•RESUMES•RESUMES•RESUMES•RESUMES
•RESUMES•RESUMES•RESUMES•RESUMES•RESUMES•RESUMES•RESUME
S•RESUMES•RESUMES•RESUMES•RESUMES•RESUMES•RESUMES•RESUM
ES•RESUMES•RESUMES•RESUMES•RESUMES•RESUMES•RESUMES•RESU
MES•RESUMES•RESUMES•RESUMES•RESUMES•RESUMES•RESUMES•RES
UMES•RESUMES•RESUMES•RESUMES•RESUMES•RESUMES•RESUMES•RE
SUMES•RESUMES•RESUMES•RESUMES•RESUMES•RESUMES•RESUMES•R
ESUMES•RESUMES•RESUMES•RESUMES•RESUMES•RESUMES•RESUMES•
RESUMES•RESUMES•RESUMES•RESUMES•RESUMES•RESUMES•RESUMES
•RESUMES•RESUMES•RESUMES•RESUMES•RESUMES•RESUMES•RESUME
S•RESUMES•RESUMES•RESUMES•RESUMES•RESUMES•RESUMES•RESUM
ES•RESUMES•RESUMES•RESUMES•RESUMES•RESUMES•RESUMES•RESU
MES•RESUMES•RESUMES•RESUMES•RESUMES•RESUMES•RESUMES•RES
UMES•RESUMES•RESUMES•RESUMES•RESUMES•RESUMES•RESUMES•RE
SUMES•RESUMES•RESUMES•RESUMES•RESUMES•RESUMES•RESUMES•R
ESUMES•RESUMES•RESUMES•RESUMES•RESUMS•RESUMES•RESUMES•R
ESUMES•RESUMES•RESUMES•RESUMES•RESUMES•RESUMES•RESUMES•
RESUMES•RESUMES•RESUMES•RESUMES•RESUMES•RESUMES•RESUMES
•RESUMES•RESUMES•RESUMES•RESUMES•RESUMES•RESUMES•RESUME
S•RESUMES•RESUMES•RESUMES•RESUMES•RESUMES•RESUMES•RESUM
ES•RESUMES•RESUMES•RESUMES•RESUMES•RESUMES•RESUMES•RESU
MES•RESUMES•RESUMES•RESUMES•RESUMES•RESUMES•RESUMES•RES

# INFORMATION SYSTEMS

UMES•RESUMES•RESUMES•RESUMES•RESUMES•RESUMES•RESUMES•RE
SUMES•RESUMES•RESUMES•RESUMES•RESUMES•RESUMES•RESUMES•R
ESUMES•RESUMES•RESUMES•RESUMES•RESUMES•RESUMES•RESUMES•
RESUMES•RESUMES•RESUMES•RESUMES•RESUMES•RESUMES•RESUMES
•RESUMES•RESUMES•RESUMES•RESUMES•RESUMES•RESUMES•RESUME
S•RESUMES•RESUMES•RESUMES•RESUMES•RESUMES•RESUMES•RESUM
ES•RESUMES•RESUMES•RESUMES•RESUMES•RESUMES•RESUMES•RESU
MES•RESUMES•RESUMES•RESUMES•RESUMES•RESUMES•RESUMES•RES
UMES•RESUMES•RESUMES•RESUMES•RESUMES•RESUMES•RESUMES•RE
SUMES•RESUMES•RESUMES•RESUMES•RESUMES•RESUMES•RESUMES•R
ESUMES•RESUMES•RESUMES•RESUMES•RESUMES•RESUMES•RESUMES•
RESUMES•RESUMES•RESUMES•RESUMES•RESUMES•RESUMES•RESUMES
•RESUMES•RESUMES•RESUMES•RESUMES•RESUMES•RESUMES•RESUME
S•RESUMES•RESUMES•RESUMES•RESUMES•RESUMES•RESUMES•RESUM
ES•RESUMES•RESUMES•RESUMES•RESUMES•RESUMES•RESUMES•RESU
MES•RESUMES•RESUMES•RESUMES•RESUMES•RESUMES•RESUMES•RES
UMES•RESUMES•RESUMES•RESUMES•RESUMES•RESUMES•RESUMES•RE
SUMES•RESUMES•RESUMES•RESUMES•RESUMES•RESUMES•RESUMES•R
ESUMES•RESUMES•RESUMES•RESUMES•RESUMES•RESUMES•RESUMES•
RESUMES•RESUMES•RESUMES•RESUMES•RESUMES•RESUMES•RESUMES
•RESUMES•RESUMES•RESUMES•RESUMES•RESUMES•RESUMES•RESUME
S•RESUMES•RESUMES•RESUMES•RESUMES•RESUMES•RESUMES•RESUM
ES•RESUMES•RESUMES•RESUMES•RESUMES•RESUMES•RESUMES•RESU
MES•RESUMES•RESUMES•RESUMES•RESUMES•RESUMES•RESUMES•RES
UMES•RESUMES•RESUMES•RESUMES•RESUMES•RESUMES•RESUMES•RE
SUMES•RESUMES•RESUMES•RESUMES•RESUMES•RESUMES•RESUMES•R
ESUMES•RESUMES•RESUMES•RESUMES•RESUMES•RESUMES•RESUMES•
RESUMES•RESUMES•RESUMES•RESUMES•RESUMES•RESUMES•RESUMES

# Melanie Sussman

46 Briarwood Court
Indianapolis, IN 58919
Phone: (317) 329-3027
Fax: (317) 822-9082

## OBJECTIVE

Key management position in the application of innovative development solutions, where strengths in analysis, design, and evaluation can improve the quality and productivity of human performance.

## QUALIFICATIONS

Extensive experience in managing program design development, and implementation, using a variety of technologies, in entrepreneurial, industrial, and academic settings, including

— Computer-based systems
— Testing and measurement
— Return on investment
— Strategic planning

— Standard operating procedures
— Vendor selection and evaluation
— Sales/management training
— Product feasibility

## EXPERIENCE HIGHLIGHTS

**New Century Education Corporation**                            **June 1994–present**

*Director, Instructional Systems*

— Directed a major division within an educational software development house with nine full-time and two part-time direct reports.
— Defined, monitored, and controlled departmental budgets up to $750,000.
— Defined the curriculum and testing components for long-range strategic plans.
— Managed large-scale multimedia basic skills product development projects, with budgets up to $1 million each.
— Developed concept of computer-based diagnostic/prescriptive "test preparation program," which is the corporation's distinguishing feature in its marketplace.

**Bristol-Myers Squibb Company, Squibb College**                **January 1990–June 1994**

*Director, Instructional Technology*

— Established the College function with three full-time and two part-time direct reports.
— Defined, monitored, and controlled operation budgets up to $500,000.
— Managed multimedia training development projects, with budgets up to $500,000 each, involving extensive approval processes and external production agencies.
— Developed the customer service portion of the College's long-range strategic plan.
— Coordinated the design of return-on-investment measures.
— Managed the design and implementation of networked office computer systems.
— Established a vendor system task force that developed standards and a computer-based system for registering vendors, soliciting a proposals, selecting vendors, and evaluating vendors' performance, to streamline the process, improve product quality, and realize cost savings.
— Developed an interactive-video employee information program and disseminated it to six corporate sites.
— Designed and developed an on-line "college catalog."

**Bristol-Myers Squibb Company, Squibb College (cont.)**

— Contributed to a Worldwide Forum on Salesforce Automation and Productivity, resulting in action plans for automation at the local level, and showcasing innovative interactive-video and computer-based sales training products that were adapted by international operations.

— Coordinated a Worldwide Training Forum for 50 management and sales trainers to develop skills to improve their training effectiveness in their home operations.

— Designed a sales management aptitude testing program incorporating personalized feedback with monitored developmental activities; implemented it with a pilot group of 40 high-potential sales representatives.

— Created a proposal, designed to reduce turnover, for the continuous assessment and development of the sales force and sales management team.

— Conducted the analysis of a corporate Quality/Productivity curriculum to ensure that it would continue to meet the changing needs of the corporation.

**University of Maryland, Baltimore County**              October 1986–December 1989

*Assistant Professor, Instructional Systems Development*

— Coordinated Computer-based Instructional Systems and Training Systems tracks.

— Designed, developed and delivered a complete graduate curriculum in Computer-based Instructional Systems, in response to changing market needs.

— Coordinated two-year, collaborative technology project in Baltimore middle schools, training teachers to integrate the use of computers into problem-solving and mathematics instruction.

— Member, Academic Computing Committee, assessing computer systems needs.

— Founding and continuing member of Training Systems Advisory Board, which ensures effective liaison between the graduate program and the marketplace.

**Dynametrics**              October 1979–December 1989

*President; Publishing and Education Consultant; Author*

— Founded and managed a long-term consulting business with a stable client base.

— Conducted product feasibility studies and provided liaison with government approval agencies.

— Managed large-scale product development projects, with budgets up to $1 million each, involving both in-house approval processes and external producers.

— Coauthored two best-selling mathematics textbooks series, including innovative instructor guides, problem-solving manuals, and other ancillary materials.

**Copp Clark Pitman; Gage Publishing; McGraw-Hill Ryerson  Summer 1974–October 1979**

*National Mathematics Consultant; Mathematics Editor; Technical Editor*

## EDUCATION

Ph.D. 1986     Syracuse University (Instructional Design, Development, and Evaluation)
M.Ed. 1981     University of Toronto (Curriculum Development)
B.A. 1974      York University (Mathematics)

# ELLEN BUKOVICH

96 VAN ALLEN DRIVE
FARGO, NORTH DAKOTA 58103
(701) 235-8767

**OBJECTIVE**   To contribute my programming knowledge to a corporation that will encourage technical and professional growth.

**TECHNICAL SUMMARY**

*HARDWARE*   IBM 3090, IBM-Compatible PC 386/486

*SOFTWARE*   Mainframe:  COBOL, COBOL II, MVS/JCL, MVS/ESA, CICS, DB2, Assembler, PL/1, OS Utilities, VSAM, IDCAMS, TSO/ISPF-PDF

PC:  MS-DOS 6.2, Windows 3.1, Paradox 4.5 for Windows, WordPerfect 5.1, Word for Windows 6.0, C, MircoFocus COBOL

*CONCEPTS*   Problem Analysis, Basic and Advanced Programming Designed Techniques in On-line and Batch Processing, Dumps Debugging and Management Utilities, System Maintenance, Multiple Error Analysis

**EDUCATION**

1995   **Chubb Institute**, Jersey City, New Jersey
Diploma in Computer Programming
Honors Student, Programming Tutor

1989   **Belarussian State University**
B.S. in Mathematics and Computer Science

**EXPERIENCE**

1989–1993   **AGATE** Scientific-Research Institute
**Programmer**
- Wrote, tested, and debugged individual parts of application for scientific purposes
- Developed and coded programs with on-line file updating, menu, and browse with batch reporting
- Provided on-site support during installation of new releases, maintenance, and user training
- Improved efficiency of existing programs for Personnel Department
- Designed and corrected system and project documentation

## *Thomas A. Jamison*

1401 Mopac Expressway • Austin, Texas 78731
*Home:* (512) 343-9875 • *Office:* (512) 795-1841

**HARDWARE**    IBM 3090, 3033, 3030, 4341, 4381

**SOFTWARE**    OS/MVS, COBOL, CICS (Command Level), DB2, SQL, QMF, VSAM, TSO/SPF, OS/UCL, and UTILITIES

### EXPERIENCE
*Consulting assignments with the following organizations:*

**8/90–present        Consolidated Securities Association, Austin Texas**
Participate in the development and implementation of the Payment Extension System, which allows the stock exchange to grant credit to customers endorsed by a brokerage firm. Designed, coded, and tested CICS portion (Maps, Menus, Inquiries, and Updates) and batch portion (Reports, Tapes, Microfiche). Also responsible for creation of views and loading of DB2 test table, cluster definition, move to production, and documentation. This system was written in CICS/DB2-SQL/VSAM/COBOL/COBOL II.

**10/88–7/90        Manufacturer's Bank, Austin Texas**
Participated in the project life cycle of the Check Processing System. This system was responsible for the preparation, recording, and sending of cash letters to the Federal Reserve Bank. The system was also responsible for managing timely and accurate receipt of deposits at the Federal Reserve. Specific responsibilities included
— design and coding of programs in CICS and batch environment accessing VSAM and DB2 database
— creation of views and loading of DB2 test tables
— creation of batch reports, tapes, and microfiche
— parallel testing of new and existing systems
— installation and move to production
— Disaster Recovery Testing
— user interface
— programmers' and users' documentation

**7/84–9/88        Booz-Allen Hamilton, Dallas, Texas**
Participated in the development and implementation of an on-line Security Inventory Trading System. Was responsible for designing and coding Bond Trading Subsystem that displayed inventory in traders' accounts and allowed then to enter trades from the same screen. Also designed, coded, and implemented Trade Inquiry Subsystem that provided traders with the ability to do an inquiry and correction of trades based upon different selection criteria. This system was written in COBOL/CICS/VSAM.

**1/84–6/84        Northeast Bank Association, Fort Worth, Texas**
Participated in the design, coding, enhancement, and maintenance of the following credit card applications:
*Collections*—This CICS/VSAM/batch system was designed to keep track of default Visa/MasterCard accounts.
*Data Capture*—This system was used to identify, record, and process Visa/MasterCard cash/letter transactions for bank merchants.

**EDUCATION**    1985—B.S., UNIVERSITY OF TEXAS, Austin, Texas
*Major:* Information Systems

# TOM WILSON

94 ELM PLACE • KANSAS CITY, MISSOURI 64033

| *Home* (816) 493-9868 | *Work* (816) 654-0274 | *Internet* YKRP95@prodigy.com |

## SUMMARY OF QUALIFICATIONS

Senior manager with 16 years' financial information systems experience. Including domestic and international operations expertise, technical marketing, staffing, project management, and technical support. Highly skilled in managing existing and start-up international/domestic operations and computer and telecommunications networking.

## EXPERIENCE

**FIRST MISSOURI STATE BANK**, Kansas City, Missouri                1995–present
Capital Markets Division, which contributes $100+ million in revenue, the result of planning, revising, and implementing overall enterprise network services for global customers via 600+ PC workstations and multiple UNIX trading floor platforms.

*Vice-President*
Accountable for the design, support, administration, and overall technology strategy of domestic and six international locations. Applications utilized Novel 4.1, Lotus Notes, ccMail, UNIX, Marketvision, Windows for Workgroups, Windows '95, NT, and various other off-the-shelf products.
- Development of network standards that meet the needs of the firm and the enterprise systems architecture.
- Provide day-to-day support, track all system and technology problems with a view to providing "one-stop" support for the organization.
- Organized, defined, and implemented the internal structure of a Lotus Notes–based helpdesk necessary to meet this objective.
- Redefined and streamlined process for maximum efficiency and customer satisfaction.
- Managing the reengineering of primary server structure into a superserver configuration for enhanced operation and management.
- Established a working coalition with 13 departments and users to identify needs and provide cost-effective technical solutions.

**NATIONAL DATA PROCESSING, INC.**, St. Louis, Missouri                1994–1995
Brokerage Information Services Division, which supplies 92,000+ customers with electronic information via 800+ node LAN networks used in banks and brokerage houses in the global marketplace.

*Senior Operations Analyst*
Designed network administration processes for division and acquisitions. Enhanced capacity, performance, change, and project management practices.
- Directed design and implementation of a PARADOX-based, problem-tracking, and change management database that monitored chronic problems and modifications across organizations international/domestic.
- Managed the redesign of an ACCESS database to control Alpha, Beta, Migration, and other aspects of project administration in a LAN, WAN, Mainframe, and Micro environment.
- Designed, managed, and implemented operational practices for the MarketMax LAN, WAN, and Appletalk network, a San Francisco-based ADP entity.
- Coordinated and implemented projects, minor and major, hands-on, at all levels world-wide.
- Redesigned and implemented operations, escalation, and contingency process and procedures for a seven-day, 24-hour operations team.
- Coordinated E-mail implementation across multiple international/domestic locations.

**EQUITIES SYSTEMS, INC.**, Columbia, Missouri                    1979–1994
Major supplier of electronic stock quotations utilized in banks and brokerage houses world-wide.

### *Director, Central Systems*                                    1990–1994
Manage all aspects of computer operations, engineering, maintenance, project change control, long-term planning, and related support functions. Overall accountability for supervision of personnel involved in a seven-day, 24-hour operation, along with responsibility for delivery of on-line services to clients and for maintaining database integrity.

- Successfully relocated London-based systems to Maryland, reducing fixed costs by $2 million per year.
- Maintained service quality levels domestically and internationally at 99.8% with 20% fewer staff.
- Supported more than 200 minicomputers and their associated networks, which served 50,000 end-users world-wide.
- Implemented a team management style with specific objectives and service quality focus.
- Started system upgrade from mini- to microcomputers, utilizing RS 6000 systems, LANs, WANs, routers, and terminal servers.

### *General Manager, Computer Operations, London, England*        1988–1990
Directed central and regional international computer centers, installation, operations, and planning. Key involvement in relocation of operational facilities from New York to London and start-up of new international data collection/processing systems and procedures.

- Successfully replaced a third-party vendor feed of international equities with our own directly processed feeds.
- Recruited, trained, and supervised a staff of 43 and managed the construction project creating the data center through to production, within deadline.
- Established a 24-hour helpdesk operation.

### *Assistant to the Vice-President, International Operations*      1983–1988
Managed international business operations. Traveled extensively to branch offices, assisting with technical and marketing efforts; monitored sales functions; and acted as the interface for domestic national accounts doing business outside the United States.

### *System Support Engineer Technician*                            1979–1983

## EDUCATION AND TECHNICAL EXPERIENCE

Mercy College, Dobbs Ferry, New York
*Major:* Management Information Systems

Lakeland Trade & Technical School, Joplin, Missouri
*Major:* Electric Wiring

## OTHER TECHNICAL EXPOSURE

| | | |
|---|---|---|
| Real Time Systems | X.25 | SUN Workstation |
| Modems | Internet | MICROVAX |
| Voice Com | Sync | Proprietary (Mini) |
| Troubleshooting | Bisync | PC applications |
| Telephony Hardware | Gateways | PC AT/XT/OS2 |
| LANs | TCP-IP | AIX |
| Multiplexes | SUN OS | UNIX |
| WANs | IBM RISC 6000 | XENIX |

# Brian Lassiter

*1432 West Main Street*
*Aspen, CO 81611*
*(303) 278-9030*

## GOAL

Design and development of microcomputer software

## EMPLOYMENT HISTORY

*1992–present*    CBS INTERACTIVE LEARNING, Boulder, Colorado

*Manager, College Product*

- Designed and implemented an innovative program of college-level software development and marketing.

- Analyzed the college software market and presented a systematic approach to lowering development costs to better fit the budgets of a college publisher.

- Directed the software development efforts of Holt, Rinehart, and Winston; Dryden Press; and Saunders College Publishing.

- Design software; supervise programmers; develop with editors and marketing managers, marketing plans; and negotiate licenses to educational versions of commercial software.

*1988–1992*    RANDOM HOUSE, New York, New York

*Director of Software Development, College Division* (1990–1992)

- Designed and supervised a side-ranging program of college-level educational microcomputer software.

- Prepared for upper management a report that analyzed the potential of the college software market and outlined a unique strategy for approaching that market. Over the next two years, oversaw the entire life cycle of more than 30 separate projects and one series of more than 45 titles. These projects varied widely, ranging from software for accounting students to a new, low-cost word processing program. The majority of these projects were conceived and in varying degrees designed by me. Others were chosen by me from submissions by authors.

- Conceived and designed the product, analyzing markets, conceptualizing products, preparing profit-and-loss analyses, preparing high-level design, choosing developers, overseeing the full life cycle of the products, assisting developers in choosing languages and software tools, supervising the programming, supervising the writing and production of documentation, presenting products to the sales staff and to customers, demonstrating products at conventions, supervising an in-house staff of three, and coordinating and supervising outside developers and freelancers.

*Microcomputer Specialist, College Division* (1989–1990)

Planned and implemented automation of the division. Analyzed the needs of the division and conceived an office automation strategy, chose hardware and software, updated the facility to meet growing user needs, and provided minor maintenance of the facility. Also provided appropriate training and served as last resort for user problems.

*Project Coordinator, College Division* (1988–1989)

Coordinated workings of the Production and Editorial Departments. Developed a computerized project tracking system in dBase. This program allowed for computer-assisted generation of schedules and tracking variations from original plan for projects with up to 45 stages. Upon request, the program would generate a revised schedule, allowing for variations from the plan.

1986–1988    ROCKY MOUNTAIN BOOKS, Denver, Colorado

Responsible for cost estimation and the production of books, from manuscript to bound books, including titles from the Special Projects, Juvenile, and Trade Paperback areas. Designed and maintained a computerized scheduling system for tracking book production.

### EDUCATION

*Graduate Studies in Philosophy*, Katholieke Universiteit te Leuven, Louvain, Belgium (1982–1986)
All but thesis in Philosophy. Specializations in Theory of Knowledge, Logic, and Structuralist theories of causality.

*Bachelor's Degree in Philosophy* granted magna cum laude, Katholieke Universiteit te Leuven (1980–1982)

*Undergraduate Studies*, St. Vincent's College, Latrobe, Pennsylvania (1978–1980)

**L. James Warner**  •  706 Monroe Street, Carthage, IL 62321  •  (217) 357-4919

## EXPERIENCE

**Self-Employment**
January 1989–present
Operate systems consulting and installation business
*Duties:*
- Hardware, software, and network installations
- CD-ROM installation and demonstration
- Software instruction and program design in Lotus, Quattro Pro, dBASE, Paradox, WordPerfect, and desktop publishing

**Good Apple, 1204 Buchanan Street, Carthage, Illinois**
June 1990–present
*Title:* Assistant Programmer
*Duties:*
- COBOL programming in minicomputer environment
- Microcomputer hardware and software installation
- Spreadsheet and database design for end users

**Hancock Central District #338, Carthage, Illinois**
September 1985–May 1990
*Title:* Bus Driver

**Midwest Carbide Corporation, Carbide Lane, Keokuk, Iowa**
March 1980–January 1985
*Title:* Maintenance mechanic
*Duties:* Maintained hydraulic and automatic machine systems

**Methode Electronics, 110 Buchanan Street, Carthage, Illinois**
December 1977–December 1979
*Title:* Setup/Maintenance
*Duties:* Mold setup; automatic systems maintenance

**Morse Rubber Division, Main Street Road, Keokuk, Iowa**
September 1974–January 1977
*Title:* Lab Technician
*Duties:* Materials testing and research and development

## OTHER EXPERIENCE

U.S. Army, May 1969–January 1972, X-ray technician, honorably discharged
Several periods of self-employment operating a construction company

## EDUCATION

B.S., Western Illinois University, Macomb, Illinois
*Major:* Industrial Technology
*Minor:* Computer Science
Graduated December 1990

A.S., Southeastern Community College, Keokuk, Indiana
*Major:* Applied Science

Currently: Graduate student, Western Illinois University
*Major:* Computer-Integrated Manufacturing

RESUMES•RESUMES•RESUMES•RESUMES•RESUMES•RESUMES•RESUMES
•RESUMES•RESUMES•RESUMES•RESUMES•RESUMES•RESUMES•RESUME
S•RESUMES•RESUMES•RESUMES•RESUMES•RESUMES•RESUMES•RESUM
ES•RESUMES•RESUMES•RESUMES•RESUMES•RESUMES•RESUMES•RESU
MES•RESUMES•RESUMES•RESUMES•RESUMES•RESUMES•RESUMES•RES
UMES•RESUMES•RESUMES•RESUMES•RESUMES•RESUMES•RESUMES•RE
SUMES•RESUMES•RESUMES•RESUMES•RESUMES•RESUMES•RESUMES•R
ESUMES•RESUMES•RESUMES•RESUMES•RESUMES•RESUMES•RESUMES•
RESUMES•RESUMES•RESUMES•RESUMES•RESUMES•RESUMES•RESUMES
•RESUMES•RESUMES•RESUMES•RESUMES•RESUMES•RESUMES•RESUME
S•RESUMES•RESUMES•RESUMES•RESUMES•RESUMES•RESUMES•RESUM
ES•RESUMES•RESUMES•RESUMES•RESUMES•RESUMES•RESUMES•RESU
MES•RESUMES•RESUMES•RESUMES•RESUMES•RESUMES•RESUMES•RES
UMES•RESUMES•RESUMES•RESUMES•RESUMES•RESUMES•RESUMES•RE
SUMES•RESUMES•RESUMES•RESUMES•RESUMES•RESUMES•RESUMES•R
ESUMES•RESUMES•RESUMES•RESUMES•RESUMS•RESUMES•RESUMES•R
ESUMES•RESUMES•RESUMES•RESUMES•RESUMES•RESUMES•RESUMES•
RESUMES•RESUMES•RESUMES•RESUMES•RESUMES•RESUMES•RESUMES
•RESUMES•RESUMES•RESUMES•RESUMES•RESUMES•RESUMES•RESUME
S•RESUMES•RESUMES•RESUMES•RESUMES•RESUMES•RESUMES•RESUM
ES•RESUMES•RESUMES•RESUMES•RESUMES•RESUMES•RESUMES•RESU
MES•RESUMES•RESUMES•RESUMES•RESUMES•RESUMES•RESUMES•RES

# LEGAL

UMES•RESUMES•RESUMES•RESUMES•RESUMES•RESUMES•RESUMES•RE
SUMES•RESUMES•RESUMES•RESUMES•RESUMES•RESUMES•RESUMES•R
ESUMES•RESUMES•RESUMES•RESUMES•RESUMES•RESUMES•RESUMES•
RESUMES•RESUMES•RESUMES•RESUMES•RESUMES•RESUMES•RESUMES
•RESUMES•RESUMES•RESUMES•RESUMES•RESUMES•RESUMES•RESUME
S•RESUMES•RESUMES•RESUMES•RESUMES•RESUMES•RESUMES•RESUM
ES•RESUMES•RESUMES•RESUMES•RESUMES•RESUMES•RESUMES•RESU
MES•RESUMES•RESUMES•RESUMES•RESUMES•RESUMES•RESUMES•RES
UMES•RESUMES•RESUMES•RESUMES•RESUMES•RESUMES•RESUMES•RE
SUMES•RESUMES•RESUMES•RESUMES•RESUMES•RESUMES•RESUMES•R
ESUMES•RESUMES•RESUMES•RESUMES•RESUMES•RESUMES•RESUMES•
RESUMES•RESUMES•RESUMES•RESUMES•RESUMES•RESUMES•RESUMES
•RESUMES•RESUMES•RESUMES•RESUMES•RESUMES•RESUMES•RESUME
S•RESUMES•RESUMES•RESUMES•RESUMES•RESUMES•RESUMES•RESUM
ES•RESUMES•RESUMES•RESUMES•RESUMES•RESUMES•RESUMES•RESU
MES•RESUMES•RESUMES•RESUMES•RESUMES•RESUMES•RESUMES•RES
UMES•RESUMES•RESUMES•RESUMES•RESUMES•RESUMES•RESUMES•RE
SUMES•RESUMES•RESUMES•RESUMES•RESUMES•RESUMES•RESUMES•R
ESUMES•RESUMES•RESUMES•RESUMES•RESUMES•RESUMES•RESUMES•
RESUMES•RESUMES•RESUMES•RESUMES•RESUMES•RESUMES•RESUMES
•RESUMES•RESUMES•RESUMES•RESUMES•RESUMES•RESUMES•RESUME
S•RESUMES•RESUMES•RESUMES•RESUMES•RESUMES•RESUMES•RESUM
ES•RESUMES•RESUMES•RESUMES•RESUMES•RESUMES•RESUMES•RESU
MES•RESUMES•RESUMES•RESUMES•RESUMES•RESUMES•RESUMES•RES
UMES•RESUMES•RESUMES•RESUMES•RESUMES•RESUMES•RESUMES•RE
SUMES•RESUMES•RESUMES•RESUMES•RESUMES•RESUMES•RESUMES•R
ESUMES•RESUMES•RESUMES•RESUMES•RESUMES•RESUMES•RESUMES•
RESUMES•RESUMES•RESUMES•RESUMES•RESUMES•RESUMES•RESUMES

# ROWENA SCOTT, Esq.

111-46 96TH DRIVE
FOREST HILLS, NY 11375
HOME: (718) 793-2063     BUSINESS: (718) 840-8151

## GOAL

Corporate Counsel or equivalent-level business position

## BACKGROUND

**Associate Counsel**                                    MANDELBAUM & SCHWEIGER, Esqs.
1990–present                                                   New York, New York

- Prepared agreements and corporate documents, commercial and personal real estate transactions, litigation, and some estate work in general practice, with emphasis on corporate, commercial, and international business law

**Associate Counsel/Assistant Corporate Secretary**     SEIKO WATCH COMPANY, INC.
1985–1990                                                   Jackson Heights, New York

*INTERNATIONAL RELATIONS*
- Handled all matters related to international marketing, manufacturing, and intercorporate relationships
- Negotiated and prepared contracts and distribution agreements
- Set up and later divested operation in American Samoa, including all negotiations with Samoan government, U.S. Departments of Commerce and Interior
- Represented company in problems involving customs and tariffs

*RESEARCH/DEVELOPMENT*
- Established and was member of Patent Policy Committee to study development of new products and improvements in order to determine whether to file patent applications
- Screened ideas for new products submitted to company, negotiated with inventors, and prepared legal documents for contractual arrangements

*LICENSING/PROTECTION*
- Initiated in-house patent licensing and trademark licensing
- Supervised preparation of and managed litigation in infringement matters

*CORPORATE COMMUNICATIONS/GOVERNMENT RELATIONS*
- Approved all press releases and advertising
- Conducted media interviews; assisted CEO in conducting others
- Assisted CEO in public appearances on problems of multinational corporations and corporate case history
- Wrote speeches and articles for CEO
- Maintained contact with legislators and administrative and trade agencies on national and local levels in all matters affecting watch industry
- Represented company in legislative and administrative hearings

*JOINT VENTURES*
- Performed all legal work in connection with joint ventures and establishment of subsidiaries, both in United States and abroad
- Negotiated all agreements, including shareholders' agreements

*MARKETING*
- Studied competition (in cooperation with marketing survey specialists) on matters of product quality and brand image, dealer and consumer acceptance

*ASSISTANT SECRETARY*
- Served as officer of parent corporation and various subsidiary and affiliated corporations
- Attended all meetings of Board of Directors

*REAL ESTATE*
- Negotiated real estate transactions, including leases, property sales, and sale/leaseback contracts; prepared legal documents

*EMPLOYEE RELATIONS*
- Negotiated and prepared employment contracts; interacted with all departments in personnel relations
- Represented company's legal position in contact with human rights agencies
- Maintained legal aid service for employees
- Served as Director of Seiko Credit Union

*GOVERNMENT CONTROLS AND REGULATIONS*
- Monitored compliance with trade regulations, including antitrust, FTC, and Wage/Price Control

*LITIGATION*
- Represented company in proceedings and hearings before administrative agencies—for example, Human Rights Commission and Environmental Protection Agency
- Supervised counsel in multimillion-dollar litigation (antitrust, contracts, and general business problems); handled some of own trial work

*INSURANCE*
- Handled all legal matters related to insurance, including directors' and officers' liability

**Associate Counsel**　　　　　　　　　　　　　　　　　　　　　　　HART & IRVIN, Esqs.
1982–1985　　　　　　　　　　　　　　　　　　　　　　　　　　Long Island City, New York

- Full range of trial practice: all aspects of pleading and practice, client interview, negotiation of settlements, pretrial, appeals

## EDUCATION

Brooklyn Law School, Brooklyn, New York
1982—L.L.B.

Hunter College, New York, New York
1978—B.A., Political Science

## BAR STATUS

Admitted to practice in New York State, U.S. Eastern and Southern District Courts, U.S. Customs Court

# BRUCE BONDURANT

35 Nob Hill Avenue
Bridgeport, CT 06610
Home: (203) 335-9077

**OBJECTIVE**    To employ tax, legal, and business experience in a position with growth potential in a corporate legal department or a law firm.

**SUMMARY**    — More than two and one-half years' general legal experience, involving real estate contracts and titles, estate planning and administration, personal injury litigation, and criminal law.
— Experienced in analyzing matters involving personal income taxation.
— Contributed, by invitation, material for 1987 edition of *Connecticut Practice Book*, by Kaye and Effron (West Publishing Company).
Admitted to the Connecticut Bar and U.S. District Court for the District of Connecticut, 1986.

## EXPERIENCE

June/1987–
present

STEWART S. KLEIN, Attorney-at-Law, Bridgeport, Connecticut
*Associate Attorney*

- Interview, advise, and represent clients in matters pertaining to civil and criminal litigation, collections, and domestic relations.
- Draft real estate contracts and leases; negotiate real estate sales/purchase agreements; conduct title searches.
- Research and prepare pleadings and memoranda.
- Generate new business for firm.

January/1986–
June/1987

FRANK A. GRIFFITH, Attorney-at-Law, Darien, Connecticut
*Associate Attorney*

- Worked on matters pertaining to personal income taxation, estate planning, and administration; prepared wills.
- Prepared real estate contracts.
- Generated new business; represented clients in criminal, civil, and probate court; researched and prepared pleadings and memoranda.

May/1985–
January/1986

LAWSON & GRIFFITH, Attorneys-at-Law, Darien, Connecticut
*Legal Assistant*

- Conducted title searches; prepared contracts, pleadings, and wills; interviewed clients; and performed legal research.
- Joined Frank A. Griffith upon dissolution of partnership.

1981–1982

TAX MAN, INC., Cambridge, Massachusetts
*Income Tax Consultant*

- Interviewed and advised clients on matters relating to personal income taxes; prepared tax returns of varying complexity.
- Clients included students and employed and self-employed individuals.

**ADDITIONAL EXPERIENCE (while attending school), 1983–1985**

UNIVERSITY OF LOUISVILLE, SCHOOL OF LAW, Louisville, Kentucky
*Research Assistant*
- Researched questions pertaining to estate law, commercial law and domestic relations.
- Performed legal research of issues involving criminal law and procedure and constitutional law.
- Selected by law professors for this job during last three semesters before graduation.

GEORGE MUNSING, Attorney-at-Law, Bridgeport, Connecticut
*Legal Clerk*
- Conducted legal research, answered court calendars, performed title searches, and prepared pleadings.

FAIRFIELD COUNTY LEGAL SERVICES, Bridgeport, Connecticut
*Legal Assistant*
- Researched and prepared memoranda for cases involving indigent clients.

## EDUCATION

University of Louisville School of Law, Louisville, Kentucky
1985—J.D.

Boston University College of Business Administration, Boston, Massachusetts
1982—B.S., Business Administration/Economics, Dean's List

Member, Society for Advancement of Management
Representative to Student Government

## MEMBERSHIPS

Connecticut Bar Association
American Bar Association
ABA Section of Real Property, Probate, and Trust Law
ABA Young Lawyer's Section
Stamford-Darien Bar Association
Greater Bridgeport Bar Association

# DIANE LOVENDAHL
304 Brooklyn Avenue
Brooklyn, New York 11213
(212) 493-6053

**OBJECTIVE**   *LABOR RELATIONS ATTORNEY*

**SUMMARY**   Experienced and deeply interested in EEO and other personnel considerations, with demonstrated ability to arrive at equitable solutions through intense investigative and interpretative procedures. Proven expertise in drafting, developing, and amending pension plans; drafting and developing language for group annuity contracts; and research/analysis of federal regulations from point of view of employee/management relations. Effective in communication; perceptive of and sensitive to socio/job-related problems. Work well under pressure.

**EDUCATION**   University of Akron School of Law, Akron, Ohio
1985—J.D.

Brooklyn College, Brooklyn, New York
1982—B.A., Political Science/English, Economics

## RELEVANT EXPERIENCE

*1985–1987*   NORTH AMERICAN PHILLIPS CORPORATION, New York, New York
*Labor Relations/EEO Department*

- Prepared and handled employment discrimination cases
  — Mounted full investigation of each case; interviewed supervisors, department managers, and other employees
  — Examined personnel records and documents, researched applicable areas of law, and filed briefs and affidavits with appropriate State Administrative Hearings and Appellate Review Boards
- Charged with responsibility for writing affirmative action plans, assisting personnel managers during on-site audits by government agents, and acting as consultant in re Federal Maternity Act, Age Discrimination in Employment Act, and effects of 1978 ADEA Amendments on Company Benefit and Pension Plans
- Effected reversal of unfavorable charge by compliance officer during one on-site audit, based on alleged violation of Equal Pay Act in regard to female employees (one of several such instances)
  — Researched problem, represented company at hearing, and produced documents and records showing that female employees requested certain jobs requiring less facility in English
  — Designed program to instruct non-English-speaking employees in English to provide position upgrading and chances for promotion
  — Instituted craft-apprenticeship programs for women
  — Company was awarded government contract; affirmative action program was approved
- Designed and implemented techniques for maintaining personnel records

*Fall 1984*  SUMMIT COURT PRETRIAL RELEASE PROJECT, Akron, Ohio
*Legal Intern*
• Performed interviewing research and counseling; made recommendations

SUMMIT COUNTY PROSECUTOR'S OFFICE, Consumer Fraud Division, Akron, Ohio
*Investigator*
• Investigated consumer complaints; prepared detailed reports

*Spring 1984*  SUMMIT COUNTY LEGAL AID SOCIETY, Akron, Ohio
*Interviewer/Researcher*
• Worked in Family Law, General, and Housing Divisions; interviewed petitioners, researched relevant matters
• Assisted in writing briefs and filing motions and affidavits

*Fall 1983*  APPELLATE REVIEW OFFICE, University of Akron, Akron, Ohio
*Staff Member*
• Performed research; wrote briefs

*Summer 1981*  NEW YORK CITY DEPARTMENT OF CONSUMER AFFAIRS, New York, New York
*Volunteer Complaint Counselor*

## OTHER EXPERIENCE

*1987–present*  BOWNICK, INC., Brooklyn, New York (family-owned enterprise)
*Assistant Manager*
• Supervise operations and personnel; enforce company policies and procedures
• Provide on-the-job training for employees, process weekly payroll and unemployment insurance claims, and maintain excellent employee relations
• Resolve customer relations problems

## PROFESSIONAL AFFILIATIONS

Association for Black Women Attorneys
Bedford-Stuyvesant Lawyers Association
Council of New York Law Associates

# MARILYN GARBER

344 West 52nd Street, #9R  •  New York, NY 10023  •  (212) 873-6320

**OBJECTIVE**  Seeking position in social service agency.

**SUMMARY**  Knowledgeable about legal aspects of community-oriented services and institutions. Experienced in counseling in a variety of situations, including drug abuse, mental health, prisoner welfare, retarded adults, and income maintenance for public assistance applicants.

**EDUCATION**  Yeshiva University, Benjamin Cardozo School of Law, New York, New York 1995—J.D.

Cornell University, College of Arts and Sciences, Ithaca, New York 1991—B.A., History (Dean's List), New York State Regents Scholarship

**EXPERIENCE**

*Summer 1994*  OFFICE OF THE DISTRICT ATTORNEY, KING'S COUNTY, Brooklyn, New York

*Intern* (Eugene Gold, District Attorney)

• Assigned to aid Assistant District Attorneys in investigations, Supreme Court, Criminal Court, and Sex Crimes Bureaus
— Researched legal issues, drafted motions and bills, wrote memoranda of law, helped prepare cases for trial, and contacted and interviewed witnesses and complainants

• Participated in research/writing of *Methods of Obtaining Physical Evidence from the Defendant* (published Fall 1994)

*Fall 1993*  FAMILY COURT, BRONX COURT HOUSE (Honorable Gertrude Mainzer), Bronx, New York

*Judicial Clerkship*

Took notes of trial testimony; did legal research; summarized and cataloged current domestic relations case law

BENJAMIN CARDOZO SCHOOL OF LAW, New York, New York

*Law Library Assistant*

• Assisted students in use of library, microfilm, and microfiche

*Summer 1993*  HOFFINGER, FRIEDLAND & ROTH, Attorneys-at-Law, New York, New York

*Legal Assistant*

• Researched and wrote memoranda regarding criminal, matrimonial, and health law; drafted and served motions

*1991–1992*  TOMPKINS COUNTY DEPARTMENT OF SOCIAL SERVICES, Ithaca, New York
*Social Welfare Examiner*
- Interviewed public assistance applicants; determined welfare, food stamp, and Medicare eligibility; supervised income maintenance for 100-household caseload

*1989–1991*  THERAPIST/YOUTH WORKER/COUNSELOR, Ithaca, New York
(while attending school)

*Crisis Counselor*, Mainline Drug Center—walk-in and phone-in

*Youth Worker*, Ithaca Youth Bureau—coordinated street theatre group

*Therapist*, Tompkins County Mental Health Clinic—counseled jail inmates and long-term clinic patients

*Aide*, Meadow House Center for Retarded Adults—directed dance movement in music

**INTERESTS**  Singing, sewing, dancing, cooking

**PROFESSIONAL AFFILIATIONS**

New York Women's Bar Association
American Bar Association
Rochester Folk Art Guild (clothing design)

RESUMES•RESUMES•RESUMES•RESUMES•RESUMES•RESUMES•RESUMES
•RESUMES•RESUMES•RESUMES•RESUMES•RESUMES•RESUMES•RESUME
S•RESUMES•RESUMES•RESUMES•RESUMES•RESUMES•RESUMES•RESUM
ES•RESUMES•RESUMES•RESUMES•RESUMES•RESUMES•RESUMES•RESU
MES•RESUMES•RESUMES•RESUMES•RESUMES•RESUMES•RESUMES•RES
UMES•RESUMES•RESUMES•RESUMES•RESUMES•RESUMES•RESUMES•RE
SUMES•RESUMES•RESUMES•RESUMES•RESUMES•RESUMES•RESUMES•R
ESUMES•RESUMES•RESUMES•RESUMES•RESUMES•RESUMES•RESUMES•
RESUMES•RESUMES•RESUMES•RESUMES•RESUMES•RESUMES•RESUMES
•RESUMES•RESUMES•RESUMES•RESUMES•RESUMES•RESUMES•RESUME
S•RESUMES•RESUMES•RESUMES•RESUMES•RESUMES•RESUMES•RESUM
ES•RESUMES•RESUMES•RESUMES•RESUMES•RESUMES•RESUMES•RESU
MES•RESUMES•RESUMES•RESUMES•RESUMES•RESUMES•RESUMES•RES
UMES•RESUMES•RESUMES•RESUMES•RESUMES•RESUMES•RESUMES•RE
SUMES•RESUMES•RESUMES•RESUMES•RESUMES•RESUMES•RESUMES•R
ESUMES•RESUMES•RESUMES•RESUMES•RESUMS•RESUMES•RESUMES•R
ESUMES•RESUMES•RESUMES•RESUMES•RESUMES•RESUMES•RESUMES•
RESUMES•RESUMES•RESUMES•RESUMES•RESUMES•RESUMES•RESUMES
•RESUMES•RESUMES•RESUMES•RESUMES•RESUMES•RESUMES•RESUME
S•RESUMES•RESUMES•RESUMES•RESUMES•RESUMES•RESUMES•RESUM
ES•RESUMES•RESUMES•RESUMES•RESUMES•RESUMES•RESUMES•RESU
MES•RESUMES•RESUMES•RESUMES•RESUMES•RESUMES•RESUMES•RES

# MARKETING

UMES•RESUMES•RESUMES•RESUMES•RESUMES•RESUMES•RESUMES•RE
SUMES•RESUMES•RESUMES•RESUMES•RESUMES•RESUMES•RESUMES•R
ESUMES•RESUMES•RESUMES•RESUMES•RESUMES•RESUMES•RESUMES•
RESUMES•RESUMES•RESUMES•RESUMES•RESUMES•RESUMES•RESUMES
•RESUMES•RESUMES•RESUMES•RESUMES•RESUMES•RESUMES•RESUME
S•RESUMES•RESUMES•RESUMES•RESUMES•RESUMES•RESUMES•RESUM
ES•RESUMES•RESUMES•RESUMES•RESUMES•RESUMES•RESUMES•RESU
MES•RESUMES•RESUMES•RESUMES•RESUMES•RESUMES•RESUMES•RES
UMES•RESUMES•RESUMES•RESUMES•RESUMES•RESUMES•RESUMES•RE
SUMES•RESUMES•RESUMES•RESUMES•RESUMES•RESUMES•RESUMES•R
ESUMES•RESUMES•RESUMES•RESUMES•RESUMES•RESUMES•RESUMES•
RESUMES•RESUMES•RESUMES•RESUMES•RESUMES•RESUMES•RESUMES
•RESUMES•RESUMES•RESUMES•RESUMES•RESUMES•RESUMES•RESUME
S•RESUMES•RESUMES•RESUMES•RESUMES•RESUMES•RESUMES•RESUM
ES•RESUMES•RESUMES•RESUMES•RESUMES•RESUMES•RESUMES•RESU
MES•RESUMES•RESUMES•RESUMES•RESUMES•RESUMES•RESUMES•RES
UMES•RESUMES•RESUMES•RESUMES•RESUMES•RESUMES•RESUMES•RE
SUMES•RESUMES•RESUMES•RESUMES•RESUMES•RESUMES•RESUMES•R
ESUMES•RESUMES•RESUMES•RESUMES•RESUMES•RESUMES•RESUMES•
RESUMES•RESUMES•RESUMES•RESUMES•RESUMES•RESUMES•RESUMES
•RESUMES•RESUMES•RESUMES•RESUMES•RESUMES•RESUMES•RESUME
S•RESUMES•RESUMES•RESUMES•RESUMES•RESUMES•RESUMES•RESUM
ES•RESUMES•RESUMES•RESUMES•RESUMES•RESUMES•RESUMES•RESU
MES•RESUMES•RESUMES•RESUMES•RESUMES•RESUMES•RESUMES•RES
UMES•RESUMES•RESUMES•RESUMES•RESUMES•RESUMES•RESUMES•RE
SUMES•RESUMES•RESUMES•RESUMES•RESUMES•RESUMES•RESUMES•R
ESUMES•RESUMES•RESUMES•RESUMES•RESUMES•RESUMES•RESUMES•
RESUMES•RESUMES•RESUMES•RESUMES•RESUMES•RESUMES•RESUMES

# BASIL LANGHART

102 Templeton Road, Fitzwilliam, NH 03215 • (603) 934-8662 (Office) • (603) 663-1173 (Home)

**SUMMARY**    Sales/marketing executive with 20 years' successful experience. Exemplary record of customer retention, while consistently exceeding revenue and growth goals. Extensive plant-level profit-and-loss responsibility. Skilled and motivational manager, with virtually no turnover of employees personally hired. Strong background in strategic planning.

**EXPERIENCE**

*1993–present*    **ANODYNE ADHESIVE, Keene, NH**
(A Division of Sandoz Chemicals, Inc.)
*Northeast Regional Manager*

- Direct marketing and sales operations of 13-state region, supervising 8 sales representatives and 4 support people
- Turned around stagnet region with no growth in preceeding 6 years to increase revenues by 37% (from $6.5 million to $9 million) over 3-year period, utilizing innovative marketing techniques and reconstructing sales operation (see attached sheet for year-by-year performance record)
- Supervised operations of 35-employee Peterboro manufacturing facility (in addition to current responsibilities) for 2 years before regional reorganization.

*1992–1993*    **MULTINATIONAL JOINT VENTURE, Lebanon, NH**
*General Manager*

- Set up joint venture between two manufacturers, including business plan, pro formas, funding strategies, and design of physical plant

*1977–1992*    **H. B. FULLER COMPANY, St. Paul, MN**
*National Account Manager* (1992)
*Business Manager* (1987–1991)
*District Manager* (1983–1986)
*Sales Representative* (1977–1982)

- Fifteen years of consistent contributions to corporate revenue and profit growth, resulting in three promotions to positions of increasing responsibility
  — Held profit-and-loss responsibility for discrete business units over a 5-year period, both as Business Manager and as National Account Manager
  — Responsible for dramatic sales and profit increase 14 out of 15 years (see attached sheets for year-by-year performance record), including doubling sales in 4-year period and growing one account from $60,000 to $7 million over same period of time

*1975–1977*    **AVERY INTERNATIONAL CORPORATION, Pasadena, CA**
*Sales Representative*

- Met all sales goals

*1973–1975*    **HAMPDEN COLOR AND CHEMICAL, Amherst, MA**
*Sales Representative*

- Met all sales goals

*1972–1973*    **SOUTHWORTH PAPER COMPANY, Acton, MA**
*Sales Representative*

- Met all sales goals

**EDUCATION**    AMERICAN INTERNATIONAL COLLEGE, Springfield, MA
1971—B.A., Economics and Sociology

## ARTHUR BERTUZZI

66-25 100th Street • Forest Hills, NY 11375
(212) 897-7311

### SALES MANAGEMENT (TEXTILES)

1984–present    *President,* SPECIAL IMPRESSIONS
Flushing, New York

- Achieved $800,000 average annual sales
- Supervised manufacture of T-shirts, including selling, financing, marketing, and establishing overhead
- Responsible for all personnel, including
  production manager
  shipping manager
  bookkeeping department staff
  accountant
  5 salesmen
  50 employees of the Cutting and Sewing Department
- Improved working relationships with mills and Cutting and Sewing staff, resulting in reduced cost of manufacturing by approximately 10%
- Developed working relationships with wholesale distributors, chain stores, department stores, media sales promotion situations, sales reps, individually owned T-shirt retailers, and boutiques
- Managed and extended credit, when warranted, to customers
- Promoted independent contractor reciprocation
- Liquidated company July 1989

1983–1984    *Sales Manager,* GOTHAM KNITTING MACHINERY
Glendale, New York

- Handled in-house sales
- Gained 35 to 40 new accounts, at an average billing of $50,000 each
- Maintained gross sales of $5 million
- Delegated work to 4 to 5 salesmen world-wide
- Traveled to mills throughout country to evaluate machinery needs and to update and service existing system
- Established long-lasting customers through goodwill and public relations
- Worked part-time during senior year in college
- Resigned from firm to go into business for myself

### EDUCATION

B.S., Sociology/Psychology, Queens College      1983

Far Rockaway High School      1978
Dean's List, 2 years
Student adviser to school newspaper, the *Phoenix*

### SPECIAL INTERESTS

Languages: French—read/speak; Spanish—read

Member, New York City Chamber of Commerce Board

1983–present:   Basketball Coach for last 4 years, Forest Hills Jewish Center Basketball League for 17-year-olds

# MARY ELLEN BOLLINGER

171 North Crestway
Bellevue, WA 98171
(206) 741-9040

## OBJECTIVE

Consumer Marketing Management

## EXPERIENCE

*Book Product Marketing, Microsoft Press 1995–present*

- Manage and implement a yearly co-op advertising program with a budget of $850,000. This entails working closely with the national accounts manager, book distributors, commissioned sales reps, major accounts, and independent bookstores to determine the best use of co-op dollars, books to advertise, and creative execution.

- Create all business communications and trade sales materials, including trade catalogs, corporate catalogs, book back-jacket copy, trade show collateral, education account materials, and point-of-sale merchandising.

- Advise wholesale, retail, and computer trade accounts on product positioning, marketing strategies, and merchandising.

- Attend Microsoft Press sales conferences and all major computer and book industry trade shows to staff booths and meet with major accounts, wholesalers, and regional bookseller associations.

- Write a yearly Communication Plan that provides a clear analysis of the competitive market and details objectives, strategies, and tactics for Microsoft Press public relations, direct marketing, and merchandising.

*Corporate Programs, Microsoft Public Relations 1993–1995*

- Managed all photo and film shoots for Bill Gates and other Microsoft executives, working with programs and publications such as *20/20, ABC News, Business Week, Forbes, New York Times*, and *San Francisco Chronicle*.

- Provided staffing, creative, and logistical support at all industry tradeshows and Microsoft product launches.

- Managed and implemented the Third-Party Publishers Program. Identified book opportunities for computer book publishers, connected authors with publishers, and worked with internal product marketing to get information on products for publishers. Within four months of starting this position, I had analyzed and reorganized the Publishers Program, spoken on a panel on behalf of Microsoft at a book publishing conference, and planned and executed a publisher briefing at Microsoft

*Marketing Communications, Microsoft Corporate Communications 1991–1994*
- Worked with internal clients and account management to plan advertising and marketing strategies and tactics.
- Developed concepts with designers and presented these to clients.
- Wrote copy for brochures, data sheets, packaging, catalogs, promotional campaign materials, direct mail pieces, and newsletters for Microsoft programs and products.

### EDUCATION

University of Washington, Seattle, Washington, 1995–1996
Writing Certification Program, Fiction

University of Oregon, Eugene, Oregon, 1987–1991
Bachelor of Arts, Journalism

Faculté des Lettres, Avignon, France, 1990
Foreign Study, French Language and Art

### HONORS

Society of Technical Communications Award of Excellence—Microsoft Press Brochure

Society of Technical Communications Award of Merit—Microsoft Press 1996 Trade Catalog

Oregon Education Association Scholarship

Women's Auxiliary Scholarship

Oregon Business Scholarship

# JOHN R. BENNETT

781 Manhasset Drive • Salt Lake City, UT 84103
(801) 371-8176

*OBJECTIVE*  Marketing Sales Management

## *PROFESSIONAL EXPERIENCE*

### 1995–present  TANDY CORPORATION, SALT LAKE CITY, UTAH

*Vice–President, Sales*

Responsible for the sales and marketing of the company's interactive, VCR-based educational products in the Western United States. Developed all sales and marketing plans for the region. Responsible for the generation and control of the sales budget. Directed all training and customer support for the region.

Accomplishments:
*   Achieved assigned sales goal in every year
*   Established dealer sales network for computer products
*   Sold first district accounts in Western Region

### 1992–1995  ACTV, INTERACTIVE, SALT LAKE CITY, UTAH

*National Director of Sales* (1993)

Responsible to the President/CEO. Participated in the development of company policy and planning. Responsible for the sales and marketing activities of the company's LAN-based integrated learning system. Directed and implemented corporate-level sales plans. Managed product pricing and packaging requirements. Developed and managed sales budget. Organized field staff training programs. Assisted Operations in the completion of all customer installations. Jointly directed the sales support staff.

Accomplishments:
*   Increased total revenue from $8 million to $14.5 million
*   Reduced sales cost as a percentage of revenue by 15%
*   Reduced overall sales budget by 25%
*   Increased production per sales representative by 30%
*   Developed third-party and dealer distribution network for stand-alone products

*Regional Sales Manager* (1993)

Responsible for the direct supervision of five sales representatives. Coordinated the activities of field consultants. Directed the development of sales plans. Provided sales training and support to field staff. Monitored and controlled regional sales budget. Responsible for providing timely field communication to Home Office.

Accomplishments:
*   Increased regional revenue by 15%
*   Secured first regional district-wide sale in Alaska for $250,000
*   Established forecast system to improve revenue reporting by 20%
*   Reduced sales expense by 15%

### 1990–1993  WASATCH EDUCATION SYSTEMS, SALT LAKE CITY, UTAH

*Major Account Manager*

Responsible for the marketing of GRiD Systems products to major accounts in the states of Utah and Idaho, with a focus on the educational marketplace. The products marketed included laptop, desktop computer systems and conductivity products for network environments. Developed and implemented systems designs for LANS, Mainframe connection, and application software compatibility.

## WASATCH EDUCATION SYSTEMS (cont.)

Accomplishments:
- Achieved sales goal of $1 million
- Sold Idaho State Police RDT system for patrol vehicles for $850,000
- Directed sales activities to gain listing on Idaho State contract
- Sold GRiD as vendor of choice to National Semiconductor

### *Branch Manager*

Responsible for the retail and direct sales and marketing of WASATCH computers through WASATCH Business Products Division. Provided systems analysis and design support for all configurations. Recruited, hired, and trained all sales personnel. Supervised a staff of 7 marketing representatives. Maintained control of profit and loss of operation with an inventory of $200,000.

Accomplishments:
- Increased revenue by 20%
- Generated the first profitable year since 1984
- Increased revenue by direct sales representative by 40%
- Reduced inventory costs by 28%
- Reduced overall budget expense to revenue by 15%
- Listed WASATCH products on Utah State Approved List
- Installed five LANs in Salt Lake City School District

## 1988–1990    FOLLETT PUBLISHING COMPANY, CHICAGO, ILLINOIS

### *Division Sales Manager*

Managed the sales of Follett educational materials in the Eastern United States and Western Europe. Established the European sales organization and distribution network. Supervised 2 district managers and 15 sales representatives. Each sales district exceeded its quota during my tenure. Responsible for initial and ongoing sales training.

Accomplishments:
- Exceeded all sales goals each year from 1988 to 1990
- Developed European sales and distribution network
- Formulated the initial PC-based software for Follett mathematics series
- Organized and implemented all sales training

## 1986–1988    Assistant Principal, CAPISTRANO USD, CAPISTRANO, CALIFORNIA

## 1983–1986    Teacher, BELLFLOWER USD, BELLFLOWER, CALIFORNIA

### *ACADEMIC BACKGROUND*

1993–present   Westminster College, Salt Lake City, Utah: Adjunct Professor, Sales/Marketing Management

1990–1992      Illinois Benedictine College, Lisle, Illinois: M.B.A., Marketing and Finance

1979–1983      Brigham Young University, Provo, Utah: B.S., Sociology

# ROBERTO SEPULVEDA

150 East 40th Street, Apt. 7J
New York, NY 10020

Home: (212) 997-8738      Business: (212) 687-9000, Ext. 250

**OBJECTIVE**   *INTERNATIONAL BOOK PUBLISHING LINE MANAGEMENT*

A line management position in international book publishing with general management responsibilities

**SUMMARY**   More than 20 years' experience in sales management and administration in domestic and international book publishing with maior publishing houses. Heavy experience in hiring, training, and motivating successful salesmen, new market development, advertising, and promotion.

**EXPERIENCE**

*1981–1996*   **OPTIMUM INTERNATIONAL BOOK COMPANY**, New York, New York

*Group Marketing Director, Asia* (based in Tokyo, 1988–1996)

- Responsible for sales of all book company products
- Hired, trained, motivated, and supervised sales and promotion staff of 30 people
- Supervised local sales managers and representatives; coordinated sales activities in offices in Tokyo, New Delhi, Singapore, Karachi, Hong Kong, Bangkok, Manila, Jakarta, and Nairobi
- Created and established sales promotion and advertising campaigns for Asia and East Africa; calculated and established budgets and expenses
- Became first known U.S. publishing representative to open negotiations with Mainland China; sales there increased from $0 in 1984 to $500,000 in 1987
- Analyzed potential new markets and established new sales territories in Hong Kong/Taiwan, Thailand/Burma, East Africa, Indonesia, and Korea
- Increased sales by average of 20% annually since assuming sales management position

*Manager of Editorial Optimum LatinaAmericana*
(based in Bogotá, Colombia, 1987–1988)

- Responsible for sales and distribution of Spanish language books throughout South America, except Brazil, and in the Caribbean and Central America
- Supervised and coordinated 60 warehouse personnel, salesmen, editors, and order service people
- Supervised publishing of 40 university-level Spanish language textbooks
- Attained annual sales of $2 million during both years as Manager

*cont.*

### OPTIMUM INTERNATIONAL BOOK COMPANY (cont.)

*Manager, International Book Co.* (based in Singapore 1983–1986)

- Set up Sales and Distribution Center, which was responsible for sale of all book company products to Asian, East African, and some Middle Eastern countries
- As sales manager, also directed and coordinated efforts of 10 sales representatives for these areas
- Achieved 25% increase in sales in each of four years in position

*Sales Manager/Export* (based in New York 1982–1983)

- Hired, trained, and supervised 12 resident sales representatives to sell to markets primarily in Asia, Africa, and Middle East
- Planned, organized, and conducted sales meetings
- Directed promotion and advertising from New York into those export areas
- Established credit and pricing policies in export market covering 45 countries and 600 accounts
- Increased sales volume by 15%

*1975–1981*  **JOHN WILEY & SONS**, New York, New York
*Sales Manager, Mexico* (1979–1981)
*Sales Representative, Northern California* (1975–1978)

*1971–1975*  **ALLYN & BACON INC.**, Boston, Massachusetts
*Regional Sales Manager, College Division* (1974–1975)
*Sales Representative, Northern California* (1971–1973)

*1967–1971*  **THE MENNEN COMPANY**, San Francisco, California
*Sales Representative*

*1964–1967*  **COLGATE-PALMOLIVE COMPANY**, St. Louis, Missouri
*Sales Representative*

**EDUCATION**  St. Louis University, St. Louis, Missouri
1964—B.A., Political Science/History

**LANGUAGES**  Fluent in Spanish
Speak Japanese

# LUTHER BURNS

300 East Anson Road, Apt. 25C  •  Memphis, TN 72304  •  (901) 532-3707

**OBJECTIVE**   *DIRECTOR OF SALES/MERCHANDISING—FASHION INDUSTRY*

**SUMMARY**   Ten years' experience in successful buying and selling of fashions for men and women at wholesale and retail. Highly knowledgeable about European designs for the American market, with proven ability to forecast trends and educate customers to changes in styles. Experienced at working with designers to create selling collections. Have traveled to Italy and France several times a year to study collections and make astute purchases.

## PROFESSIONAL HIGHLIGHTS

1991–1995   RAFAEL FASHIONS, Memphis, TN

*Sales/Merchandising Manager* (1993–1995)

- Supervised five-person sales force in developing major accounts for men's and women's fashions ($10 million annual sales)
- Instigated and implemented intensive customer relations program to improve company's position with store buyers
- Worked with designers to create sales-oriented designs
  — Established procedures for controlling design expense
- Accurately projected sales/volume to exercise control over fabric purchases
  — Reduced fabric inventory through program of special cuttings and sales to selected outlets for piece goods
- Effected increase in profit-cost ratio through increase in markup
- Established advertising program in cooperation with stores
- Improved coordination of fabric delivery to factory and finished orders to stores
- Exercised quality control over line design, manufacturing, and overall company performance

*Merchandise Manager* (1992–1993)

- Supervised three people handling key accounts in establishing quality control of designer lines and factory performance
- Acted for company in liaison with manufacturers of piece goods in Italy to exercise control over manufacturing and distribution
- Instigated and implemented records systems for piece goods to coordinate delivery with projected date of manufacture of finished product
- Worked with pattern cutters, technicians, and production personnel to ensure excellence of product and on-time readiness of sample line for showing to buyers
- Worked closely with owner-designer to create salable product at good price for most favorable profit-cost factor

(cont.)

RAFAEL FASHIONS (cont.)

*Salesman* (1991–1992)

- Opened and developed major accounts with high-ticket stores (Saks, Neiman Marcus, I. Magnin, and Bloomingdale's)
- Responsible for increase in volume from $2.5 million to $8 million
- Guided clients in merchandise selection; projected sales for more effective production

1989–1990     BARNEY SAMPSON, Lexington, Kentucky

*Salesman*

- Opened and developed major accounts, doubling sales volume to $3 million — Brought in Bonwit Teller, Saks, and Bergdorf Goodman
- Educated customers to styling and design of European clothing
- Studied collections in Europe and selected parts of collections for the American market

1985–1989     TYRONE MEN'S APPAREL, Cedarhurst, New York

*Salesman*
(Started as stockboy while in high school and emerged as top salesman while in college)

- Learned men's European clothing business at retail level, giving me opportunity to judge customers' tastes and reactions to style and style changes

*EDUCATION*   Hofstra University, New York, New York
1985—History/Political Science

Speak Italian

# Marlene Parks

725 Ocean Parkway, Apt. 1C
Brooklyn, New York 11218

(212) 941-9759
(212) 870-8210

**Objective**

To employ expertise in clinical chemistry in a position as a technical representative for a pharmaceuticals or laboratory equipment manufacturer

**Summary**

More than ten years' experience as a graduate biochemist, with in-depth knowledge of clinical laboratory procedures and equipment. Proven capability in establishing and implementing work flow processes for expedited, integrated hospital record keeping. Specialist in accurate testing techniques.

**Primary Instruments Used**

Gamma Counting Spectrometer
Flame Photometer
Atomic Absorption
Micro Sampler Spectrophotometer

Auto Analyzer
Microcentrifugal Analyzer
Blood Gas Machine

## Highlights of Experience

*1984–present*

ST. LUKE'S HOSPITAL, New York, New York

*Laboratory Technologist*

- Developed and established standards for accuracy of hospital tests and quality control of special procedures
- Assisted with development and implementation of successful installation of Gamma Counter for use in radioimmunoassay procedures
  — Trained staff; established standards for use of Gamma Counter
- Perform standard and special clinical tests, including analyses of whole blood, serum, fluids, and urine, using both manual and automated methods
- Trained and supervise staff of five technicians, maintain good relationship with coworkers, and distribute daily workload in high-pressure atmosphere
- Troubleshoot equipment and serve as consultant on new procedures
- Conduct drug-identification tests
- Member of IV team

*1983–1984*

ELIZABETH SEATON'S HOSPITAL, Cochabamba, Bolivia

*Biochemist*

- Established and implemented laboratory procedures in new hospital
- Assisted in introduction of new manual methods, set up laboratory equipment, and prepared reagents
- Performed routine tests in hematology, chemistry, urine, bacteriology, and serology and for blood bank

| | |
|---|---|
| *1982–1983* | **MINISTRY OF PUBLIC HEALTH, CENTRAL LABORATORY,** Cochabamba, Bolivia |

*Biochemist Trainee*

- Worked under supervision of group leader
- Performed routine detailed tests in hematology, serology, parasitology, and bacteriology

*Concurrent* **FARMACIA COCHABAMBA,** Cochabamba, Bolivia

*Pharmacist Trainee*

- Organized and filled prescriptions
- Prepared special compounds not available from manufacturer: tablets, suppositories, suspensions, solutions, and lotions

**EDUCATION**

University of St. Simon, Cochabamba, Bolivia
1984—Degree in Biochemistry/Pharmacy
(Annual Best Student Award with 4.0 GPA throughout five-year program)

Hunter College, New York, New York
1979—Course in Histology

The American Institute, Cochabamba, Bolivia
1977—Graduated among five top students

**CERTIFIED**

Biochemist and Pharmacist
Laboratory Technologist

**LANGUAGES**

Trilingual: Spanish/English/German
Working knowledge of Italian

# BARRY ROGERS

25-25 Parsons Boulevard
Whitestone, NY 11357
(212) 445-5300

**OBJECTIVE**    *SALES/TECHNICAL REPRESENTATIVE*

**SUMMARY**    Experienced as wholesale and retail salesperson, buyer, and technician. Extensive knowledge of photographic market, product lines, and product maintenance. Excellent sales track record. Familiar with sales, promotion, merchandising, and forecasting of market trends.

**EXPERIENCE**

1988–present    L. J. CRANSTON CORPORATION, New York, New York
(Rep organization for manufacturers of photographic equipment)

*Manufacturers' Representative*

- Represent the following manufacturers in Connecticut and Westchester County, New York

  — Holson, photo albums
  — M. W. Carr, photo frames
  — Amphoto, photographic books
  — Harwood, movie and video lighting equipment
  — Taprell Loomis, picture folders

- Opened up 37 new accounts, increasing sales volume by $100,000

- In first year, sold $300,000 in supplies and equipment

1985–1988    MACY'S DEPARTMENT STORES, New York, New York

*Assistant Buyer*

- Purchased photographic products and equipment for 15 Camera Departments with $7 million combined annual volume

- Researched and evaluated new products; identified and defined changing trends in consumer preference

- Analyzed sales figures; planned advertising and sales promotions

- Conducted weekly personal visits to stores to check inventory; supervised display and merchandising

- Maintained extensive vendor contact

1980–1985    MACY'S DEPARTMENT STORES, Rego Park, New York

*Camera Department Manager, 1985*

- Managed Camera and Calculator Departments; supervised and motivated staff of 19

- Purchased bulk of camera department inventory; monitored stock levels

- Advised management on changes in customer preferences and buying trends

MACY'S DEPARTMENT STORES (cont.)

*Book and Stationery Department Manager, 1981–1984*
- Managed staff of 9
- Purchased and merchandised 95% of all books and stationery; made all merchandising and ordering decisions
- Showed consistent 10% seasonal increase in sales; demonstrated success in targeting merchandise to the needs of the community

*Camera Salesclerk, 1980–1981*
- Sold cameras and accessories to retail customers

1971–1977   HOFSTRA UNIVERSITY, Hempstead, New York

*Audiovisual Technician/Photographer/Darkroom Technician*

1977–1980   *Elementary School Teacher*

**EDUCATION**   Hofstra University, Hempstead, New York
1974—B.A., English/History
1981—M.S., Education

**EXTRACURRICULAR ACTIVITIES**

Hofstra University—Photo Club, Campus Newspaper, Yearbook and Radio Station

Member of Fresh Meadows Camera Club, New York

# EARL ORR

150 Lark Court
Marietta, GA 30067

(404) 453-0705 (home)
(404) 266-8259 (office)

**EXPERIENCE**    TRAVELERS INSURANCE CO.                October 1986–present

*Regional Assistant Vice-President/Marketing Operations Officer*
Southeast Region, Atlanta, Georgia, 12/94–present

Management responsibility for General Managers of regional branch offices; areas of supervision include marketing, underwriting, claims handling, and administrative support.

Directly accountable for results in 7 of region's 13 branch offices; offices produce $125 million in revenues, require operating budget of approximately $20 million, and employ 750 people.

- Youngest in company to hold position of Marketing Operations Officer.
- Initiated management actions necessary to change and upgrade ineffective leadership in critical branch offices.
- Maximized revenue opportunities through successful producer management actions.
- Minimized expense deterioration by developing and implementing needed expense control actions.
- Analyzed product and pricing needs, state by state, and worked successfully with technical staff to achieve desired filings, particularly in commercial lines.
- Effectively represented assigned offices in the annual negotiations with Regional Headquarters.

*Regional Assistant Vice-President, Management Services*
Southeast Region, Atlanta, Georgia, 12/92–12/94

Responsible for all administrative support functions, including budgeting, expense control, credit and collections, internal audit, manual and computer processing operations, employee relations, training and development, purchasing and real estate.

Provided support to 13 branch offices in 11 Southeastern states; offices produced $225 million in revenues, required operating budget of approximately $30 million, and employed 1,300 people.

- Established decentralized regional operation; management had been centralized prior to 12/92.
- Selected as top region in 1993 and 1994 from an overall administrative support perspective.
- Directly responsible for the corporate-wide implementation of a more effective compensation program.
- Developed and implemented computerized monitor and control system for all regional training and developmental activities.

*Manager Administrative Operations*
White Plains Service Office, White Plains, New York, 10/86–12/92

Comprehensive management responsibility for Financial Services, Administrative Operations, and Personnel.

Prepared, allocated, and distributed office operating budget in excess of $1 million.

Directed personnel in Collections, Data Processing, Filing, Mail, Supply, Telecommunications, and Typing Departments.

Supervised all employment activities, included recruiting, screening, and testing for staff of 120.

- Consistently exceeded assigned productivity standards.
- Functioned as in-house management consultant for General Manager.
- Reduced outstanding receivables from $100,000 monthly to only $1,500, without any adverse effect on sales.
- Created a formal orientation program for new employees.

**EDUCATION**    M.B.A., 1987, Iona College
Major: Organizational Behavior
Graduated cum laude

B.S., 1976, University of Bridgeport
Major: Marketing
Attended on athletic scholarship

**REFERENCES**    Provided upon request

**R. D. GRANEY** • 35 East 46th Street • New York, New York 10016 • (212) 889-9920

**OBJECTIVE**     *MANUFACTURING/MARKETING COORDINATOR*

**SUMMARY**      Fourteen years' experience in competitive design and marketing of brand-name clothing for boys and girls. Highly expert in close coordination of marketing and manufacturing divisions. Demonstrated excellence in supervision of design staff and management of showroom. Possess conceptual acuity in interpreting buyer ideas into salable designs.

**EXPERIENCE**

*1988–present*      PERKY PRINT TEXTILES, INC., New York, New York

*Corporate Design Director, Showroom Manager* **(1/88–present)**

- Direct design and merchandising of domestic and international line of childrenswear, with corporate volume of $60 million
- Maintain close and constant communication with marketing executives in establishing achievement of marketing plans
- Coordinate manufacturing and marketing divisions for most effective production of seasonal and standard merchandise
- Manage New York office, including showroom, Design Department, and all administrative functions for International Division
- Maintain retail-client relations in the field in determination of local and regional taste and demand
- Initiate use of available machinery to produce new lines
- Helped company maintain strong market position in recessional climate
- Also carried full responsibilities of Senior Design and Merchandising Coordinator (see below)

*Senior Design and Merchandise Coordinator* **(7/86–12/87)**

- Researched market for merchandise mix and capacity for introduction of Perky Print products in particular stores and locales
- Established and implemented systems to improve design, color, and fabrics of line

*Design and Merchandise Coordinator* **(1/86–7/86)**

- Dealt directly with national chain store accounts in development of private-label lines
- Established input into models and colors from results of market research
- Designed children's garments for mass production for private-label accounts
- Designed line of children's clothing (models, colors, fabrics) for Infants' to Girls' 7–14 and Boys' 8–16

| | |
|---|---|
| *7/85–12/85* | COLONIAL CORPORATION OF AMERICA, New York, New York |

*Consultant*
- Set up coordinates program for line of boys' and youths' garments from conception to final production
- Structured division based on the development processes of the program for private-label sales to J. C. Penney and Kmart
- Participated in design of men's knit and woven shirt line
- Conducted market research for colors, models, stripes, and plaid formations

| | |
|---|---|
| *10/82–6/85* | GARAN, INC., New York, New York |

*Head Designer, Girls' 7–14 Division* (7/83–6/85)
- Designed and merchandised Garanimal line
- Designed four collections annually (400,000 dozen—$35 million in retail sales)
- Improved coordination between Design, Production Planning, and Manufacturing Divisions
- Developed new size specifications to increase marketability
- Expanded previously minimal girls' line through development of more feminine silhouettes

*Associate Designer, Girls' 7–14 Division* (10/82–7/83)
- Assisted Head Designer in all areas listed above

**EDUCATION**    Fashion Institute of Technology, New York, New York
1981—A.A.S., Major, Apparel Design; Specialization, Childrenswear

**CERTIFICATIONS**  Dale Carnegie Institute: Dale Carnegie Personal Development Course
Diploma, July 1985

# MICHAEL REMINGTON

2 Franklyn Avenue, East Brunswick, NJ 08816 • (201) 238-6201

**OBJECTIVE**   *SALES/MARKETING or DIVISION MANAGEMENT*

**SUMMARY**   Record of significant contributions to profit levels and productivity in every position held. Capable leader and motivator, with broad overview of sales and marketing. Adept at market analysis and conceptualization. Able product spokesman.

## PROFESSIONAL ACHIEVEMENTS

1989–1996   **FEARON CORPORATION**, Piscataway, New Jersey

*Vice-President, Fearon Tool Group Division* (1995–1996)

- Control sales, marketing, profit and loss, inventory, and purchasing for five tool lines with annual sales of $22 million and staff of 250
  — Developed and managed nation-wide sales organization of 92 manufacturers' rep firms, 10 direct sales managers, and 35 interoffice personnel
- Established sales incentive program, resulting in 13% increase in annual sales and previously unparalleled gross profit levels
- Reorganized Marketing and Creative Departments, resulting in increased efficiency and improved market analysis
- Through analysis of item costs, market, and competition, increased gross profit share of three assumed lines by 10% in one year
- Resolved marketing difficulties through reorganization to encourage total market penetration
- Expanded merchandising productivity almost 200% through analysis and redesign of merchandising aids after studying competitive aids and consumer acceptance
- Established new product concept and conducted market tests; supervised design, pricing, item selection, and selling program

*Vice-President, Delco Division* (1992–1995)

- Directed division with annual sales of $13 million; oversaw inventory, quality control, sales, and marketing of two tool lines
  — Managed 45 rep firms, 5 direct sales managers, and 20 interoffice personnel
- Established and organized national advertising campaign to penetrate all markets
- Increased gross profit share 5% through market analysis and reformulation of marketing program
- Improved product quality and expanded all categories for favorable competition with domestic tool manufacturers, raising sales by 25%

*National Sales Manager, Delco Division* (1991–1992)

- Directed sales force of 45 rep organizations
- Upgraded Delco image from small import to top quality line, permitting favorable competition with domestic manufacturers; formulized and marketed Pro-Mate as secondary line

*Western Regional Sales Manager, Delco Division* (1989–1991)

- Directed 8 rep organizations throughout 12 states
- Ranked no. 1 in regional sales during 1989 and 1990; sales volumes more than doubled between 1989 and 1991
- Originated merchandising aids and pricing structure ideas that were adopted by home office for implementation throughout company

1983–1989    **ALBERTO CULVER COMPANY**, New York, New York

*District Sales Manager* (1987–1989)

- Supervised 1 assistant and 7 salespeople working throughout seven Northwestern states
- Awarded President's Cup for highest district sales increase in 1988; in 1989, scored within top third of total districts in company
- Ranked No. 1 District Salesman between 1985 and 1987
- First manager in company to hire saleswoman to represent women's health and beauty products

*Assistant District Sales Manager* (1985–1987)

- Supervised 5 salespeople and headed Len Dawson (Kansas City Chiefs quarterback) promotion program

*Sales* (1983–1985)

- Represented company among drug wholesalers, food trade, mass merchandisers, and rack jobbers in Kansas City, Missouri

1979–1983    **SHEAFFER PEN COMPANY**, Fort Madison, Indiana

*Sales*

- Called on retailers and wholesalers in Oklahoma, Kansas, and Missouri

**EDUCATION**    B.A., Business, Northeast Missouri State University

Professional Seminars:
     Dale Carnegie Sales/ Management Program
     American Management Association

**PROFESSIONAL AFFILIATIONS**

     American Management Association
     National Association of Service Merchandisers
     General Merchandise Distributors Conference
     Automotive Service Industries Association
     Automotive Warehouse Distributors Association

*Willing to relocate and free to travel*

## PETER CHEUNG

32 Burton School Avenue
Westport, CT 06880
(203) 226-7721

**OBJECTIVE**

To employ expertise and experience in international marketing in a senior management position for a manufacturer of industrial or consumer goods

**SUMMARY**

— More than 20 years' experience in international marketing between Asia and United States–Europe, including industrial and farm equipment and consumer goods

— Thirteen years as manager for consumer goods exporter in Hong Kong

— Expert in locating markets in Asia, negotiating contracts, and expediting shipping details and government documentation

— Completely fluent in English, Mandarin Chinese, Shanghai. and Cantonese

— Have M.B.A. in International Business

— Possess intimate knowledge of entire East Asian marketplace with specific knowledge of China

**BUSINESS HIGHLIGHTS**

*1983–present*

C. K. CHAN CO.,INC.
Westport, Connecticut
**President**

• Developed market for tannery equipment, chemicals, and raw materials in Taiwan, Hong Kong, Bangkok, Singapore, and Malaysia

• Conduct market analysis surveys through personal contact with buyers and agents and on-site exploration in trading countries

• Negotiate contracts with suppliers and buyers

• Exploring markets in China proper; negotiations proceeding

• Maintain financial intelligence through correspondence and personal investigation relevant to exchange rates and credit requirements

• Maintain excellent customer service relations through correspondence and in-plant visits

• Transact shipping details: letters of credit, freight forwarding, customs clearances, and delivery verification

*1979–1983*

SHANGHAI TRADING CORPORATION
New York, New York
**Vice-President/Executive Manager**
- Charged with responsibility for shipment of materials to Vietnam and Cambodia under U.S. Government Aid Program
  - Machinery shipped included textile fabrication machinery, tractors, and tractor-drawn implements for small farms
  - Tools included digging and chopping tools for farmers hand tools for factory and construction workers
  - Raw materials included farm chemicals, fertilizers, and plastics for use in manufacturing
  - Full range of consumer products
- Directed all export procedures and processing of U.S. government documents

*1966–1979*

WELLMING TRADING CO., LTD.
Hong Kong
**Export Manager**
- Exported products manufactured in Hong Kong to importers in United States, England, West Germany, Belgium, Italy, and France
  - Products included men's and women's garments, gift items, costume jewelry, and toys
- Analyzed markets, negotiated sales, maintained customer relations through correspondence and personal visits, and processed shipping documents

**EDUCATION**

Hong Kong University
1971 — M.B.A., International Business

Regional College, Hong Kong
1966 — B.A., Philosophy

*Able and willing to travel extensively*

## STACY HALL
42 Knot Road · Tenafly, NJ 07670
(201) 567-6987

**OBJECTIVE**    *ADVERTISING ACCOUNT EXECUTIVE*

**SUMMARY**    Ten years' experience in advertising with direct client contact throughout and three years in account management. Demonstrated expertise in budget management. Creative copywriter on variety of industrial, consumer, and corporate campaigns, including print ads, direct mail, and collateral material. Proven ability to supervise production, assist in new business development, and maintain excellent client relations with all levels of management.

Clients included Conrac Corporation, Maserati Automobiles, McGraw-Hill Publications Company, North American Philips Corporation, Thomas J. Lipton Company, "21" Brands, U.S. Industries, Xerox Corporation, and Zeiss-Ikon.

**EXPERIENCE**

1992–1996    DOBBS ADVERTISING COMPANY, INC., New York, New York

**Account Executive** (1994–1996)

- Successfully planned and administrated advertising and promotion for several clients, in many cases maximizing limited funds through knowledge of media and production (for example, utilizing free media publicity to support insertions, negotiating most advantageous rate structures, and getting the most efficiency from production expenditures)
- Conceived, developed, and directed advertising and promotion programs for numerous industrial and consumer accounts
- Planned and supervised selection and purchase of print and broadcast media
- Wrote or directed copy on all accounts handled

**Copy Director** (1992–1994)

- Created concepts and wrote copy for print and broadcast media as well as collateral, sales material, direct mail literature, and publicity releases
- Supervised all in-house and freelance copywriting
- Served as client contact on several accounts
- Recommended media schedules

*Highlights*

- During tenure as account supervisor and head writer, one account experienced 20% sales increases on numerous products
- Developed print ad for leading surveying equipment manufacturer that completely repositioned client in the market, increased sales, and influenced the "look" of future advertising in publication in which it appeared
- Created and directed a campaign that reaffirmed client, the Bank of Toms River, as the no. 1 bank based in Ocean County, New Jersey

1987–1992    MULLER JORDAN HERRICK/N.J., Inc., Fort Lee, New Jersey and New York, New York
(Formerly Richard James Associates)

**Copywriter and Assistant Account Executive**
- Conceived and wrote advertising and promotion copy for print ads and collateral material for industrial and consumer accounts
- Served as account executive for numerous clients
- Planned and purchased media advertising

*Highlights*
- Created a coupon-response newspaper campaign for retail tire dealer; as a result, client had to restaff and reorganize to handle increased business
- Produced print ad for new account that generated more inquiries from the first insertion than former agency's year-long campaign had achieved

1985–1987    KALMAR ADVERTISING, INC., Englewood Cliffs, New Jersey

**Copywriter**
- Wrote advertising and promotional copy for consumer and industrial accounts
- Served as copy contact
- Recommended and purchased print and broadcast media
- Developed numerous public relations programs for clients

1984–1985    PRENTICE-HALL, INC., Englewood Cliffs, New Jersey

**Assistant Production Editor**
- Planned and coordinated book production, from manuscript to completed bound book
- Copy-edited and supervised same
- Acted as liaison with authors, suppliers, and internal personnel
- Checked galleys, page proofs, and blues
- Generated advertising copy for book jackets

**EDUCATION**  Fairleigh Dickinson University, Teaneck, New Jersey
1984—B.S.

**LANGUAGE**  French

# JOHN POWELL

154 East 49th Street • New York, NY 10011 • (212) 684–8820

**OBJECTIVE**   *CORPORATE ADVERTISING DIRECTOR*

**SUMMARY**   Proven track record in creating and developing comprehensive advertising campaigns, with special emphasis on sales promotion materials, direct response advertising, and direct mail. Experienced in negotiation for cooperative advertising. Ability to design and coordinate trade show activities. Highly skilled in all production techniques, creative direction, account management, and media selection.

## PROFESSIONAL HIGHLIGHTS

**1988–present**   MKP, INC., New York, New York (Graphics Studio)

*Manager*

- Direct, coordinate and exercise quality control of production activities
  — Four creative departments: Design, Art, Typesetting, and Color Proofing

Clients include United Technologies, Hearst Publications, Union Carbide

**1986–1988**   INTERSIGHT DESIGN, INC., New York, New York (Packaging Design)

*Art Director*

- Charged with responsibility for studio production and final art for product packaging
- Selected and coordinated outside services: typesetting, photography/retouching, printing, color proofing
- Knowledgeable about product packaging and marketing

Clients include Bristol Myers, Pillsbury, Mennen, Hoescht

**1983–1986**   WENK ORGANIZATION, INC., New York, New York (Advertising Agency)

*Creative Director/Account Executive*

- Managed, directed, and supervised creative production
  — Specified and purchased outside support services: typography, photography, printing, mailing lists, and media
  — Provided creative concept and direction to 15-member staff, including in-house and freelance artists; supervised and personally designed and produced material; edited and wrote copy and headlines
- Assumed management of Media Department
  — Upgraded department operation through initiation of improved production/traffic systems and contract negotiations
  — Handled an increase in media sales of approximately 200% without additional staff
  — Developed media budgets with most effective allocation for radio, print, and some TV

(cont.)

WENK ORGANIZATION, INC. (cont.)
- Managed direct response and coupon advertising campaigns
  — Developed campaigns for various clients, targeted audiences, suggested appropriate media, and made account presentations
  — Followed through with total production after client approval
- In-depth experience in direct mail
  — Targeted audiences based on specific criteria
  — Researched list companies; purchased lists for test markets and full-scale efforts
  — Designed printed material to be mailed, including personalized letters
  — Monitored responses and fulfillment of campaigns, ranging from 5,000-piece test market to 500,000-piece general mailing

Clients included Chase Manhattan Bank, Mego Toys, New School, Parsons School of Design, New American Library

1981–1983  TYPE FACTORY, New York, New York (Advertising and Graphic Design Studio)
- Directed all creative activities: print campaigns, catalogs, trade show exhibits, and sales promotional material

Clients included R. R. Bowker Company, Library Bureau Division of Sperry, New Process Steel

1981  OTTINO/SOLOMON, INC., New York, New York (Design and Typography Studio)
- As Studio Manager/Designer, was responsible for production, including concept, design, type direction, board work, and process lettering

1976–1978  BOROGRAPHICS, INC., New York, New York (Design and Typography Studio)
- Instituted, directed, and promoted growth and operation of full-service graphics and typography studio

EDUCATION  John Jay College, New York, New York—Marketing Major
Served apprenticeship in graphics in several art and graphics studios in New York and Los Angeles

# GEORGE HALKIADES

100-55 77 Drive • Forest Hills, NY 11375
(212) 896–3275

**OBJECTIVE**   *MANAGEMENT - RETAIL OPERATIONS*
To apply my experience and expertise in retail management, organization and merchandising in a position with growth potential to general management/executive management level

**SUMMARY**   More than 15 years' experience in retail/customer service management with 4 years' definitive experience in full management responsibility and accountability. Skilled in selection of merchandise to attract local customers, merchandising and cost control. Creative in traffic-stopping displays and promotion with keen eye to profitability. Excellent in customer and employee relations.

## HIGHLIGHTS OF PROFESSIONAL EXPERIENCE

**1988–present**   MAXI-DISCOUNT DRUGS, Richmond Hill, New York
*Manager*

- Solved problem of confusion over price changes by proposing price-coding system to be circulated to managers of eight stores in chain
  - Proposal, adopted by general management, has developed into orderly presentation of imminent price changes on merchandise to provide all store managers with a method of putting changes into effect simultaneously
- Developed creative merchandising plan for Christmas sales
  - Proposed codification of Christmas display setup to enable local managers to effect same or similar merchandising displays
  - Personally supervised setup for five of the eight stores
  - Through grouping of Christmas items for easy access, merchandise is moving well in every store in chain with profitable outlook anticipated

**1981–1988**   F. W. WOOLWORTH COMPANY
*Manager, Rego Park, New York* (1986–1988)

- Instigated, developed, and maintained fluid merchandising policy to meet the demands of a changing neighborhood
  - Stocked merchandise to attract different ethnic groups
  - Improved profit picture to turn around operation, which was scheduled for closing
- Recommended removal of lunch/fountain operation, which was losing money through poor sales and high maintenance costs
  - Instituted expansion of horticultural, Shoe and Hosiery Departments that produced large increases (25% to 50%) for the year
- Initiated merchants' committee of 40 local store managers to install special Christmas lighting to improve night traffic, which had declined considerably over four-year period
  - Night business showed large increase over previous year, with minimal cost to all concerned

(cont.)

F. W. WOOLWORTH (cont.)
*Manager, Rye, New York* (1985–1986)
- Hired dynamic individual to replace retiring operator of lunch fountain that had been steadily losing sales over long period
  — Lengthened hours of operation; hired additional competent help
- Developed reputation of being "the place to eat" in Rye, especially at breakfast; sales took upward turn and increased dramatically

*Positions of Increasing Responsibility, Various Stores* (1981–1985)
- Was accepted into Management Trainee Program, which included training in merchandising, office procedures, lunch operations, and overall management of store
- Was steadily promoted to Assistant Manager, Advanced Assistant Manager, and Specialized Assistant Manager prior to official appointment as Manager of Rye Store

1977–1981    GLATT TRAVEL, Hicksville, New York
*Tour Coordinator*
- Managed arrangements for world-wide tours of 20–30 people
  — Scheduled tours, booked members into hotels, and dealt directly with carriers for most timely and economical travel accomodations
- Interacted with people at all levels on a one-to-one basis
- Booked in excess of $20,000 per year in general and customized tours

## EDUCATION

Queens College, Flushing, New York
  1977—Major: History

## SPECIAL INTERESTS

Reading, stamp collecting, sports events

# STEPHEN FURMAN

150 West End Avenue
New York, NY 10023

*Home:* (212) 873-6512 • *Messages:* (212) 787-4900

**OBJECTIVE**     *INFORMATION INDUSTRY: MARKETING REPRESENTATIVE*

**SUMMARY**     Eleven years of sales and merchandising experience, including technical products. Consistent track record of sales volume increases. Ability to train sales staff.

**EXPERIENCE**
1992–1995     ANDREW'S DEPARTMENT STORE, INC.
NEW YORK, NEW YORK

*Assistant Buyer, Appliance Department*
- Purchased appliances for retail chain; $7 million annual appliance volume
- Assisted with store merchandising to create additional departmental traffic for 15 stores
- Followed up on delivery of merchandise
- Monitored distribution of goods to various stores
- Checked competitive retailers for comparative pricing
- Acted as troubleshooter in solving store management problems pertaining to appliances

1984–1992     *Assistant Manager of Radio and Television*

Promoted to *Manager of Calculator Department*
- Responsible for operation of Calculator Department
- Quadrupled the department's sales, from $125,000 to $500,000, during period of sharp price competition
- Increased sales volume each year as Manager
- Trained commission team with high morale and low turnover
- Personally sold more than 15,000 calculators during an eight-year period
- Made recommendations to buyers on merchandise selection
- Sold programmable calculators (priced as high as $500) to end users, including business and technically oriented customers

**EDUCATION**     AMERICAN INTERNATIONAL COLLEGE, SPRINGFIELD, MASSACHUSETTS
1984—B.A., History

Additional Skills and Interests:
| | |
|---|---|
| Logic Seminar | Mechanics |
| Philosophy | Statistics |
| Communications | Financial Research—gold, foreign currency markets |

**PERSONAL**     Will travel

## *Betty Ames*

24-54 Lancaster Avenue, Jamaica, New York, NY 11432 • (212) 521-7240

**OBJECTIVE**  Product management position utilizing diversified marketing experience and strong analytical skills

**EXPERIENCE**
1995–1996

STATLER-MORRISON, INC., New York, New York
**Account Executive**
Supervised marketing and advertising of two major accounts:

### HAIRCARE, INC.

- Developed and implemented $10 million advertising budget
- Created new product, "Le Monde," and new color line, "Corsage D'Amour," increasing both market share and profitability
- Supervised research, media, creative, and production staffs
- Designed media plans for placement of print and network advertising
- Developed all necessary production estimates and cost analyses for advertising campaigns
- Prepared and presented product strategy statements to senior management

### STILL SPIRITS, INC.

- Prepared and implemented $3 million advertising budget
- Planned, positioned, and launched major new product "Bourbon Royal," in response to market need, including packaging, pricing, and merchandising
- Developed promotional packages, point-of-purchase displays, and sales force incentive programs

SIMMONS AND STERNS INC., New York, New York
1994–1995
**Senior Research Analyst**
Formulated and implemented quantitative questionnaire to forecast marketing trends
- Based on survey findings, prepared and presented marketing recommendations to clients
- Based on qualitative and quantitative analyses of consumer response, predicted potential market share for new product entries

CHESEBROUGH POND'S INC., Greenwich, Connecticut
Summer
1993
**Research Analyst**
- Conducted design testing for product packaging
- Developed and prepared commercial evaluation reports

**EDUCATION**  UNIVERSITY OF PENNSYLVANIA, Wharton School
1993—B.S., Marketing
1993—B.A., Psychology
- Dean's List, 1991–1993

HARVARD UNIVERSITY, Graduate Program in Clinical Psychology
1992—Study of Small-Group Communication

**PERSONAL**
- President, Juvenile Diabetes Foundation
- Extensive travel throughout Europe and Middle East

# WAYNE PENDERGRAFT

4121 Seaview Avenue   •   Baltimore, MD 21830   •   (301) 469-4725

**OBJECTIVE**   *SALES/SALES MANAGEMENT*

**SUMMARY**   Solid experience in sales and production management, with effective, low-key approach to promotion of business appreciation. Demonstrated expertise in staff motivation for quality production of product in highly competitive industry. Strong ability to establish and maintain excellent customer relations in turnaround of company image. Fully knowledgeable about account management, from point of initial contact to impact on bottom-line profitability.

**EXPERIENCE**

1989–1996   ALL PURPOSE IDENTIFICATION, LTD., Kingston, Jamaica

*Sales Manager*

- Charged with effecting turnaround of company that, because of poor image, was losing sales and revenue
- Established and maintained excellent customer relations program
  - Heeded customer complaints on product quality and took steps to institute major quality control system
  - Negotiated contracts to ensure adherence to orders by the customer and delivery by the company
- Directed activities of five salesreps in promotion of identification badges
  - Motivated, routed, and monitored staff efforts; established incentive system for surpassing set quotas
  - Traveled with each rep on periodic basis to assess performance and customer acceptance of personality and sales presentation; offered suggestions for improvement where needed
- Instituted and systemetized sales call program to ensure regular visits by representatives with positive service attitude
  - Customers responded through increased orders
- Administered collection process
  - Worked with slow-pay customers to establish reasonable base for time payments
  - Improved collections by 45%
- Opened several new major accounts
- Improved overall sales volume by 35% each year
- Set incremental pricing policy to cover constantly rising costs of imported materials
  - Sold policy to customers who agreed to abide by it
- Developed effective advertising campaign, with ads in local papers and on radio; wrote all copy

(cont.)

ALL PURPOSE IDENTIFICATION, LTD. (cont.)

*Production Manager*

- Charged with reestablishing rapport with customers having serious complaints regarding quality of product
- Called on each dissastifled customer; ascertained problem customer was having with product and/or company performance
- Quietly persuaded each customer to "bear with us"; promised that as new Production Manager I would take necessary steps to improve quality and delivery times
  - Initiated, established, and maintained systems for improving quality of product and high degree of quality control on a continuing basis
  - Initiated, established, and maintained shipping systems to ensure on-time delivery to customers
  - Program resulted In keeping the accounts in-house and recelvlng larger and more frequent orders and referrals to new customers
- Increased productivity and efficiency of production staff
  - Set clear standards of performance in regard to punctuality and responsibility
  - Established incentive program for adherence to rules
  - Attracted higher quality of personnel to work in plant
- Improved performance; again, resulted in increased sales volume and better customer relations

| | |
|---|---|
| 1988–1989 | GOODYEAR TIRE, LTD., Kingston, Jamaica |

*Sales Manager* (while attending school)

- Directed activities of three salesmen; set sales quotas and performance standards
- Personally opened 14 new accounts (local firms and gas stations)

**EDUCATION**  College of Art, Science and Technology, Kingston, Jamaica
Personnel Management

Jamaica School of Business, Kingston, Jamaica
Accounting

**SKILLS**  Knowledge of laminating and pouching machinery, embosser, Polaroid Land ID-2, and four-way ID cameras

# JANICE WHITE

205 BUSHNELL AVENUE, HARTFORD, CT 06103
*HOME:* (203) 522-2193    *OFFICE:* (203) 241-4202

**OBJECTIVE**    *SENIOR BUYER FOR AGGRESSIVE, MULTISTORE RETAIL OPERATION*

**SUMMARY**    Highly motivated buyer, with nine years' domestic and import experience in various retail furniture departments. Strong color and design sense, with ability to identify market winners. Creative and effective merchandiser; good advertising and budgeting skills. Nation's youngest casegoods buyer.

**EXPERIENCE**
1987–present    STERN AND COMPANY, Hartford, Connecticut
*Buyer, Bedroom, Dining Room, Occasional, and Lifestyle Furniture*
- Purchase for and manage $2 million inventory throughout eight stores, representing average of $22 million in annual revenues
    — Supervise all aspects of retailing, from product purchasing through merchandising, to floor presentation
    — Hire, train and supervise Assistant Buyer and sales staff of eight
    — Formulate and administer departmental objectives; prepare long-range plans
- Increased volume of Lifestyle Department from $200,000 to $800,000 in one year (Ranked No. 1 Lifestyle Buyer for all Stern and Company stores)
- Personally selected program for importing profitable, high-volume line of European chairs, with assistance of Head Marketing Representative for Stern and Company
    — Visited nine Italian factories to ensure best product and value, with goal of achieving additional $3 million in sales
- Organized cooperative publicity venture with Museum of Modern Folk Art in conjunction with marketing effort for new casegoods line
    — Worked up seminar/slide show that was conducted by Museum Director of collection on which product line was based and that attracted 50 potential customers
- Promoted from Assistant Buyer to Buyer after only three months on job

1986–1987    W. & J. DOANE, New York, New York
*Assistant Buyer*
- Assisted Buyer for Bedroom and Dining Room, Mattresses and Sleep Sofas, and Contemporary and Occasional Furniture Departments
- Promoted from Trainee Assistant Buyer after only four months on job, as part of University of Massachusetts Internship program

1985    W. & J. DOANE, San Francisco, California
*Floater* (summer, junior college year)
- Assigned to various departments: Advertising, Accounts Payable and Accounts Receivable, Personnel, Decorating Studio, and Executive Offices

1983    STERN'S DEPARTMENT STORE, Boothbay Harbor, Maine
*Salesperson, Women's Specialty Operation* (summer, freshman college year)

1983    CLOTHES CORNER, Acton, Massachusetts
*Salesperson, Women's Discount Operation* (between high school and college)

**EDUCATION**    UNIVERSITY OF MASSACHUSETTS, Amherst, Massachusetts
1987—B.S., Retail Merchandising

**INTERESTS**    Photography, Sailing

# DAVID BENCKE · 300 East 93rd Street · New York, NY 10028 · (212) 737-6620

**OBJECTIVE** *MEDIA SALES—PRINT/BROADCASTING*

**SUMMARY** Results-oriented salesman with proven ability for productive effort. Broad background in self-education through employment in different types of industries as well as extensive travel throughout United States, the Caribbean, Latin America and Europe. Excellent verbal skills. Proficient in French. Strong in interpersonal relations.

## RELEVANT EXPERIENCE

*1988–present* TREND NEWSPAPERS, INC., Boston, Massachusetts
*Account Executive*
- Service established accounts; contact and sell new accounts
- Present prestige concept of publication to prospects; assist clients in ad design and composition
- Work with clients in establishing new format for ads when publication changed size from tabloid to magazine
- Maintain excellent customer relations with established accounts through reinforcement of magazine concept
- In first week, brought in 2 important accounts
- Responsible for servicing 6 of the paper's largest advertisers

*Concurrent* TIME/LIFE LIBRARIES, INC., Boston, Massachusetts
*Telephone Sales Representative*
- Developed sales of Home Improvement Series through phone contact with people in their homes
  — Established 19 new accounts in four days (200 calls, 50 pitches—working four hours per day)

## OTHER EXPERIENCE

*1987* 73 MAGAZINE, INC., Peterborough, New Hampshire
*Book Production Assistant*
- Edited manuscripts and other copy, proofread and corrected galleys, selected type, produced rough pasteups, and participated in research

*1980–1986* SUMMERTIME AND PART-TIME JOBS WHILE GOING TO SCHOOL
  — Lumber Industry, Missoula, Montana—sawmill assistant
  — Management Consulting Firm, Durham, New Hampshire—groundskeeper
  — Construction Industry, Lee, New Hampshire—swimming pool installation
  — Laundry Industry, Portsmouth, New Hampshire—delivery driver
  — Prescott Park Arts Festival, Portsmouth, New Hampshire—art instructor
  — Also: crewed on 65-foot ketch; housepainter, Alaska; landscape gardener; grape harvester in France

**EDUCATION** UNIVERSITY OF NEW HAMPSHIRE, Durham, New Hampshire
1986—B.A., English; Minor: French

ALLIANCE FRANÇAISE, Paris, France
1984—French

# RUSSELL CARTER

2-20-4 KUDAN KITA, CHIYODA-KU  •  TOKYO 102, JAPAN
Home Phone: (011 81 03) 262 3412

## OBJECTIVE

### MAGAZINE MARKETING CONSULTANT/SALES MANAGEMENT

## SUMMARY

More than 20 years of high productivity in sales, sales management, and marketing for major magazine/book publisher. Demonstrated expertise in direction of Far East operations, with in-depth knowledge of Australasian business practices and procedures. Highly successful track record in creation, training, and motivation of sales force. Proven ability to generate exceptional increases in circulation and advertising sales.

## HIGHLIGHTS OF EXPERIENCE

1972–1995     UNIVERSAL INDUSTRIES, INC, New York, New York

UNIVERSAL PUBLICATIONS CORPORATION, Tokyo, Japan
**Director of Asia Pacific Operations** (1992–1994)

Directed all business operations in Japan, Australia, Singapore, the Philippines, Taiwan, Hong Kong, and South Korea, supervised space sales and circulation for 28 publications, investigated and researched business and joint venture potential throughout Asian and Australian markets

- Managed definitive sales effort, resulting in 21% ($500,000) increase in advertising space, during first year in Japan
  — Supervised staff of 20 sales, promotion, and clerical personnel, conducted regular motivational meetings to establish and examine strategies for deeper market penetration
  — Accompanied Japanese sales reps on calls to customers and prospects in making direct sales presentations to top management; traveled throughout Asian and Australian territories to work with independent sales representatives in Hong Kong, Melbourne, and Sydney

- Investigated, researched and drew up presentations of potential acquisition or joint venture investments for corporate consideration
  — Met with scores of other publishers, entrepreneurs, writers, and correspondents throughout Asia to assess publishing ideas
  — Determined value of and recommended four new Asian ventures worthy of presentation (two are pending; two others, tabled for future reference)
  — Interfaced with executives of two major Asian joint ventures: Nikkei Universal, Tokyo, and the *American Industrial Report,* Hong Kong (monthly publication directed to People's Republic of China)

- Met periodically with Japanese counterparts to advise them on promotion tactics, circulation development, and advertising sales strategies; advised Hong Kong group on special projects (personal efforts helped Japanese associates generate $100,000 in current new business)

- Facilitated closer cooperation between corporate office in New York and Far Eastern/Australian representatives (was first person from Universal management Australian representatives had seen in seven years)
  — Assessed problems in Australia; instituted new procedures, resulting in $100,000 new business
  — Advised corporate management on advertising/promotion programs for *Business Week's* new Asian Edition (programs covered both advertising and circulation strategies)

(cont.)

UNIVERSAL PUBLICATIONS CORPORATION (cont.)
- — Successfully assisted and advised Hong Kong representatives with special *Business Week* sections featuring Korea and Taiwan
- — Instrumental in contributing to sales increases in Hong Kong, Singapore, Melbourne, and Sydney
- Explored circulation problems and opportunities throughout Asia in relation to all 28 Universal magazines, with particular emphasis on *Business Week*
  - — Consulted with customers, sales organizations, distributors, and air freight companies; improved delivery service through elimination of shipping bottlenecks
- Selected by United Nations, Geneva, to participate in Singapore seminar (1985); discussed advertising, sales promotion and research with export management

UNIVERSAL (*Business Month*), Houston, Texas
**Account Manager** (1974–1982)

- Successfully sold both product and corporate advertising campaigns in tough, competitive market, including South Texas, Louisiana, and Mississippi
  - — Demonstrated outstanding achievement in face of strong competitors—*Fortune, Forbes, Wall Street Journal, Time, Newsweek, U.S. News and World Report*

UNIVERSAL PUBLICATIONS COMPANY, Houston and Dallas, Texas
**Advertising Sales Representative** (1969–1974)

- Sold space in as many as 28 different publications, covering such fields as power, construction, electronics, aviation, computers, mining, and electric utilities
  - — Uncovered technical equipment martufacturers serving specific industries (presented them with marketing data to aid them in marketing their products)

## EDUCATION

University of Illinois, Urbana, IL (Attended on merit scholarship)
1969—B.S., Journalism, Advertising
Member of Alpha Delta Sigma (Advertising Fraternity) and of Illini Marketing Club

## PROFESSIONAL AFFILIATIONS

| | |
|---|---|
| Tokyo | American Chamber of Commerce in Japan (Served on China Trade Committee; directed Publication Advertising Committee) |
| | Foreign Correspondents Club of Tokyo |
| | Forum for Corporate Communications |
| | Tokyo American Club |
| | Pacific Area Travel Association |
| Hong Kong | Hong Kong Press Club |
| | American Chamber of Commerce in Hong Kong (Served on China Trade Committee) |
| Other | Chamber of Commerce, Houston, Texas |
| | Houston Advertising Federation |
| | Business and Professional Advertising Association |
| | Houston Illini Club (University of Illinois alumni); President four years |

# ESTHER BURNS

300 37th Avenue
San Francisco, CA
(415) 795-1657

**OBJECTIVE**   *BROADCAST MEDIA BUYER*

**SUMMARY**   Experienced buyer in both national and local radio and TV. Skilled in negotiations, client relations, planning, and market analysis.

## HIGHLIGHTS

**1987–present**   ZEA MARKETING COMMUNICATIONS, San Francisco, California

*Media Director*

- Planned and selected media campaigns in agency with billings of 3 million annually. Client list included
  — FSC Corporation
  — ABC-FM-owned stations
  — Fall's Poultry
  — Handleman's Garden Center

- Participate in all phases of planning, including client contact, negotiations with media, and payment of affidavits

- Successfully negotiate client-media relations:
  — Obtain favorable rates for clients
  — Convince well-known media personalities to endorse client services
  — Secure favorable positioning of announcements during prime time at no extra cost

- Planned and administer all details of $40,000 Yellow Page budget for a national telecommunications client

- Established in-house specialty trade research library that ensures speed and accuracy of information delivery to client companies

- Perform continuing and ongoing liaison between agency, media, and clients, resulting in excellent rapport and improved service

**1984–1987**   FOOTE, CONE AND BELDING, San Francisco, California

*Broadcast Buyer*

Client list included
  — Bristol-Meyers
  — Noxell Lestoil
  — Frito-Lay
  — Campbell Soup Company

- Monitored rate, affiliate, and programming changes

- Negotiated favorable radio and television rates and buys

- Developed improved reporting system to provide clients with faster GRP information (system was adopted by buying group and remains in current use); this significantly improved client relations

(cont.)

FOOTE, CONE AND BELDING (cont.)

- Worked closely with clients to coordinate contests and merchandising promotions
  — Coordinated 40+ stations for Long & Silky promotion
- Established format for facilitating the provision of aircheck and GRP information to clients; "sold" new procedure to both stations and clients, cementing client-agency relations
- Organized contract book and monitored buys for clients and agency
- Charged with approval of make-goods and spot preemptions

*Estimator Print/Broadcast*

- Coordinated buys and issued media estimates that contained
  — Total gross dollars spent
  — Number of stations used
  — Total GRPs
  — Length of announcements
  — Scheduled flight dates
- Issued discrepancy reports; maintained continuing rapport between station reps and Billing Department
- Organized various computer reports and distributed finished estimates to clients

1983    KENYON AND ECKHARDT, Los Angeles, California

*Accounts Payable Clerk*

- Disbursed payments and processed vouchers

1980–1982    WILLIAM ESTY ADVERTISING, INC., Los Angeles, California

*Print Estimator*

- Coordinated planners' insertion orders and compiled print estimates through use of Standard Rate and Data books
- Checked tearsheets, made lineage adjustments, and facilitated payment of invoices
- Handled rebates and short rates and compiled final lineage reports

**EDUCATION**    Junior College of Albany
Business Marketing

# JOSEPH WANG

822 North Sixth Street
Orlando, Florida 33710
Home: (407) 387-5420     Business: (407) 763-9571

*OBJECTIVE*     *SALES/MARKETING—CABLE TV/TV SYNDICATION*

To employ time sales/marketing experience in a position with growth potential in the industry

*SUMMARY*     Extensive experience in broadcasting industry as account executive in sales and service of major accounts. Successful track record in acquiring direct accounts as well as additional business through advertising agencies. Adept at creation of advertising campaigns to sell sponsor's product. Worked extensively with TGI, Simmons, and Scarborough market research.

## PROFESSIONAL HIGHLIGHTS

1984–present     WYZO/AMERICAN GENERAL, Orlando, FL

**Account Executive**

- Beginning at zero base, created list of accounts with annual billing of $250,000

- Presented marketing studies and created campaign that brought Berdorf Goodman to the use of radio advertising for the first time
  - Designed special Columbus Day coat sale promotion (proved more successful than sponsor had anticipated)
  - Consulted with Berdorf Goodman executives; advised on buying time on other radio stations in New York, Chicago, and Philadelphia

- Deal with account people at all levels of advertising management, in both client and agency contact

- Communicate promotional ideas to retailers utilizing radio/in-store promotion tie-ins
  - Created successful radio campaign and commercial for La Mode Fashion; designed co-op campaign for Minolta, Polaroid and Goodyear; developed major campaign for Macy's Shoe Department

- Established major cooperative advertising programs between manufacturers and dealers

- Design marketing research to position station demographics (specifically to the 18–34 age-group)

- Developed and presented marketing research to Westinghouse
  - Resulted in first buy of a contemporary radio station

1982–1984    KRMI RADIO, Oakland, CA

**Account Executive**

- Beginning at zero base, developed account list with $100,000 annual billing
- Designed marketing research and evaluated merchandising concepts for client use
- Worked with clients in determining marketing problems; provided successful promotional ideas

1981–1982    KRAC RADIO, Alameda, CA

**Account Executive**

- Handled all record industry accounts and major advertising agencies in San Francisco Bay Area
  — Increased billing by 120%

1980–1981    JACK WODELL & ASSOCIATES (Advertising Agency)
San Francisco, CA

**Mailroom Supervisor**

*EDUCATION*    UCLA, Los Angeles, CA
1980—Graduate courses in Marketing and Advertising

University of Denver, Denver, CO
1980—B.A., History, Political Science

Golden Gate University, San Francisco, CA
1981–1982—Marketing courses

# SANDRA NURENBERG

1817 Forest Avenue
Des Allemands, LA 71128
(504) 734-2648

**OBJECTIVE**    *TRAVEL SALES/SALES PROMOTION*

To apply broad knowledge of and experience in the travel industry to a position in sales or sales promotion with a solid energetic operation in the travel field.

**SUMMARY**    Wholly knowledgeable about the travel industry. Experience includes positions in sales and sales promotion in varied phases of the industry. Have lived, worked, and traveled in Europe, Latin America, Asia, Africa, and 40 of the 50 United States (including Alaska and Hawaii), providing priceless, firsthand knowledge about much of the world.

## RELEVANT EXPERIENCE

*1992–1996*    INTERNATIONAL WOMEN'S CLUB OF COPENHAGEN,
Copenhagen, Denmark

**President**

- Founded the organization in 1985; founded club magazine in 1986
- Responsible for all financial affairs of the organization; raised in excess of $300,000 for philanthropic purposes
- Worked with embassies, tourist offices, and airlines to arrange monthly programs and philanthropic projects throughout the world
- Organized and arranged all tours throughout Scandinavia and Eastern Europe
- Chaired meetings of 10-member board and monthly meetings for 250 general members; addressed various organizations and associations regarding functions of club
- Sold 90% of all advertising to and received donations from major international corporations and organizations
- Coordinated editing, proofreading, and layout of magazines with staff and printers
- Wrote press releases for use on TV and radio and in magazines and newspapers

*1990–1992*    AMERICAN WOMEN'S CLUB IN DENMARK, Copenhagen, Denmark

**President**

- Functions similar to those performed with International Women's Club
- Worked with universities and foundations in Denmark and the United States to further club's scholarship program
- As a member of Danish-American Committee, coordinated activities with Danish Foreign Affairs Office
- Personally presented club's book to the Queen of Denmark prior to her departure for the United States
- Raised funds for and assisted in planning (including housing) of student group tour of United States

*1991–1992*    ECOLE SUPERIEURE D'AFFAIRES ET DE SECRETARIAT, Brussels, Belgium

**Business English Lecturer**

- Taught American business techniques, from letter composition to filing systems, to 80 women students from 16 countries
- Gave private consultations to individual students and to interested employers

**1989–1990**    BELTZ WORLD TOURS, San Francisco, California

**Travel Consultant**

- Met with retail accounts and individual clients and formulated plans, and made arrangements for transportation, hotel accommodations and tours for business and pleasure
- Sold Asian travel packages, including cruises and steamship lines
- Top sales representative for three consecutive months with fewest cancellations
- Traveled extensively to Europe and Latin America; coordinated tours with competitive travel agencies

**1988–1989**    JAPAN EXTERNAL TRADE ORGANIZATION, Chicago, Illinois

**Administrative Assistant**

- Supervised Chicago showrooms and displays
- Arranged special promotions and exhibits for trade shows, state fairs, and exhibitions in the Midwest promoting Japanese products
- Hired personnel to work special exhibits
- Worked with management of various hotels in setting up conferences, banquets, and receptions
- Created, administered and arranged for public reaction questionnaires to be given out to people viewing products and exhibits
- Worked special assignments in Tokyo, Osaka, and Vienna

**1986–1988**    NORTHWEST ORIENT AIRLINES, Chicago, Illinois

**Reservation Sales/Service Agent**

- Processed reservations and tickets for domestic and international flights; maintained passenger manifests
- Handled cancellations; investigated passenger complaints

**1981–1986**    HERTZ CORPORATION, Chicago, Illinois

**Station Manager**

- Supervised 12 employees
- Coordinated all office procedures, including processing of monthly accounts and acquisition of office supplies and equipment, with the main office

**EDUCATION**    Northwestern University, Evanston, Illinois
1983–1984, Liberal Arts/European History

Loyola University, Chicago, Illinois
1982–1983, Liberal Arts/European History

Florence Utt Business School, Indianapolis, Indiana
1980–1981, Business Administration

**LANGUAGES**    Danish, German, French (read and write)

# LEAH GARST

1182 HANCOCK STREET
WASHINGTON, D.C. 20008
(202) 345-7787

## OBJECTIVE

Organizational fund-raiser for a recognized nonprofit organization or foundation or for a privately endowed educational institution, possibly entailing some travel.

## SUMMARY

More than seven years' experience in direct fund-raising. Demonstrated expertise working with governmental and nongovernmental agencies. Traveled extensively in Europe, Latin America and the United States.

## EXPERIENCE

EPICURES CLUB OF NICE, FRANCE

*1989–1996*   **President-Founder**

Responsible for all financial affairs; raised $300,000+ for philanthropic purposes.

Worked with embassies, tourist offices, and airlines to arrange monthly programs and philanthropic projects throughout the world; organized and arranged all tours.

Addressed various organizations regarding club functions.

Wrote press releases for use on TV and radio and in magazines and newspapers.

HELEN TOURS, Aspen, Colorado

*1987–1989*   **Travel Consultant**

Top sales representative for two consecutive years with fewest cancellations.

Traveled extensively throughout Europe and Latin America; coordinated tours with competitive travel agencies.

## EDUCATION

Vassar College, Poughkeepsie, New York
B.A., Literature/History, 1987

## LANGUAGES

Fluent in French, German, Italian, and Spanish

## REFERENCES

Provided upon request

# OPERATIONS

# KENNETH CANNON

*2403 Needham Street, Brooklyn, NY 11235*
*(718) 646-7522*

**OBJECTIVE**      INVENTORY CONTROL MANAGER

To employ expertise in inventory control with a multi-national corporation in a position with growth potential to Operations Manager

**SUMMARY**      More than seven years' experience in inventory control and production planning. Strong ability to gain confidence and cooperation of production management to alleviate inventory problems. Knowledgeable about BASIC and COBOL languages and the use of computers. Multilingual—fluent in Swedish, Polish, and Russian, with working knowledge of German and Norwegian.

## EXPERIENCE HIGHLIGHTS

1987–present      WHALEDENT INTERNATIONAL (Dental Products)
New York, New York

*Production Controller/Planner*

- Charged with the detail planning and release of work orders to four production departments in accordance with Master Schedule
  — Plan material requirements
  — Requisition purchases
  — Interface with production supervisor and materials manager
- Improved planning system through use of MRP principles; introduced use of more efficient instruments for shop floor control
- Pinpointed inventory management problems through use of ABC analysis in estimation of excess inventory

1984–1987      THORN LIGHTING DIVISION AB (Subsidiary of Thorn Electrical Industries, London) Stockholm, Sweden

*Inventory Control/Purchasing Supervisor*

- Charged with responsibility for purchasing $5 million to $6 million/year of lighting equipment, reporting directly to Financial Controller
- Established inventory levels for four regional warehouses
  — Implemented and assisted in designing control system
  — Decreased value of inventory with 40% (approximately $250,000) saving per year
  — Increased inventory turnover and service level
- Controlled procedures for Purchasing Department
  — Set up and followed yearly supplies budget
  — Purchased products from Thorn's factories in England

THORN LIGHTING DIVISION AB (cont.)

- Worked with Data Division to computerize order processing procedures with subsequent savings in manpower
  — Implemented ABC analysis
  — Member of select management team to implement integrated MIS

(Parent company has annual gross of 1 billion pounds sterling)

1982–1984    SIEMENS AB, Stockholm, Sweden (Subsidiary Siemens AG, West Germany)

*Inventory Control Planner, Lighting Fixtures Division*

- Charged with planning for sales and manufacturing, setting inventory levels for six regional warehouses, and planning for future production based on marketing forecasts and production capacity
- Established inventory control system through use of computer reports
- Implemented Master Production Schedule for local factory
- Generated sales statistics for Marketing and Sales Departments
- Promoted from Office Clerk within six months of employment in recognition of my analytical ability and studies
  — Worked full-time while attending school

(Parent company is sixth largest in world in its field, with annual gross of approximately $16 billion)

**EDUCATION**    Stockholm University, Stockholm, Sweden
1986—B.A., Business Administration

Quantitative Methods for Business Decisions
— Marketing/Management

**MEMBER**    American Production-Inventory Control Society

# BRUCE FREEMAN

720 Ocean Parkway
Brooklyn, NY 11218
Home: (718) 436-9928    Office: (718) 689-7523

---

*OBJECTIVE*    SENIOR MANAGEMENT—CONSUMER PRODUCTS

*SUMMARY*    — More than 20 years of bottom-line responsibility in manufacturing, marketing, and merchandising consumer products

— Creative and innovative in product management, encompassing purchase of raw materials, design, production, merchandising, and sales

— Aggressive and energetic salesman with discerning ability to analyze market trends and forecast consumer demands

— Strong motivator of merchandising team, able to spark imagination and productivity

— Capable of producing quality merchandise in competitive market with excellent cost-profit ratio

### CAREER HIGHLIGHTS

**1975–present**    SHAPIRO & SON CORPORATION, New York, New York

*Vice-President/Director of Purchasing and Production*    (1981–present)

• Developed cost reduction apparatus and profit improvement systems and set annual production budget

— Implemented and tightened procedures, effecting increase in percentage of net profit

— Researched and managed installation of computer system components facilitating sophisticated forecasting of piece goods requirements, production scheduling, and sales volume

• Created new products and designs, some of which remain as staples in company's line

• Controlled sales of special promotions to major retailers, national chains, and catalog houses

— Maintained close and active contact with top buyers

— Created products for specific promotions, negotiated sales, and worked up sales proposals for account executives

— Realized $3.5 million in "plus" sales from three orders

• Devised system for merchandising discontinued styles, turning projected losses into net profits exceeding $250,000

• Established more effectual control system over packaging and distribution to more than 3,000 outlets, reducing claim rate to less than 0.5%

SHAPIRO & SON CORPORATION (cont.)

- Improved control systems of record keeping, retention scheduling, and perpetual inventory
- Developed recruitment and training programs; heightened employee interest through education about company services and products

*Production Manager* *(1978–1981)*

- Responsible for planning, scheduling, and coordinating production for all factories employing more than 700 people
  — Purchased raw materials and scheduled production cycles in relation to marketing trends, consumer demand, and seasonal aspects
- Effected 10% cost reduction through restructure of converting department procedures and in-house printing of greige goods
- Controlled activity of outside contractors

*Purchasing Manager, Raw Materials* *(1977–1978)*

- Negotiated contracts with mills, involving $12 million to $15 million
  — Established and administered systems resulting in 5% economies
  — Scheduled current and future orders of greige goods and printed materials to coincide with production requirements, thereby reducing warehouse inventory costs

*Purchasing Agent, Piece Goods* *(1975–1977)*

- Effective handling of this department was directly responsible for assignment to positions of greater accountability

**Prior** GREYWOOD KNITWEAR INDUSTRIES, New York, New York

*Production Manager*

- Hired as Assistant to Production Manager; promoted after two years to Production Manager
- Was responsible for purchase of raw materials, plant scheduling in a cut-and-sew operation, sales and production forecasting, and liaison with factory management

*EDUCATION* Queens College
1971—B.S., Math/Science

*PERSONAL* Free to relocate

# ETHEL BURKS

300 EAST 24TH STREET, APT. 4RW
NEW YORK CITY, NY 10009

---

HOME (212) 477-6525
WORK (212) 751-6216

**OBJECTIVE**    *OFFICE MANAGEMENT*

**SUMMARY**    Departmental manager with strong corporate administrative background. Experienced in purchasing, budget forecasting, salary planning and personnel evaluation. Expert at anticipating problems and effecting their resolution. Excellent writing and production skills. Knowledge of telecommunications and word processing software.

**EXPERIENCE**    MEDICARE DIVISION OF HUMANA, INC., New York, New York

1988–present    *Manager, Secretarial Services* (1990–present)

- Supervise 13 secretaries and typists in completion and daily updating of all medical records and tests for patient base of 17,000
  — Prepare all correspondence to parent company and physician clientele
  — Responsible for departmental budget forecasting, salary planning, and personnel evaluation
- Trained and supervised five additional typists to accommodate dramatically increased workload over four-month period
  — Created and implemented double shifts to ensure completion of extra work volume on time and without sacrifice of quality; appointed interim supervisors for both shifts

*Executive Administrative Assistant* (1988–1990)

- As right hand to company CEO, responsible for coordination of executive office functions
  — Assisted President with confidential matters affecting all company activity and managed office during his absences; scheduled meetings and appointments
  — Maintained ongoing contact with nation-wide sales force, monitored activities of managers reporting to President, and prepared schedules and recommendations for his consideration
  — Prepared executive correspondence and composed internal administrative correspondence, composed and distributed minutes and other pertinent documents, and prepared legal forms, statistical reports, and contracts
- Developed methods to streamline office repair and maintenance functions affecting comfort and efficiency of 100 employees

3M COMPANY, New York, New York

1984–1988    *Publicity Assistant*

- Composed product and news releases, feature stories, and quarterly reports; supervised printing and photography; and coordinated national mailings to consumer and trade media

- Made arrangements for press events—researched and selected sites, designed press kits and invitations, monitored responses, and prepared guest lists

CORE COMMUNICATIONS IN HEALTH, INC., New York, New York

1981–1984    *Script Coordinator/Assistant Director of Program Development*

- As first employee in new organization, assisted in start-up and office management, including purchase of all supplies

- Assisted in creating and updating library of audiovisual education programs; researched and edited program material

- Typeset and assisted in design of educational print materials

**EDUCATION**    QUEENS COLLEGE, Queens, New York
1981 B.A., English, Writing
- — Phi Beta Kappa and magna cum laude
- — Honors in English and Creative Writing
- — John Golden Award for Creative Writing, 1972
- — Fiction Editor, College literary magazine

*Professional Programs*
Buffalo University, Seminar on Management Tools
Katherine Gibbs Entry Program
Betty Owen Word Processing Program
Dale Carnegie Public Speaking Course

**SALVATORE ORAZIO**  •  21 Pine Street  •  Cresskill, NJ 07626  •  (201) 568-8770

**OBJECTIVE**    *OPERATIONS MANAGEMENT*

**SUMMARY**    Operations specialist with excellent track record in coordination of sales and production. Adept at analysis and reformulation of systems to increase profits. Able to establish effective rapport with superiors, colleagues, and subordinates. Hands-on knowledge of computer services.

**ACHIEVEMENTS IN OPERATIONS MANAGEMENT**

> **BURLINGTON INDUSTRIAL FABRICS**, Rockleigh, New Jersey
> *Administrative Supervisor, Inventory and Reconciliations* (1995–1996)
> *Sales Coordinator* (1995)
> *Planning Coordinator* (1988–1994)
> *Production Planning Manager/Assistant Planner* (1987–1988)

*Sales/ Production Coordination*

During period of fifteenfold sales expansion, balanced plant production with sales requirements while overseeing planning, scheduling, sales, and customer service, distribution, and R&D functions

Increased sales 25% to 50% by improving liaison between sales and production

- Instituted control sheets, with daily updates for individual sales reps
- Developed easy-to-read, open contract status record book to aid control, scheduling, and sales
- Initiated operations to accommodate on-the-spot requests

*Production Planning*

Increased sales and production 25% through careful production scheduling and close liaison with Sales Department

- Allowed for new business in production scheduling
- Ensured customer satisfaction through communication with sales on load conditions and possible substitute orders during heavy load periods
- Instituted daily flow of inventory contracts and coordinated salable inventory with Sales Manager

*Contracts Administration*

Instituted measures resulting in same-day service for rush orders and quicker processing of entire order volume

Decreased composition and transmittal period for typed contracts by 50%

- Established capability for telephone credit approval on rush orders
- Set priorities for transmittal of contract and corrections between Northern and Southern Offices, improving liaison

Developed capability for daily processing of sales notes, cutting four to six days from original procedure; set up system eventually taken over by clerical staff

*Inventory Control/ Purchasing*

Through timely purchases of greige goods, saved 540,000 and maintained better control of inventory

Increased efficiency of inventory process, decreasing time required by 66% while effecting one of division's best-audited inventories on record

| | |
|---|---|
| *Computer Operations/ Records* | Worked closely with programmers to set up weekly computerized status reports on contracts, inventory available for sale, and case listings |
| | Set priorities for computer services; developed accurate manual and computerized records |

**H.W. LOUD MACHINE WORKS, INC.**, Pomona, California
(Division of Menasco Manufacturing Co.)
*Supervisor* (1986–1987)
*Material and Systems Control Supervisor* (1981–1986)
*Scheduling and Records Supervisor* (1972–1980)

| | |
|---|---|
| *Personnel Training* | Eased overload conditions and increased output by 50% to 66% by cross-training personnel in purchasing, traffic, stock, shipping, and receiving |
| *Production Planning* | Coordinated purchasing, outside production, and production liaison with Montebello and Burbank Plants; supervised Production Control Office |
| | Increased work flow control, eliminated overissuance of plant and outside production work orders, and promoted planning flexibility |

- Created simple, accurate location control system for thousands of components in process

Upgraded production coordination

- Instituted system for establishing assembly priorities
- Created procedures for nightly status reports on all components of open orders

| | |
|---|---|
| *Computer Operations* | Developed accurate shop load computer reporting system; worked with outside consultant, computer programmer, and in-house personnel to set up input and completion data |

**BURLINGTON INDUSTRIES**, New York, New York and Teterboro, New Jersey
Assistant Department Head Office Services (1980–1982)
*Warehouse Supervisor* (1974–1980)

| | |
|---|---|
| *Office Services Management* | Coordinated and supervised 15-member staff responsible for office moves and services, prepared budgets, and directed outside contractors |
| | Developed system for timely delivery of mail between five major New York City office buildings |
| *Warehouse Supervision* | Set up inexpensive and effective location control system for thousands of piece goods in process |
| **EDUCATION** | *Professional Courses and Seminars* |
| | AMERICAN MANAGEMENT ASSOCIATION, New York, New York |
| | Various eight- to ten-week courses in Supervisory Management, Planning, Organization, Standards and Appraisals, Communication, Motivation, Decision Making |

*Free to travel*

197

*Alan Toulouse*     150 East 71st Street • New York, NY 10021 • (212) 838-7777

**OBJECTIVE**  *GENERAL MANAGEMENT/OPERATIONS*

**SUMMARY**  Experience in day-to-day administration at management level in import/distribution industry. Highly expert at initiating and implementing systems, including data processing, for inventory and cash control. Capable of start-up of major installations, including warehousing, from point-of-site selection to full operation. Excellent in recruitment and supervision of personnel and in customer relations.

### HIGHLIGHTS OF EXPERIENCE

1985–present  INTERCO PARTS CORPORATION, Syosset, New York

*General Manager*

Charged with start-up of parts distribution business in 1985; administer all phases of business (accounting, inventory control, data processing, and enhancement of management information capability of computer operation)

- Achieved growth to $6 million/year
- Participated in preparation and administration of annual budget
- Installed and implemented in-house computer to perform inventory control, accounts receivable, and sales and product analyses
- Created and implemented warehouse operating procedures with internal controls (current 13-man staff); established and maintain paper flow procedures and internal audit control

1979–1985  GEON INTERCONTINENTAL CORPORATION, Woodbury, New York

*General Manager, Operations, Woodbury, New York* (1984–1985)

Had direct responsibility for data processing and transition to in-house MIS capability for company now at $38 million level

- Served as project leader for installation of IBM System 3 computer
  — Participated in system design, wrote operating manual, trained operators
  — Scheduled procurement of hardware and software
  — Delivered eighteen-month project (IBM estimate) on-line in seven months
- Administered New York headquarters with staff of 80 in the office and 130 at warehouses

Concurrent  *General Manager, Operations, Richmond, Virginia/Los Angeles, California* (1983–1985)

Had control over two warehouses (280,000 square feet), with 130 personnel and more than $20 million/year in sales

- Controlled budget, daily operation and planning (except sales), warehousing, customer service, data collection/transmittal, and union negotiations
- Reduced expenses by 30% to 40% overall through efficient management of employees and information
  — Instituted uniform training program to strengthen first-line and middle management
- Carried over expense control systems from Richmond operation to Los Angeles warehouse with same success
- Recalled to New York to head up computer project

continued

*General Manager, Richmond Warehouse, Richmond, Virginia (6/83–12/83)*

Line responsibility for $10 million profit center

- Administered all operations (except sales)
- Instituted cost accounting system to control expense; reduced operating expenses by 40% while maintaining sales level and improving order turnaround time

*Assistant to President, Woodbury, New York (1981–1983)*

Member of Office of the President

- Maintained liaison between administration and department managers
- Helped prepare and controlled budget; implemented corporate policies and procedures
- Appointed project manager in movement of warehouse from New York to Virginia
  — Located site, negotiated for purchase, negotiated favorable contract for construction, supervised recruitment of personnel, and developed and implemented warehousing procedures
- Assisted in union contract negotiations

*Manager, Data Entry, Woodbury, New York (1980–1981)*

- Supervised staff of 32 data entry operators feeding to outside service bureau
- Helped establish and implement inventory control system for 102 wholly owned branches
- Developed data reporting systems (sales analysis, stock status, and forecasting) in concert with other department managers and service bureau

*Customer Service Manager, Woodbury, New York (1978–1980)*

- Established goodwill and maintained clientele during period of extreme competition
  — Resolved customer complaints; reduced response time from eight to ten weeks to two weeks
  — Established returns authorization and other procedures for issuance of credits to customers

**EDUCATION** New York University, New York, New York (On scholarship)
1979—M.A., Latin American History
SUNY, Buffalo, New York
1978—B.A., History (Dean's List)
National Honor Society and Dean's List at Jamaica (New York) High School
American Management Association: Writing of Administrative Manuals

**LANGUAGES** Spanish

# EMILE BERGSON

220 West 76th Street, New York, NY 10020
(212) 761-2571

**OBJECTIVE**  SENIOR-LEVEL OPERATIONS MANAGEMENT

**SUMMARY**  Direct management responsibility in proposal management, cost estimating, contract administration, scheduling and cost control, quality assurance, engineering, and technical and new product development. Expertise in domestic and international technical and commercial operations, including air pollution control systems, fuel cell and solar energy devices, semiconductors, ceramics, and catalytic materials.

Principal customer industries: electric utilities, petrochemical, pulp and paper, combustion equipment, coal, and federal, state, and local governments.

Published in numerous technical journals; author of various device-oriented patents.

**EXPERIENCE**  FLAKT, INC., Old Greenwich, Connecticut (American Group company of AB Svenska Flaktfabriken, Stockholm, Sweden) Annual Revenues: $40 million

1988–present  *Director of Precontract Operations*

- Direct all Proposal Management, Applications Engineering, Cost Estimating, Project Planning, and Sales Support
- Develop and implement technical, pricing, and commercial strategies for proposals
- Manage all precontract negotiations (bid approximately $300 million, capturing approximately $70 million)
- Convinced management of need for series of procedures manuals; authored Proposal Managment and Cost Estimating Operations Manuals

1983–1988  UOP AIR CORRECTION DIVISION, Norwalk, Connecticut

*Manager of Project Services (1986–1988)*

- Created department to serve as support group to Project Management, at request of management
- Directed activities related to Cost Engineering, Scheduling (Multilevel, CPM), Contract Administration (Contract Interpreting, Claims Preparation and Negotiation) and Project Administration
- Authored company Project Control Manual
- Formulated division Cost Code of Accounts, remedying lack of adequate cost definition that was seriously hampering cost control efforts

*Manager of Quality Assurance (1985–1986)*

- Created Quality Assurance Department at request of management
- Formulated and directed total division quality program, including Planning, Inspections, and Reliability
- Created division Operations Auditing Program for identifying and solving systematic organization and procedural problems, encompassing all departments
- Formulated Quality Cost Monitoring Program to identify and eliminate significant and recurring avoidable costs (resulted in 70% reduction of such costs associated with Engineering, Manufacturing, and Construction)
- Authored division Quality Assurance Manual

*Manager of Engineering* (1984–1985)

- Directed all Engineering activities of department of approximately 100 engineers and 60 drafters
- Managed entire company product line of Flue Gas Desulfurization Systems, Electrical Precipitators, and Multicyclone Collectors
- Reorganized department from Functional Organization to Matrix Management organization, to better utilize limited personnel resources; productivity increased by 26% as a result
— Authored and developed Engineering Drafting Manuals

*Manager of Precipitator Technology* (1983–1984)

- Created department to eliminate performance liability situations
- Directed field diagnostic studies and corrective action programs
- Invented and developed proprietary designs for new ancillary product lines, now marketed (sales approximately $15 million)
- Conducted world-wide survey, including site visits to Europe, Asia, and Australia; evaluated licensing potential for a rigid frame-type precipitator (In lieu of licensing, recommended proprietary design field-tested in 1983)
- Invented, developed, and marketed new products

1978–1982     UOP CORPORATE RESEARCH CENTER, Des Plaines, Illinois

*Research Administrator*

- Served as Air Correction Liaison with Corporate Research, directing field studies and developing annual division R&D programs
- Administered and directed research projects in auto emission control, energy conversion, and materials development
- Issued nine patents

**EDUCATION**   CITY UNIVERSITY OF NEW YORK, New York, New York
1978—Ph.D., Physics
1975—M.A., Physics
1972—B.A., Physical Sciences

UOP Management Development Program
AMA Seminar on Project Planning and Control
American Society for Quality Control Seminar on Managing for Quality
Lincoln Electric Company Seminar on Welding
EPA Seminar on Gaseous Emission Control
Working knowledge of French and Hebrew

**HONORS**     Guest speaker at ASME regional conference, Air Pollution Engineering
Guest speaker at ASQC Energy Division annual conference
President of employees' Federal Credit Union
Recipient of company award for Outstanding Support of Sales

# ARTHUR RINEHART

1050 Maple Avenue
Bronx, NY 10475
(718) 994-2770

**OBJECTIVE**  *EXPORT MANAGER/INTERNATIONAL TRADE SPECIALIST*

To obtain a position as export manager for energetic, high-volume exporter of consumer or industrial goods or services.

**SUMMARY**  Broadly experienced in all phases of export and domestic operations. Demonstrated expertise in new market development, sales forecasting, budgeting, inventory control, warehousing, and shipping. Knowledgeable about medical and publishing industries specifically.

**EXPERIENCE**

**1976–present**  NORTHWESTERN PUBLISHING COMPANY, Brooklyn, New York

*Export Manager, Eastern Division* (1987–present)
($15 million annual revenues)

*Operations Manager* (1976–1987)

- Charged with full responsibility for developing marketing strategies, operations management, and the management of combined sales and support staff of 17 for this major branch

**MARKETING**
- Expanded foreign sales from base of $150,000 (1976) to $3 million (1987)
- Research and analyze potential markets; project forecasts on which sales are based
- Travel extensively to Puerto Rico, Mexico, Central and South America, and Africa studying educational systems and determining potential textbook markets
  — Initiate contacts and work out agreements with distributors to promote and distribute products
  — Work out all sales contracts, including sales conditions, credit terms, banking, discounts, and promotion
- Most recently, selected and set up marketing/distribution organizations in Liberia and Nigeria, as well as South America

**OPERATIONS**
- Prepare annual transportation and distribution budgets (in excess of $1.25 million/year)
- Determine quarterly sales needs; prepare appropriate stock requisitions
- Coordinate physical inventory (2 million units monthly)
- Establish agreements with warehousing concerns for consolidation with other publishers for overseas shipments
- Organize special Container/Consolidation Programs with major airlines at reduced rates
- Work closely with U.S. Postal Service in simplifying mail classification and requirements for mailing to foreign countries

NORTHWESTERN PUBLISHING COMPANY (cont.)

- Was instrumental in getting the limit of Custom Free Import Entry amount increased from $250 to $500
- Develop major sales promotions for teachers and educational groups through direct mail and specially designed seminars and workshops

**1970–1976**  NATIONAL SURGICAL SUPPLY, INC., Westchester, New York
(Major manufacturer of surgical instruments—$25 million annual sales)
*Assistant Service Manager*

- Responsible for all customer service aspects, including problem solving and handling of customer complaints of highly technical nature
- Instructed members of medical profession in proper methods of maintenance, sterilization, and application of instruments
- Personally inspected repaired instruments to ensure quality control
- Supervised technical and secretarial staff

**1968–1970**  STUDENT'S TUTORING INSTITUTE, Larchmont, New York
*Instructor*

- Taught Italian and Spanish to businessmen, doctors, and lawyers on individual and group basis

**EDUCATION**  Istituto Magistrale Lucrezia Della Valle, Cosenza, Italy
B.A., Secondary Education/Foreign Languages

Hunter College, Bronx, New York
42 credits in English, History, Marketing, Spanish, and Italian

**AFFILIATIONS**  Tri-State Traffic Management Association (Secretary)
Bronx-Westchester Traffic Club
Latin American Chamber of Commerce
Modern Language Association

**LANGUAGES**  Fluent Italian; excellent Spanish; working knowledge of French and Portuguese

## ERNEST CAWLEY

125 Forest Lane
Radnor, PA 19087
(215) 293-0151

**OBJECTIVE**

To establish, develop, and direct an export division or subsidiary for a manufacturer new to exporting

**SUMMARY**

— Astute evaluator of foreign market potential for U.S.-manufactured consumer products

— Proven organizer of export activities for manufacturers that lack previous overseas sales experience

— Strong connections with world-wide business community through extensive travel and personal contact

— Broad experience in corporate development and financing, investment analysis, venture capital, and business management

**BUSINESS HIGHLIGHTS**

1984–present

TREMONT INTERNATIONAL
Bryn Mawr, Pennsylvania

**Founder and Managing Director**

• Develop export sales for "new-to-export" U.S. manufacturers; successful sales in more than 100 countries on 5 continents
   — Thoroughly research the industry, product, competition, and client manufacturer, including definitive profitability assessment of potential overseas markets
   — Make convincing presentation to acquire client manufacturers' export distribution or representation rights
   — Expertly handle all export procedures, from creating the sales through distribution, transportation, and collection
   — Effectively represent dozens of client companies concurrently

• Personally generate export business and develop overseas markets
   — Sell diverse lines of products (mainly consumer), including safety and security equipment, laser-engraved prestige advertising specialties and corporate awards and gifts, specialty housewares and hardware, building materials and interior architectural products, and micro-electronic ceramic subassemblies
   — Process more than 100 pieces of correspondence per week, plus telexes, cables, and overseas telephone calls
   — Participate in trade shows and exhibits in market countries

• Established export activities for two corporations and currently serve on their Boards of Directors

*(cont.)*

| 1978–1984 | **HORNBLOWER & WEEKS, HEMPHILL NOYES & CO.**<br>Bala Cynwyd, Pennsylvania |
|---|---|

**Account Executive**

- Managed portfolios of my individual and institutional accounts
- Consistently produced high profit margin business for the firm; responsible for millions of dollars in investments
- Consulted with and did exhaustive investment analysis research for my clients in matters of investment banking, venture capital, and corporate development
- Selected to this nation-wide firm's Management Advisory Board (1980) in recognition of consistent professionalism and competence

| 1968–1978 | **NEWBURGER & CO.**<br>Philadelphia, Pennsylvania |
|---|---|

**General Partner**     (1974–1978)

- Among my investment banking responsibilities, structured and raised venture capital for two manufacturing corporations and was cofounder of each; continued the activities below

**Investment Analyst**     (1968–1974)

- Managed investment portfolios for my own clients and the firm's investment advisory clients, conducted investment analyses, and created venture capital plus merger and acquisition opportunities
- Restructured Research Department to reflect current methods and practices
- Wrote regular research reports on attractive investment opportunities and edited the monthly bulletin

| 1967–1968 | **SHEARSON, HAMMILL & CO.**<br>New York, New York |
|---|---|

**Investment Analyst**

- Researched and analyzed investment potential in securities of publicly owned corporations, with emphasis on electronics, aerospace, airline, shipbuilding, and other industries of similar scope; consulted on investment banking and merger and acquisition proposals

| **MILITARY** | U.S. Army and U.S. Army Reserve, 1965–1973<br>Captain, Finance Corps; Finance Regional Accounting Officer |
|---|---|
| **EDUCATION** | Wharton Graduate School, M.B.A., 1966—Finance and Investments, Real Estate<br>University of Texas, B.B.A., 1965—Finance and Banking |
| **MEMBER** | International Trade Development Association, Greater Philadelphia Region President, 1985–1986; Director, 1986–present<br>Manufacturers & Agents National Association<br>Main Line Chamber of Commerce |

# EDWARD BARTLESVILLE

920 Eastwind Drive, Westerville, Ohio 43081

Home: (614) 247-9827                                                 Office: (614) 475-5070

**OBJECTIVE**    **SENIOR MANAGEMENT IN AGGRESSIVE RETAIL ORGANIZATION**

**SUMMARY**    Retail management experience, with rapid and consistent record of growth and advancement. Conceptual and creative approach to marketing and merchandising. Sound long- and short-range planning skills. Astute motivator with ability to identify and maximize talent of subordinates.

**PROFESSIONAL EXPERIENCE**

1990–present    **FEDERATED STORES CORPORATION, Columbus, Ohio**
**Director of Merchandise Marketing**

- Advise top management regarding incorporation of innovative marketing strategies and concepts for all six divisions of $600 million corporation
- Develop marketing programs to reposition corporation as necessary
  — Created 120-store test to analyze customer buying patterns for purposes of maximizing inventory investment (testing validated program implementation in all 489 stores)
  — Initiated and implemented merchandise line plan to fully develop previously nonformalized corporate policy (concept to be layered into organization as basis for focusing merchandise purchase in second and third quarters of 1997)

1984–1990    **SAKS FIFTH AVENUE, New York, New York**

**Senior Vice-President**               **General Merchandise Manager,
                                          Sportswear and Intimate Apparel
                                          (1988–1990)**

- As member of Executive Committee and Management Board, participated fully in all marketing and merchandising decisions for $500 million organization
- Generated 22% volume increase (from $102 million to $125 million) and 1.2% gross margin increase (from 46.3% to 47.5%) through restructuring and redefinition of planning, merchandising, marketing, merchandise distribution, and training and development operations
  — Trained, developed, and managed 5 divisional merchandise managers and 21 buyers to achieve their professional goals, as well as company objectives

**SAKS FIFTH AVENUE (cont.)**

| **Vice-President** | **Divisional Merchandise Manager, Intimate Apparel (1987–1988)** |
|---|---|

- Supervised planning, management, merchandising, and marketing operations of $25 million business to achieve annual gross margin objective
- Improved division profit ranking, from tenth to first (out of 17 divisions), by broadening customer base, reorganizing resource structure, and developing effective marketing strategies
- Generated 26% sales volume increase (from $20 million to $25 million) and 2.1% gross margin increase (from 49.0% to 51.1%)

| **Divisional Vice-President** | **Managing Director, Branch Store, Fairlane Mall, Detroit, Michigan (1986–1987)** |
|---|---|

- Assumed total responsibility for start-up and opening of individual store
  — Led and managed all areas (Merchandising, Operations, Personnel, and Intercommunity Relations) to achieve sales volume and profit objectives
  — Trained, developed, and managed 1 Assistant Managing Director, 6 Operational Department Managers, and 13 Merchandising Department Managers
  — Established environment of full employee input preparatory to store opening, keeping motivation and morale at optimum levels
- Generated $14 million in sales volume and 2.6% pretax profit during first year of operation

| **Divisional Merchandise Manager** | **Men's Clothing, Boys' Clothing, and Furnishings Divisions (1984–1986)** |
|---|---|

1981–1984 **BLOOMINGDALES, New York, New York**

| **Group Manager** | **Men's Sportswear and Designer Sportswear (1983–1984)** |
|---|---|

- Promoted from two Buyer positions after starting as Staff Assistant to Divisional Merchandise Manager in 1973

_**EDUCATION**_  SOUTHERN METHODIST UNIVERSITY
1981—M.B.A.; Major: Marketing

1980—B.A.; Major: History; Minor: Economics
Dean's List, eight semesters
Sigma Phi Epsilon Fraternity

# HECTOR LOPEZ

7720 Cowne Court
Nokesville, VA 22123
(703) 594-9570

**OBJECTIVE**      GENERAL MANAGEMENT, BUILDING TRADES INDUSTRY

**SUMMARY**      Top-level manager with definitive expertise in creative marketing and sales techniques for the building trades industry. Proven ability to penetrate new markets through establishment and implementation of successful marketing strategies and initiating and maintaining highly effective distribution systems. Outstanding achievement record in start-up and growth situations.

## HIGHLIGHTS OF EXPERIENCE

1990–present      ONDULINE, U.S.A., INC. (Subsidiary of Media General, Inc.) Fredericksburg, Virginia

**Senior Vice-President**

Charged with responsibility for start-up of company in the United States, dealing with specialized building materials items

- Developed initial market analysis that led to company's establishment
- Initiated, established and implemented marketing strategies, hired and trained field and office personnel, and set corporate and financial policies (still in force)
- Directed company's sales effort from zero base in 1980 to $8.1 million in 1987
  — Established markets by selling product through most levels of distribution
  — Generate high volume through wholesale building supply and retail home centers, OEM, and agricultural cooperatives
  — Instituted Select Distribution System to permit increased distributor responsibility for product marketing
  — Increased sales volume to extent that construction of $10 million U.S. manufacturing installation was justified
  — Established record of not losing a single distributor during eight-year period
  — Personally field-trained salesmen and developed sales education program
- Developed and direct advertising programs whose success caused budget increase from $30,000 in 1990 to $600,000 in 1996
  — Achieved product recognition in the industry by trade name
- Won Drummer Award for 1983 by Building Supply News in two categories: Unique Educational Literature and Dealer Promotional Literature
- Elevated to Senior Vice-President following acquisition by Media General of 100% of stock of French parent company
  — Immediately assigned additional responsibility of starting up new product line for the residential market and managing full test-marketing campaign (still in progress)

1988 – 1990    INTERNATIONAL BOARD SALES, New York, New York

**National Sales Manager**

- Established marketing arm for European-based plastic laminate manufacturer
  — Redesigned line for U.S. market; reduced line to 40 items
  — Developed copper-clad laminates for decorative purposes (first time in United States)
- Started sales through home centers and retail stores; developed network of manufacturers' representatives for furniture, tabletop, and dinette makers to expand market
  — Sales increased from zero base to $1 million in two years
- Assigned additional responsibility to sale of imported products in Plywood and Furniture Divisions (increased sales to $4 million)

1985 – 1988    BUDD COMPANY POLYCHEM DIVISION, New York, New York

**Regional Salesman**

- Assigned failing territory; effected turnaround, with increase in sales from $300,000 to $800,000 in first two years
  — More than tripled sales to large customers, including Otis Elevator, Stuart Warner, and Republic Aircraft
- Initiated blanket order system with distributors, locking in both company and buyer on a year-by-year basis (resulted in elimination of competition and improved service)

1984–1985    ITEK CORPORATION, New York, New York

**Salesman**

- Made comprehensive studies of needs of large corporation for in-house printing plants; demonstrated specific savings in cost through use of Itek platemaker for offset work
  — Made formal presentations to corporate management, documenting accrued savings from purchase of capital items costing from $12,000 to $18,000
  — Success ratio of 80%, including such major firms as Booz-Hamilton, Gray Advertising, General Dynamics, Hooker Chemical, and Edison Electric Institute

1979–1983    JOHNS MANVILLE SALES CORPORATION, New York, New York

**Territory Salesman**

- Assigned most of New England after service as a Trainee and Inside Sales Coordinator and as a Developer of Customer Relations
- Increased sales from $17,000 to $100,000 in two years (territory had been neglected for several years)
- Received special award for formal presentation to City of Hartford introducing improved line of general building products

*EDUCATION*    Villanova University, Villanova, Pennsylvania
1979—B.S., Economics/Prelaw–Marketing

## JUSTINE SHIPLEY    107 HUDSON STREET    HOBOKEN, NJ 07030    (201) 795-9573

**OBJECTIVE**    **ADMINISTRATIVE MANAGEMENT**
Seeking management-level position in corporate administration with potential for advancement to line management.

**SUMMARY**    Strong administrator in large-volume operation possessing follow-through ability in implementing company policies and programs. Expert in departmental organization for maximum efficiency at minimum cost. Results-oriented salesperson with conceptual marketing acuity. Proven capacity for discharging increasing responsibility and accountability.

**CAREER HIGHLIGHTS**

1989–1996    *AMERICAN EXPRESS COMPANY,* New York, New York
**Administrator, Retail Sales**    (1994–1996)
- Directed flow of detail in operation of credit card retail sales contract negotiations throughout United States
  — Managed agreements, advertising and operational budgets, advertising addendum program, discount reevaluation programs, sales presentations, and repetitive sales activity
  — Administered charge account solicitation and promotional mailing campaigns throughout United States
- Wrote retail section of card-member newsletter and president's letter in addition to a variety of departmental communications
- Represented department at conventions, meetings, and other events locally and throughout United States; prepared agendas

**Senior Administrative Secretary**    (1992–1994)
- Coordinated and supervised input from offices reporting to Vice-President, Domestic Sales; directed activities to subordinate staff

**Secretary to Director, Lodging Sales**    (1990–1992)
**Secretary/Backup Assistant to Manager, Domestic Sales**    (1989–1990)

1988–1989    *PATROLMEN'S BENEVOLENT ASSOCIATION,* New York, New York
**Executive/Personal and Confidential Secretary to President**
- Maintained current intelligence on political and police activities, assisted Public Relations Manager, and prepared releases for news media

1987–1988    *MERRILL LYNCH, PIERCE, FENNER & SMITH,* New York, New York
**Secretary**
- Prepared Turnpike, Tunnel, and Bridge Association reports, financial statements, and prospectus reports

1985    *AMERICAN EXPORT ISBRANDTSEN LINES*
**Assistant to Manager, Bill of Lading Department**
- Directed functions of office personnel; maintained teletype procedures for overseas communications

1984–1985    *CASTELO & SONS, SHIPSERVICING CO., INC.,* Hoboken, New Jersey
**Assistant to Payroll Supervisor/Secretary**
- Prepared manual payroll; posted AP and AR journals

**LANGUAGE**    Bilingual, Spanish-English

**EDUCATION**    New York University, Courses in Business Administration and Personnel (1984)

# JAMES CYRUS

| 250 East 76th Street, New York, NY 10021 | (212) 879-6216 |

## OBJECTIVE

Construction Superintendent, with enough growth opportunity to permit advancement to Project Manager and ultimately to General Project Manager

## EXPERIENCE

1983–present   JPD Construction Company
New York, New York

*Construction Superintendent* (1986–present)

— Order materials, deal directly with suppliers, schedule payments for subcontractors
— Supervise electrical, painting, carpentry, masonry, HVAC, flooring, hardware, and final cleanup trades
— Deliver all materials to job sites; prepare billing and payroll reports

*Accomplishments*

• Organized front office; realigned unorganized stacks of blueprints by specific jobs
• Served as Acting General Project Manager for one month in boss's absence
• Originated uniform manner of processing each job from point of sale to final billing; recommended new equipment for field and front office
• Purchased trade manuals at own expense to improve job knowledge

*Foreman's Assistant; Estimator; Salesman* (1983, 1985)

— Started as Laborer in 1975; promoted to Carpenter's Helper; learned estimating at night school; promoted to Estimator (time out for military)

1978–1982   Zerep Construction Company
New York, New York

*Laborer*

— Drove company truck; assisted in demolition work; acted as Mason's Helper, Carpenter's Helper

## EDUCATION

Music and Art High School, New York, New York; graduated 1982
Attended Institute of Design and Construction, 1985

## Military

USMC, 1983–1985; separated with rank of Lance Corporal; honorable discharge

Demolition and Construction Specialist; Demolition Instructor; completed Basic Combat Engineer School and refresher course; instructed officers in basic land mine warfare

**JUAN S. GEISLER**     975 East 44th Street, Brooklyn, NY 11234 • (212) 645-7133

**OBJECTIVE**  *BUILDING MANAGEMENT of PRESTIGIOUS OFFICE BUILDING or CORPORATE HEADQUARTERS*

**SUMMARY**  Extensive experience in commercial building management, supervision, and administration. Excellent track record in energy conservation, cost-effective maintenance, and minimization of downtime for all systems. Able to motivate engineering and maintenance staffs and contractors to produce work of high quality. Work effectively under pressure. Solid understanding of technical details and problems.

**EXPERIENCE**

*1985–present*  DAKOTA REALTY, INC., New York, New York
Managing agents for six commercial buildings, including 720 Fifth Avenue (ICC Building) and 445 Park Avenue (MCA–Universal Pictures)

*Vice President-Director of Operations* (1989–present)

- Charged with administration of all six buildings
  — Recruit, train, and supervise personnel responsible for on-site operations and Supervisor of Operations overseeing all six sites
  — Approve interior design, decorating, signage, and maintenance and service contracts
  — Supervise energy management
  — Interface with owners and principals; assist brokers with leasing details
  — Oversee all electrical billing and surveys

- Saved thousands of dollars on selection of fire safety system through utilization of existing resources
  — Carefully analyzed all contractor bids and received variances that eliminated the need to install expensive equipment

- On a regular basis, ensure reconstruction of office space for new tenants within critically limited time schedules
  — Through careful planning, maintain revenue level and promote good landlord-tenant relationships

- Interface with city agencies, including Fire Department and Departments of Buildings, Air Resources & Environmental Protection, and Sidewalks & Highways

*Supervisor of Operations* (1988–1989)

- Oversaw daily operations of six office buildings
  — Analyzed and solved emergencies
  — Supervised six employees and trained new personnel
  — Oversaw all construction, maintenance, and repair work
  — Acted as Purchasing Agent

- Set up schedule for periodic checking of all systems to ensure interruption-free service

*Building Manager, 445 Park Avenue* (1986–1988)

- Upgraded productivity of maintenance and engineering staffs, resulting in improvement in occupancy rate from 65% to 95% and promotion of building as company showplace

- Instituted major energy management program that cut steam usage in half and resulted in
  — letter of commendation to landlord from city/administration
  — three attempts by Con Edison to control revenue losses by installing new meters

*Building Superintendent and Engineer, 720 Fifth Avenue* (1985–1986)

- Established excellent reputation for building security by instituting tenant file and ID card security system
- Operated 300-ton electrical drive centrifugal air-conditioning and heating systems and all other building systems
- Supervised six-person staff

1981–1985    WILLIAMS REAL ESTATE, New York, New York

*Building Superintendent*

- Decreased energy consumption by improving efficiency of boiler and installing fluorescent lighting
- Acted on brokers' behalf, showing space to future tenants

1979–1981    BROWN BROTHERS HARRIMAN, New York, New York

*Manager, Air-Conditioning Section*

- Planned and implemented preventive maintenance program to reduce purchases of major parts, downtime, and service costs

## MILITARY SERVICE

1974–1978    U.S. AIR FORCE
Honorably Discharged as Staff Sergeant

- Awarded Commendation Medal for Meritorious Service

**EDUCATION**    Kingsborough Community College, Brooklyn, New York
1982–1983 Liberal Arts Courses

New York City Community College, Voorhees Campus
1982 Environmental Science Courses

*Coursework for professional advancement*
Building Owners' and Managers' Institute: Real Estate Property Administrator
Apex Technical Institute: Certificate in Theory of Thermodynamics and courses in Commercial HVAC, Blueprint Reading, and Drafting

## CERTIFICATIONS AND LICENSES

Certified Fire Safety Director
Licensed Sprinkler Operator
Licensed in Standpipe Maintenance
Licensed as No. 6 Oil Burner Operator

**AFFILIATION**    Building Owners' and Managers' Association

# GREG MAXWELL

157 Charing Cross Road
Tucson, AZ 85713
(602) 771-2510

## OBJECTIVE

Security administrator or related management position

## EXPERIENCE

HAMPTON HILLS COMMUNITY ASSOCIATION, Tucson, Arizona
*Security Director*

1992–present
- Supervise approximately 30 security officers and guard personnel at a four-season recreational community
  - Implement and evaluate all security programs
  - Manage personnel
  - Act as liaison with federal, state, and local officials
  - Plan and approve all budgets

FEDERAL BUREAU OF INVESTIGATION, Washington, D.C.
*Special Agent* **(Retired)**

1964–1992
- Responsible for extensive investigative-, training-, and supervisory-level positions, covering all investigative matters and operations
  - Planned, organized, and directed investigative staff and interfaced harmoniously and effectively with executives at all levels
  - Commended for excellence in performance on numerous occasions

## MILITARY

U.S. Navy, 1957–1959 (Honorable Discharge)

## EDUCATION

Seton Hall University—Graduated with B.S. degree in 1963

## ORGANIZATIONS

Society of Former Special Agents of the Federal Bureau of Investigation
Interstate Law Enforcement Association
International Association of Chiefs of Police

RESUMES•RESUMES•RESUMES•RESUMES•RESUMES•RESUMES•RESUMES
•RESUMES•RESUMES•RESUMES•RESUMES•RESUMES•RESUMES•RESUME
S•RESUMES•RESUMES•RESUMES•RESUMES•RESUMES•RESUMES•RESUM
ES•RESUMES•RESUMES•RESUMES•RESUMES•RESUMES•RESUMES•RESU
MES•RESUMES•RESUMES•RESUMES•RESUMES•RESUMES•RESUMES•RES
UMES•RESUMES•RESUMES•RESUMES•RESUMES•RESUMES•RESUMES•RE
SUMES•RESUMES•RESUMES•RESUMES•RESUMES•RESUMES•RESUMES•R
ESUMES•RESUMES•RESUMES•RESUMES•RESUMES•RESUMES•RESUMES•
RESUMES•RESUMES•RESUMES•RESUMES•RESUMES•RESUMES•RESUMES
•RESUMES•RESUMES•RESUMES•RESUMES•RESUMES•RESUMES•RESUME
S•RESUMES•RESUMES•RESUMES•RESUMES•RESUMES•RESUMES•RESUM
ES•RESUMES•RESUMES•RESUMES•RESUMES•RESUMES•RESUMES•RESU
MES•RESUMES•RESUMES•RESUMES•RESUMES•RESUMES•RESUMES•RES
UMES•RESUMES•RESUMES•RESUMES•RESUMES•RESUMES•RESUMES•RE
SUMES•RESUMES•RESUMES•RESUMES•RESUMES•RESUMES•RESUMES•R
ESUMES•RESUMES•RESUMES•RESUMES•RESUMS•RESUMES•RESUMES•R
ESUMES•RESUMES•RESUMES•RESUMES•RESUMES•RESUMES•RESUMES•
RESUMES•RESUMES•RESUMES•RESUMES•RESUMES•RESUMES•RESUMES
•RESUMES•RESUMES•RESUMES•RESUMES•RESUMES•RESUMES•RESUME
S•RESUMES•RESUMES•RESUMES•RESUMES•RESUMES•RESUMES•RESUM
ES•RESUMES•RESUMES•RESUMES•RESUMES•RESUMES•RESUMES•RESU
MES•RESUMES•RESUMES•RESUMES•RESUMES•RESUMES•RESUMES•RES

# RESEARCH & DEVELOPMENT

UMES•RESUMES•RESUMES•RESUMES•RESUMES•RESUMES•RESUMES•RE
SUMES•RESUMES•RESUMES•RESUMES•RESUMES•RESUMES•RESUMES•R
ESUMES•RESUMES•RESUMES•RESUMES•RESUMES•RESUMES•RESUMES•
RESUMES•RESUMES•RESUMES•RESUMES•RESUMES•RESUMES•RESUMES
•RESUMES•RESUMES•RESUMES•RESUMES•RESUMES•RESUMES•RESUME
S•RESUMES•RESUMES•RESUMES•RESUMES•RESUMES•RESUMES•RESUM
ES•RESUMES•RESUMES•RESUMES•RESUMES•RESUMES•RESUMES•RESU
MES•RESUMES•RESUMES•RESUMES•RESUMES•RESUMES•RESUMES•RES
UMES•RESUMES•RESUMES•RESUMES•RESUMES•RESUMES•RESUMES•RE
SUMES•RESUMES•RESUMES•RESUMES•RESUMES•RESUMES•RESUMES•R
ESUMES•RESUMES•RESUMES•RESUMES•RESUMES•RESUMES•RESUMES•
RESUMES•RESUMES•RESUMES•RESUMES•RESUMES•RESUMES•RESUMES
•RESUMES•RESUMES•RESUMES•RESUMES•RESUMES•RESUMES•RESUME
S•RESUMES•RESUMES•RESUMES•RESUMES•RESUMES•RESUMES•RESUM
ES•RESUMES•RESUMES•RESUMES•RESUMES•RESUMES•RESUMES•RESU
MES•RESUMES•RESUMES•RESUMES•RESUMES•RESUMES•RESUMES•RES
UMES•RESUMES•RESUMES•RESUMES•RESUMES•RESUMES•RESUMES•RE
SUMES•RESUMES•RESUMES•RESUMES•RESUMES•RESUMES•RESUMES•R
ESUMES•RESUMES•RESUMES•RESUMES•RESUMES•RESUMES•RESUMES•
RESUMES•RESUMES•RESUMES•RESUMES•RESUMES•RESUMES•RESUMES
•RESUMES•RESUMES•RESUMES•RESUMES•RESUMES•RESUMES•RESUME
S•RESUMES•RESUMES•RESUMES•RESUMES•RESUMES•RESUMES•RESUM
ES•RESUMES•RESUMES•RESUMES•RESUMES•RESUMES•RESUMES•RESU
MES•RESUMES•RESUMES•RESUMES•RESUMES•RESUMES•RESUMES•RES
UMES•RESUMES•RESUMES•RESUMES•RESUMES•RESUMES•RESUMES•RE
SUMES•RESUMES•RESUMES•RESUMES•RESUMES•RESUMES•RESUMES•R
ESUMES•RESUMES•RESUMES•RESUMES•RESUMES•RESUMES•RESUMES•
RESUMES•RESUMES•RESUMES•RESUMES•RESUMES•RESUMES•RESUMES

# *Matthew Silverman*

45-59 65th Street
Woodside, NY 11377
(718) 786-3576

**OBJECTIVE**  INDUSTRIAL MANUFACTURING ENGINEER
Responsible production development opportunity with growth-oriented electronics manufacturer.

**SUMMARY**  Eight years' experience in all phases of electronics manufacturing engineering. Expertise in setup and planning for entire production process. Capable of reducing costs while simultaneously increasing quality and output. Familiar with development and introduction of new designs. Effective supervisor of engineering staff.

## RELEVANT EXPERIENCE

*1987–present*  GBC CLOSED CIRCUITS TV CORPORATION, New York, New York

**Technician**

- Repair, control, adjust, modify and test equipment used in manufacture of closed-circuit television systems; equipment includes
  - black and white and color TV receivers and monitors
  - video switchers
  - video/audio minisystems
  - black and white VTR
  - video and camcorders
  - total-darkness TV cameras
  - amplifiers and distributors
  - intercoms and talk-a-phones
  - lenses

- Was recently invited by company President to tour new production line. As a result of visit,
  - pinpointed defect in adjustment during initial product run of latest design; modification resulted in major quality improvement at no cost
  - suggested use of specialized tool that immediately reduced total assembly time by 5%
  - advised Manufacturing Department of change in electronic thermal cooking procedures, that, if adopted, could reduce processing time by more than 75%

*1981–1986*  KOZITSKY TV MANUFACTURER, Leningrad, USSR

**Chief Manufacturing Engineer** (1983–1986)

- Conceived, planned, and organized total structure of new department; planned shop layout and assembly production line; established testing and adjustment procedures; organized work flow and determined equipment and personnel requirements; and wrote production manuals

- Successfully solved technical problems in production
  - Production increased from 10 to 1,200 units per day over three-year period
  - Overall production costs were reduced by 15% in one year
  - Improved quality was achieved in manufacture of color TV sets, radio receivers, tape recorders, and other products

(cont.)

KOZITSKY TV MANUFACTURER (cont.)

- Directly supervised 10 engineers and 12 technicians in department of firm with 1,600 employees
- Through state-of-the-art production techniques, was able to reduce number of employees required from 50 in initial tests to 15 in large-scale production
- Developed technique for producing new model equipment by utilizing same production used in producing older models
- Evaluated prospective engineers for other departments
- Served as Assistant Plant Manager, monitored four production lines, and supervised experimental shop where new models were conceived

**Senior Engineer, Experimental Section** (1982–1983)

- Responsible for design, assembly, and testing of experimental TV models and radio receivers
- Supervised two Assistant Engineers

**Engineer, Experimental Section** (1981–1982)

- Participated in experimental assembly, control tuning, and testing of electronic equipment

**EDUCATION**  Leningrad Institute of Mechanical-Electronic Engineering
Leningrad, USSR
1981—M.S., Radio-Electronic Engineering

Advanced training in Manufacturing and Production Technology
(150 hours)

**LANGUAGES**  Fluent English (Native Russian)

**VISA STATUS**  Permanent resident with intent to apply for citizenship

# PETER TAGORE

480 Stillson Avenue
Montpelier, Vermont

Home: (802) 469-5971
Message: (802) 270-9630

**OBJECTIVE**

*PRODUCTION ENGINEER/PROJECT ENGINEER*

To apply skills and experience to a position as a planning and production engineer in a machine shop, fabrication shop, or foundry or as a construction site manager overseeing turnkey projects in piping, structurals, or machinery installation and commissioning.

**SUMMARY**

Highly experienced as site manager, works manager, and operations manager in directing the performance of turnkey contracts, projects, and machine shop and fabrication shop operations and inspections

**RELEVANT EXPERIENCE:**
*1992–1996*

UNIQUE BUILDERS, LTD.

*Operations Manager* (350 Employees)                    Cuttack, India

- In overall charge of Rourkela works and site in Rourkela steel plant, to direct and coordinate the complete operations of turnkey contracts in piping, fabrication erection, and commissioning of heavy structurals and equipment
  — Supervised design-to-completion (turnkey) construction of air line and oxygen line for plant expansion in Rourkela steel plant
  — Designed and supervised fabrication and commissioning of ferro-alloy addition system in steel melting shop
  — Developed door frames and door bodies with improved sealing for coke ovens
- Directed and coordinated sales, contract negotiations, planning, procurement, and sales promotion
- Directed, coordinated, and motivated personnel in all phases of manufacturing process, including design, layout, foundry, machine shop, fabrication, fitting, assembly, final erection and commissioning, and office management
- Maintained quality control of projects from inception through shakedown; provided advisory and practical assistance in the solving of problems occurring subsequent to shakedown

*1991–1992*

EAST INDIA ENGINEERING COMPANY

*Projects Manager* (300 Employees)                    Rourkela, India

- Responsible for the management of mini-steel project involving labor management, materials management, project planning, supervision, and inspection in all phases of manufacture, construction, and commissioning, including office administration
- Introduced and implemented partial subcontracting system for labor at a saving of 25% on labor costs, eliminating the problem of providing labor facilities (housing, transportation, and so on) on project sites; introduced subcontracting for projects, reducing capital investment by 50%
- Supervised and coordinated activities of 300 employees

(cont.)

EAST INDIA ENGINEERING COMPANY (cont.)

1990–1991     *Project Engineer*
- Responsible for the supervision and inspection in all shops of manufacture, erection, and commissioning; also responsible for stores' inventory and manpower planning for the economy and time schedule of the project
- Introduced and implemented incentive-bonus system for bringing projects in on time, with 20% increase in on-time execution of contracts
  — More efficient allotment of manpower resulted in saving of 20% in labor costs
  — Improved raw materials inventory, reduced waste, and saved 5% in materials cost

1988–1990     PRABHAT IRON FOUNDRY & METAL INDUSTRIES

*Planning Engineer*          Rourkela, India
- Directed department responsible for job planning for machine and fabrication shops
  — Supervised procurement of raw materials, tools, and consumables for both shops and of tools required by inspectors; supervised inspection and quality control
- Introduced incentive-bonus system for more efficient utilization of personnel, resulting in 10% increase in production
- Introduced system of stage inspections in production to improve quality control, resulting in fewer job rejections; increased profits by 15%

1982–1988     *Trainee*
- Received general training in various units of the company—planning, machine shop, GI foundry, nonferrous foundry, and pattern shop

**EDUCATION**     Regional Engineering College, Rourkela, India
1985—B.S., Mechanical Engineering

Specialized Courses:
   Industrial Organizations and Works Management
   Refrigeration Engineering (Theory)
   Automobile Engineering (Theory)

Sacred Heart College, Ernakulam, India
1979—Predegree

# PETER CHU MING
*10 Ashley Avenue • Norwich, New York 10523 • (914) 592-6320*

**OBJECTIVE**   ENGINEER—MECHANICAL/THERMODYNAMIC

Seeking staff position with opportunity to advance to consulting engineer

**SUMMARY**   Experience in design, fabrication, and installation of air-conditioning duct and equipment. Expert at taking off specs and bidding from architects' drawings. Knowledge of manufacturer equipment. Shrewd negotiator with subcontractors. Able supervisor of mechanics and junior engineers. Capable draftsman. Skilled in design and research and quality control of precision mechanical parts.

**RELEVANT EXPERIENCE**

1978–1996   BIG FOUR ENTERPRISE AND ENGINEERING COMPANY, Taipei, Taiwan

*General Manager/Mechanical Engineer*

- Operated as prime air-conditioning contractor on four textile factories
  - Bid on and negotiated contracts from specifications
  - Designed, fabricated, and installed sheet metal duct lines
  - Installed and started up air-conditioning equipment ordered from manufacturer
  - Supplied maintenance and repair service after installation and during operation
- Operated service of installation, maintenance, and repair for commercial and residential construction and service of maintenance and repair for industrial installations
- Managed plant, with supervision of sales force, office personnel, and engineering and mechanical specialists

1970–1978   RESEARCH INSTITUTE OF TECHNOLOGY (1974–1978)
PRODUCTS SERVICE, COMBINED SERVICE FORCES (1972–1974)
CHINESE GOVERNMENT ARSENAL (1970–1972)
Taipei, Taiwan

*Mechanical Engineer*

- Placed in high-security position of military research and testing
- Supervised control of inventory in factories and of material purchased from U.S. government under aid program
- Supervised quality control of manufactured precision mechanical parts for adherence to close tolerance for interchangeability, according to military specifications

**EDUCATION**   Ordnance Engineering College, Taipei, Taiwan
1968—B.S., Mechanical Engineering
Coursework included Industrial Engineering, Industrial Management, Plant Layout, and Time-Motion Studies

Taiwan Provincial Taipei First Professional Technical School
Electrical Engineering

*Willing to relocate*

# ROBERT STEVENS

1573 Palm Springs Blvd.
Miami, Florida 33182
(305) 890-5261

## *OBJECTIVE*

SENIOR ENVIRONMENTAL SCIENTIST

## *SUMMARY*

Experienced in trace element and inorganic compounds analysis in particulate and liquid samples.

Comprehensive knowledge of Atomic Absorption Spectroscopy, Ion Chromatography, X-ray Photoelectron Spectroscopy, and various wet chemical methods.

Working knowledge of EPA methods and Level I and Level II procedures.

## *EXPERIENCE*

1984–present   ENVIRONMENTAL SCIENTIST
       *APR Corporation*, Jensen Beach, Florida

- Evaluate sampling and analysis techniques used in Environmental Assessment Programs
- Design experimental programs and conduct background research on collection techniques for volatile trace metals, current uses and potential applications of ion chromatography, and the effect of ammonia on the sampling and analysis of sulfur oxides and nitrogen oxides
- Participated in design and construction of sample steam generator to simulate flue gases of varied chemical composition, temperature, and flow rate
- Principal investigator in program to characterize total suspended particularities for total volatiles and selected anions and metals
- Assisted in development of an ashing-fusion technique to prepare cellulose filter samples for analysis of silicon by atomic absorption

## *EDUCATION*

HARVARD UNIVERSITY, Cambridge, Massachusetts
1984—A.B., Engineering and Applied Physics
       Concentration in Environmental Science

# HERMAN SCHWARTZ

628 Newbridge Avenue • Staten Island, NY 10310
(718) 727-5321

**OBJECTIVE**  *ENGINEERING MANAGEMENT*

**SUMMARY**  Hands-on experience in electronic systems engineering. Innovative conceptual designer, acutely cost-conscious, with proven ability to complete project within budget limitations. Capable coordinator of interdepartmental activities. Excellent supervisor of technical personnel. Have security clearance at secret level.

## PROFESSIONAL HIGHLIGHTS

1978–present  ISRAEL AIRCRAFT INDUSTRIES, LTD.
Yahud, Israel

*Senior Project Engineer, MBT Division* (1979–present)
- Manage projects involving the design, development, production, and installation of microwave, radar, antenna, and other systems for commercial, government, and classified military use
- Designed and developed, from prototype through production, microwave system and antenna equipment for EW application in ECCM
  — Wrote proposal, sold it to government, and executed program
- Prepare PERT and long-lead programs
- Coordinate Purchasing, Design and Production Departments, effect expedited delivery of equipment, supervise staff of ten engineers and technicians
- Updated and maintain accurate testing programs and equipment

*Senior Development Engineer, Elta Electronics Division* (1978–1979)
- Charged with design and system control of two radar systems, one for ship and land base use and the other for airborne use, in X-band frequency

1975–1978  NORDEN DIVISION, UNITED AIRCRAFT CORPORATION
Norwalk, Connecticut

*Development Engineer*
- Designed Beacon receiver for A-6A radar system and AMTI equipment
- Analyzed F-111D video systems for computer-oriented go-no-go philosophy program; established final acceptance specifications for system
- Met deadlines required for delivery of equipment; executed and manufactured to specifications
- Effected saving of $100,000 in costs through judicious selection of components and vendors
- Supervised test engineers, technicians, and production personnel

| | |
|---|---|
| 1970–1975 | **LITCOM DIVISION OF LITTON SYSTEMS, INC.**<br>New York and Maryland |

*Project Engineer* (1972–1975)

- Designed and developed HF receivers
- Ran complete on-site final acceptance testing of high-performance SSB communications system and trained personnel for U.S. government installation
- Credited with saving six months' work and a year of development time through expedited procedures

*Electrical Engineer* (1970–1972)

| | |
|---|---|
| 1967–1970 | **RCA COMMUNICATIONS, INC.**<br>New York, New York |

*Electromechanical Designer*

- Designed circuits and worked on packaging and layouts (PC boards for amplifiers, transmitters, receivers, motor controls, talker hybrid units, and ARQ equipment)

| | |
|---|---|
| 1964–1967 | **WESTERN UNION TELEGRAPH COMPANY**<br>New York, New York |

*Senior Electromechanical Draftsman*

- Worked on schematics and finished wiring and assembly drawings for cabinets, carrier equipment, and switching systems

**MILITARY**  U.S. Army, 1962–1963
Sergeant, Communications

**EDUCATION**  University of Maryland, College Park, Maryland
1970—B.S.E.E.

Brooklyn Polytechnic Institute
City College of New York
Coursework toward B.S.E.E.

**MEMBER**  Institute of Electrical and Electronics Engineers

Willing to travel and/or relocate

# CAESAR HABIB

77-02 67th Avenue • Jackson Heights, NY 11372 • (718) 424-7539

## OBJECTIVE

*INDUSTRIAL CHEMIST, PHARMACEUTICALS*
A production, quality assurance, or R&D position in the pharmaceutical field

## SUMMARY

Experienced chemist involved in drugs, pharmaceuticals, and cosmetics. Expert in qualitative and quantitative analysis, with thorough knowledge of USP, NF, and nonofficial compendia.

*Instruments Used*

| | |
|---|---|
| Viscometer | Gas/water separation index |
| UV, GC, IR, TLC | Reid vapor pressure |
| ORD; CD (Cary 14, 60) | Spectrofluorometer |

## PROFESSIONAL HIGHLIGHTS

*1982–present*　　NEW YORK POLICE DEPARTMENT, New York, New York

**Chemist, Crime Laboratory**

- Charged with analysis of physical evidence for use in criminal proceedings
  — Quantitative and qualitative organic analysis of unknown street samples
  — Analysis of illicit pharmaceutical preparations
  — Analysis of intermediates, solvents, reagents, and drug products from clandestine laboratories
  — Physical comparison of evidence such as unknown tablets, trace particles, and ballistics

- Successfully defended analyses before lower and supreme courts at local and federal levels in establishing guilt or innocence of defendant

- Improved analytical procedures to produce more timely reports

- Direct work of assistant chemists, junior chemists, and technicians during periods of heavy activity

*Concurrent*　　ST. JOHN'S UNIVERSITY INSTITUTE OF PHARMACEUTICALS, New York, New York

**Pharmaceutical Chemist (Part time)**

- Performed analyses for New York State Board of Pharmacy as a consultant
  — Determined legality of dosages and conformation with USP and NF standards in both quality and quantity
  — Acted on customer complaints regarding compliance
- Developed improved analytical procedures and techniques for various nonofficial pharmaceutical preparations

*1979–1982*   PURDUE FREDERICK PHARMACEUTICAL COMPANY, Yonkers, New York

**Analytical Chemist, Quality Control Laboratory**

- Worked with vitamins, aspirin, surgical scrub solutions, laxative tablets, capsules, lotions, and ointments
  — Thoroughly familiar with all wet methods of analysis
- Ran quality assurance tests on raw materials, intermediates, and finished products
- Checked dosages and conducted stability studies

*1977–1979*   ELIZABETH ARDEN COSMETIC COMPANY, New York, New York

**Production Chemist**

- Developed formulas for lotions, creams, lipsticks, loose powder, pressed powder, and foundations
- Supervised manufacture of thousands of pounds of product on production line
- Supervised and directed technicians on problem products; personally checked the operations of large batches
- Became expert in all aspects of color matching and contrasting shades of makeup
- Worked under Director of Quality Control for six-month period, solving particular problems in color matching
- Developed solution to problem of stability in one cream

### EDUCATION

St. John's University, College of Pharmacy, New York, New York
1988—Ph.D. Candidate, Industrial Pharmacy
*Thesis:* "Microencapsulation"

St. John's University, School of Chemistry, New York, New York
1983—M.S., Chemistry
*Thesis:* "Effect of Divalent Salts (Magnesium, Calcium) on the Conformation and Configuration of Bovine Serum Albumin"

Ain Shams University, School of Science, Cairo, Egypt
1974—B.S., Chemistry

### LANGUAGES

Bilingual, English-Arabic

# JANET PIERCE

400 Schenck Avenue • Great Neck, NY 11021
(516) 487-9530

**OBJECTIVE**    Seeking position offering advancement in the field of genetics

**EXPERIENCE**
1993–1996    MONTREAL CHILDREN'S HOSPITAL, Montreal, Quebec, Canada

*Cytogenetic Technician* and *Tissue Culture Technician*

- Set up and cultured amniotic fluids; added colcemid and harvested when indicated
- Prepared, stained, and screened slides under microscope
- Photographed metaphase cells; enlarged and printed pictures
- Cut karyotype
- Used tissue culture techniques to make poor growth cultures successful, thus eliminating need for repeat taps
- Set up skin biopsies and prepared cells for biochemical analysis
- Maintained cell bank of mutant fibroblast strains and diseases, shipped world-wide on request, and thawed and froze fibroblasts
- Participated in diabetic research related to the development and morphology of the fetal pancreas
  — Assisted in removal of fetal pancreas, digested pancreas to obtain islets, cultured islets, and prepared them for electron microscopy
- Developed technique for successful growth of bloody amniotic taps
- Initiated quality control of individual bags of flasks
  — Identified cell attachment problem

1992–1993    CIRCO CRAFT, INC., Granby, Quebec, Canada

*Chemical Analysis and Quality Control Technician*

- Organized lab for testing and adjusting concentrations of metal solutions for manufacturer of printed circuit boards
- Tested thickness and quality of electroplated metals

1991–1992    McGILL UNIVERSITY, Montreal, Quebec, Canada

*Microbial Genetics Technician*

- Prepared all chemicals and maintained equipment used in 400-student-per-week laboratory
- Tested mutant bacterial strains and verified necessary calculations by conducting eight separate experiments, among them
  — UV irradiation and repair of DNA (mutagenesis)
  — mapping of genes on the *E. coli* chromosome by interrupted conjugation
- Proposed system and adapted equipment for automated method of successfully pouring agar media dishes under sterile conditions

Summer 1990     LONG ISLAND JEWISH MEDICAL CENTER, New York
                *Microbiology Technician Trainee*

**EDUCATION**     State University of New York, Stony Brook, New York
                1991—B.S., Medical Technology

                Alton Jones Cell Science Center, Lake Placid, New York
                1994—Seminar in Prenatal Diagnosis

**LANGUAGES**     French

**REFERENCES**    Available upon request

# FRANCES DAVISON
2500 YORK AVENUE
NEW YORK, NY 10021
(212) 288-7356

**OBJECTIVE**      Seeking a position employing experience in investigative drug research and project systems design

**SUMMARY**      Registered professional nurse-researcher with intensive experience in clinical administration. Adept at problem analysis, with ability to develop systems for efficient records management. Knowledgeable about testing techniques and legal requirements. Demonstrated expertise in human resource management. Highly experienced in research into drug quality control and effectiveness of recommended dosage.

## MEDICAL RESEARCH/ADMINISTRATION HIGHLIGHTS

1981–present   MEMORIAL SLOAN-KETTERING HOSPITAL, New York, New York

*Clinical Research Coordinator* (1984–present)

- Responsible for development, coordination, and human resource management of federally funded cancer treatment research project
  — Report directly to Board of Clinical Investigators; determine and initiate appropriate action based on their requests
  — Design systems for administration, record keeping, and control of experimental drug program
  — Develop procedures for patient recruitment, evaluation, dosage administration, and follow-up testing of participants
  — Organize and work in liaison with participating surgeons, clinics, and laboratories
  — Solve special scheduling, transportation, and communication problems, as well as counseling terminally ill patients and their families
  — Designed toxicity sheet, label for experimental tablet, and patient schedule cards to facilitate and simplify record keeping and communications
  — Train medical fellows as backup administrators
- Assist with clinical administration of 30 additional protocols
  — Coordinate appointments; document tests and dosages according to legal and protocol requirements
  — Monitor patients and assess dosage requirements and referrals
  — Developed systems for identification of incomplete records, indexing and chart procurement; evaluated information required for efficient usage of records desk
- Developed and administered two-year breast study
  — Wrote problem analysis and offered solutions in paper submitted to Chiefs of Staff and discussed in interdepartmental meeting
  — Initiated system for following day-to-day changes in patients' toxicity levels

*(cont.)*

228

MEMORIAL SLOAN-KETTERING HOSPITAL (cont.)

— Designed label for medication vials according to legal specifications; organized effective systems for patient follow-up

• In addition to official job responsibilities, accomplished extensive reorganization of general record keeping

— Set up log book to document work flow and staff use of time for funding

— Designed and redesigned numerous charts, forms, cards, and labels

— Reorganized responsibilities of entire staff to achieve full productivity during crisis caused by 40% personnel shortage

— Simplified reordering of supplies and drugs by preparing coded catalogs

*Clinical Research Nurse, Chemotherapy Department* (1981–1984)

• Prepared and administered experimental drug therapy; monitored and evaluated patient status both in and out of hospital

## NURSING EXPERIENCE

1977–1981    NEW YORK STATE REGISTRY, New York, New York

*Private-Duty Nurse*

KINGS COUNTY HOSPITAL CENTER, Brooklyn, New York

*Assistant Clinical Instructor* (1978–1979)

• Taught Respiratory Medicine and Respiratory Intensive Care to senior nursing students (both theory and practice); designed techniques for teaching Decision-Making Skills

• Supervised student nurses in clinical care, assessed and graded performance, conducted individual evaluation conferences

*Staff Nurse, Intensive Care Unit* (1977–1978)

• In charge of Intensive Care Unit; supervised entire night staff for 600-bed service

1975–1976    DOCTORS HOSPITAL, Freeport, New York

*Nurse's Aide, Medicine and Surgery* (while in school)

**EDUCATION**    Current—Marymount Manhattan College, New York, New York
(Earned 99 credits toward BS in Nursing, attending school part-time)

Kings County Hospital Center School of Nursing, Brooklyn, New York
1977—Nursing Diploma

Nassau Community College, Garden City, New York
1974—Liberal Arts/Nursing Program

**CERTIFICATION**    Registered Professional Nurse

# MICHAEL FRIER

120 West 86th Street, Apt. 4A
New York, New York 10025

*Home* (212) 724-6572
*Work* (212) 650-7530

***FACILITIES PLANNING*** for consulting and development, real estate, construction firm, or government planning agency

**SUMMARY**

Facilities planner with planning and development experience for major New York City medical center. Management authority over as many as ten ongoing projects, with combined budgets of up to $750,000, involving sophisticated medical and research facilities. Experienced at obtaining government approvals, certificates of need, and variances. Effective client consultant and director of architects, engineers, and general contractors.

**1979–present**

MONTEFIORE HOSPITAL, New York, New York
Office of Facilities Planning and Design

*Project Manager*

Responsible for all phases of the planning and implementation of major facility changes

*Facilities Planning*

- Create and direct construction, renovation, and space utilization projects to facilitate institutional development
  — Design programs that reconcile desires of client departments with facility objectives
  — Determine available resources and administer budgets ranging from $50,000 to $100,000
  — Review architectural and engineering proposals to achieve maximum cost-effectiveness
  — Schedule, direct, and monitor work of architects, engineers, consultants, and interior designers

- Fully knowledgeable about New York Department of Health Building codes and other state regulatory agencies and local planning regulations

*Major Building Programs*

- Assisted Director of Planning with development of major building programs
  — These included a $100 million, 500-bed hospital facility; a 30-story, $10 million residence; and a 10-story, 100-suite professional practice building

- Wrote and presented proposal to New York City Environmental Agency for a $3 million, 600-car garage
  — This was the only such proposal approved by agency since its inception

*Long-Range Planning*

- Developed currently implemented long-range plan in 1983 for future development of hospital and its building

(MONTEFIORE, cont.)

*Space Planning*
- Designed comprehensive, computerized, 2-year, $100,000 space inventory to achieve efficient space management

*Construction Management*
- Managed projects up to 15,000 square feet with budgets ranging to $750,000
  — Put projects out to bids
  — Negotiate contracts and approve changes
  — Monitor costs and schedules
  — Inspect work to ensure adherence to plans and specifications
  — Deal with general contractors and subcontractors

1978-1979    Stevens, Smith & Partners, New York, New York
Architects and Hospital Consultants

*Health Planner*

*Long-Range Planning*
Developed long-range plans for Bronx Municipal Hospital Center, New York; Norwich Hospital, Norwich, Connecticut; and Backus Hospital, Greenwich, Connecticut

- Prepared comprehensive studies, serving as basis for long-range building programs
  — Studied demography, patient origins, physician manpower, community objectives, transportation, ambulatory care, delivery systems, long-term care, and available health and community resources

1974-1978    Taught for New York City Board of Education, served in Peace Corps in India, and traveled through Mideast, Europe, and Mexico

**EDUCATION**    NEW YORK UNIVERSITY, New York, New York
1973–1974    Completed coursework for M.A., Philosophy
New York University Fellowship

KENYON COLLEGE, Gambiar, Ohio
1973    B.A., Philosophy (cum laude, with High Honors in Philosophy)
Woodrow Wilson Scholar

*Professional Courses*
New York University—Urban and Health Planning, Construction Technology and Management
New School for Social Research—Urban Planning and Real Estate

**Willing to relocate, free to travel**

# BERNARD REESE

600 Rosedale Avenue
White Plains, NY
(914) 946-7357

## OBJECTIVE

*PHARMACEUTICALS: Market Research and Development*

## SUMMARY

Diversified experience in clinical and immunological cancer research. Candidate for master's degree in Marketing. Master's degree in Immunology and bachelor's degree in Biology/Chemistry

## EXPERIENCE

INMAN INSTITUTE, New York, New York

*1977–present*　　*Senior Research Assistant* (1982–present)

- Conduct experimental immunological research (in-vivo and in-vitro)
- Write experimental papers
- Direct laboratory and staff of approximately 15 M.D.'s, Ph.D.'s, technicians, students, and volunteers
- Prepare annual budget of $250,000
- Administer $100,000 annual laboratory purchases from pharmaceutical companies
- Write grant papers
- Interview job applicants

*Research Assistant* (1977–1982)

- Developed formally adopted creative procedures for performing perfusion techniques in live animals
  — Performed immunological preparation associated with liver and pancreas transplantation surgery in dogs and cats
  — Performed microsurgery in rats
  — Ran Alpha Feto Protein Immune-Electropheresis of serum proteins from patients suspected of having liver malignancy
- Responsible for some laboratory administration

## EDUCATION

NEW YORK UNIVERSITY, New York, New York
Present—M.B.A. candidate, Marketing
1986—M.S., Immunology

BOSTON UNIVERSITY, Boston, Massachusetts
1977—B.S., Biology/Chemistry

UNIVERSITY OF ROME, Rome, Italy
1977—Summer courses at School of Medicine

FAIRLEIGH DICKINSON UNIVERSITY, Teaneck, New Jersey
1976—Summer course in Advertising

## EXTRACURRICULAR ACTIVITIES

Worker in University Hospital Volunteer Plan
Orientation Adviser and Guidance Counselor

President, Boston University International Folk Dance Club

## LANGUAGES

Italian—read/speak

# Lewis Lee Shun

200 SMITHTOWN ROAD          YORKTOWN HEIGHTS, NY 10598          (914) 245-5662

**OBJECTIVE**  To obtain a research or management position utilizing education and expertise in international economics, monetary economics, and finance.

**SUMMARY**  M.A. in Economics, with specialization in International and Monetary. Economist, Government of Republic of China. Research at University of Florida. Bilingual: English–Mandarin Chinese.

**RELEVANT EXPERIENCE**

1994–1996    **Research Assistant**, UNIVERSITY OF FLORIDA
Gainesville, Florida

— Assistant to economist Michael Connelly, performing the research function for papers and projects on Foreign Exchange, Economics, and International Studies
— Sole responsiblility for evaluation and selection of new sourcebooks for economics, international finance, and business administration for University of Florida library
— Simultaneously worked toward M.A. in the fields of International and Monetary Economics

1993–1994    **Economist** (GS-11 equivalent level)
ECONOMIC PLANNING COUNCIL OF REPUBLIC OF CHINA
Taipei, Taiwan

— For the Director, organized, wrote, and edited reports on International Trade, New Developments, and the Effect of Monetary Devaluation—much of it having to do with the United States, Canada, Asia, and Europe
— Published two reports for the Republic of China: (1) *The Effects of Devaluation* and (2) *A Comparison of Taiwan-Korean Trade Patterns*

**Instructor**, THE NATIONAL CHUNG-HSING UNIVERSITY
Taiwan

— In addition to my position as a staff economist, taught Money and Banking and International Economics courses at the university
— Developed curriculum for both courses, based upon U.S.-published texts

**OTHER EXPERIENCE**

1996–1997    **Part-time retail sales work**
Washington, D.C.

**EDUCATION**

M.A., University of Florida, 1996
*Major:* Economics, International and Monetary

Graduate work, Cornell University, 1991–1992

B.A., National Taiwan University, 1989
*Major:* Economics

**PERSONAL**  Married, no children, willing to travel, permanent U.S. resident

# 5

# Developing a Successful Marketing Plan

You have followed all the rules. Your résumé is as good as it can be, for the specific audience you had in mind. Let's now determine how to make the best possible use of it. This will depend, as mentioned in Chapter 2, on why you wrote it.

First of all, are you accelerating or changing careers? The strategies are different. Accelerating is much easier, so let's deal with it first.

## Strategies for Accelerating

If you are trying to get further faster in the same field, you probably are seeking an interview for a position you either *know* is available or think *might* be, now or in the near future. For either option, the most effective approach is to keep in mind and utilize the three levels of information listed in Chapter 3: knowledge of industry, knowledge of company, and knowledge of position.

Knowing what's out there obviously maximizes your chances of getting the job you want. Moving from the obvious to the less obvious, consider the following sources:

- Employment agencies
- Executive recruiters
- Newspaper want ads and business section display ads
- Business and trade publication articles and want ads
- Industry or function journals and newsletters
- Industry association officers
- Former colleagues and "friends of friends" networks
- Electronic job-search resources

Let's take them in turn.

### Employment agencies

Reputable agencies specializing in your field are worth contacting, but should not be depended on too heavily. Send a résumé and letter to those you've identified as the best of them, call within a decent interval for an interview (so at least one placement counselor knows you personally), and then forget about it.

Employment agencies work for the corporations and private institutions that give them job orders and therefore can't be expected to go out of their way for you. It's important to take enough time to interview with each agency to which you send a résumé, though, so that it has a data file on you in its database of applicants. Most agencies are now computerized, so it is relatively easy to do a candidate search based on skills and experience. You will be contacted if your background matches a client company's needs.

If you are in the following fields, there is likely to be one or more agencies in your metropolitan area specializing in positions appropriate for you:

| | |
|---|---|
| Accounting/Finance | Personnel |
| Advertising | Public Relations |
| Banking | Publishing |
| Brokerage | Retailing |
| Data Processing | Sales |
| Healthcare/Pharmaceutical | Technical/Scientific |
| Legal | Textile/Apparel |

## Executive recruiters

Our advice regarding "headhunters" is similar to that for employment agencies. Their allegiance is to their clients, understandably, rather than to any individual applicant.

Some of you who have been contacted by a recruiter may remember being vaguely irritated that first time to be told about a great new job just as you were beginning to enjoy the best one you ever had. That happens. Don't expect them to be there when you need them. Most recruiters lure "fast trackers" from their clients' competitors and companies with similar product/service lines to that of their clients.

Recruiters like to *solicit* résumés, not receive them unasked. If they hear from you first, you are perceived to be vulnerable with your current employer or even unemployed (even though you may not have alluded to your job status in a cover letter). The reason is not so much that you are tainted professionally by being—at worst—between jobs as that you are a tougher "sell" to the client. Most recruiters would rather not spend the extra time it takes to neutralize the negatives of pitching an out-of-work applicant or one whose job is in jeopardy. An executive who has to be pried from his or her current position is a much lower risk and a more prized commodity.

Most recruiters do accept résumés, however, and indeed keep them. And because they have to stay on top of industry/company/position trends, they can be excellent sourcepeople.

Call the recruiter for an interview a week or so after you send in a résumé and see if you can steal a half hour of time. Do enough brain picking to get a sound estimate of your intrinsic marketability and the current state of the market for someone with your background and aspirations.

## Newspaper want ads and business section display ads

Responding to a newspaper ad is much like buying a lottery ticket: The cost is low and the payoff high, but the odds of winning are even higher. The employers' screeners first scan résumés as much to exclude the unacceptable as to identify the qualified. Their instructions usually are to pick out the top 10 or 25 résumés from the hundreds they read, so that interviews can be set up accordingly.

Their checklist usually is inviolable, because they are simply following orders. So if you like the sound of the job but fall short on more than one of the stated criteria, applying will probably be a waste of your time. Papering the gap between your qualifications and the minimum listed by writing a long cover letter won't help either. Either rewrite your résumé to fit the specifications of the opening (honestly, that is—anything less will catch up to you, eventually), or keep looking until you find a better match.

As to want ads in particular, be sure you look under all the appropriate categories, and do it consistently. Some companies advertise by function, others by industry, still others by job title. A public relations writer, for example, conceivably could find openings appropriate to ability under Public Relations, Corporate Communications, Corporate Relations, Copywriter—Public Relations, Speechwriter, and Writer, as well as under the various industry and individual agency listings. Get in the habit of regularly cross-checking all categories that could pertain to you.

Be familiar with those weekdays your metropolitan papers gang their display ads in a discrete employment section. The *Wall Street Journal* lists employment opportunities and services every Tuesday, for example; the *New York Times*, on Tuesdays, Wednesdays, and Sundays.

## Business and trade publication articles and want ads

Spend a half day every week at the best public library available to you, so you can assemble an intelligence system effective enough to anticipate trends that may in turn trigger job openings.

Go through business magazines such as *Fortune, Forbes,* and *Business Week* regularly, as well as your particular trade magazines. Take notes on companies that interest you and individuals in them who may make good contacts for you someday. Check the back-of-the-book classifieds for openings you may want to follow up on.

## Industry or function journals and newsletters

Those journals and newsletters you can't find at the library, subscribe to. Use them as you would business and trade publications.

## Industry association officers

Membership directories are great sources for identifying leaders in your field who could be valuable contacts for you. If you don't know of a directory listing your industry or function membership, talk to a reference librarian or consult the *Directory of Directories* (Gale Research Company), published semiannually.

## Former colleagues and "friends of friends" networks

To draw a lead on companies where you have discovered openings or believe they are about to occur, contact former colleagues or friends in other companies to see who knows somebody in power at each target company.

Raised to its highest, most organized form, this systematic contacting is called networking. (It's an effective strategy for career changers as well, so you'll be referred back to this section if you're thinking of plunging ahead to those paragraphs.)

Most female executives and professionals are great networkers. Many males don't even know the term. One reason for this is that women as a group have had it far rougher in the business world than their male counterparts have, owing to various forms of sexual discrimination. They've been the Outs; men, the Ins. As a result, women have learned to cope and scramble in an alien world, a bit like fish learning to walk on land. So they're less reluctant to ask the right questions of anyone who can help them break down the barriers.

Male executives generally talk to a handful or so of former colleagues to see where the jobs are, but rarely do they exploit the networking technique to its fullest. Many groups of female executives meet regularly just to exchange business cards and broaden their network base.

But the technique is beginning to spread. A noted former radical, excoriated in the 1960s by a large segment of society for his antiestablishment behavior, helped broaden the networking concept in the early 1980s by taking over a large New York discotheque on off-nights. By promising both professional and social introductions to attending male and female executives, he generated the exchange of thousands of business cards, leading to proposals of various kinds—many of them for jobs.

Male reluctance to networking has been partly attributed to the eggshell egos some say go with the gender. This is probably true, although the job hunt exposes anyone—male as well as female—to vulnerability in the extreme. And this is the case even for those changing positions of their own volition. Most executives feel best about themselves when they are secure, productive, well-compensated team members. They feel worst about themselves, understandably, when this security is taken away.

## Electronic job-search resources

Among the phenomena arriving with the 1990s was "cyberspace," the term given to computer-driven information derived from telephone hookups. Not all of the implications are yet known to us—but some are already proving extremely valuable to job seekers.

It is not necessary to "be on-line" with your family personal computer to take advantage of much of the computer-assisted job-search assistance available today. Most public libraries utilize one or more of a number of services offered by the growing number of providers. Here are five of the most popular:

- *Infotrac*, a journal and newspaper article index providing data about prospective employers

- *Business Dateline OnDisc*, business articles appearing in local, state, and regional journals and newspapers and magazines and of interest to job seekers

- *ProQuest*, business articles in newspapers and magazines

- *Standard & Poor's Corporation*, listings of public and private companies as well as biographical listings

- *Ultimate Job Finder*, 4,500 sources of trade and specialty journals

**Using the Internet for employer research.** Currently, six major on-line services offer job- and career-search information. But because this is such a newly emerging and highly competitive market, several additional services may be available by the time you read this. Prices and kinds of information vary widely from service to service, however—often from one month to the next. So investigate carefully, possibly by opting for a trial membership, to be sure you've made the best decision. Here are the basics, to help get your investigative process started:

**America Online**
8619 Westwood Center Drive
Vienna, VA 22182-2285
(800) 827-6364
Fax (703) 883-1509

**Compuserve**
5000 Arlington Centre Boulevard
P.O. Box 20212
Columbus, OH 43220
(800) 848-8199
Fax (614) 457-0348

**Delphi Internet**
1030 Massachusetts Avenue
Cambridge, MA 02138
(800) 695-4005
Fax (617) 491-6642

**GEnie**
401 North Washington Street
Rockville, MD 20850
(800) 638-9636

**Prodigy**
445 Hamilton Avenue
White Plains, NY 10601
(800) 776-3449

**Résumé databases.** A number of services will store your résumé with others for a fee, to be examined by prospective employers as *their* needs become acute. Again, no firm standards yet exist in this infant industry, so expect wildly divergent parameters, as well as a wide range of charges. Neither does a performance record exist for such services, so check carefully regarding the effectiveness of any you contact so as not to waste your money.[1]

If a company interests you, learn more about it by "surfing" the Internet to gather information. Many companies have created "home pages" that provide both basic background and information about their product and service lines. Occasionally, a home page will link you as well to the company's annual report or to a directory of its senior executives, enabling you to target your job search to specific individuals. You may even be able to download your résumé and send it by E-mail to a specific executive, regardless of whether an opening exists.

The Internet is also helpful for job postings. Many universities, labor offices, and placement centers act as "bulletin boards" for listing employment opportunities. The best way to find these postings is by doing Net search using a key word such as *careers*, *jobs*, or *employment*. You can also use your job title or objective and see what turns up. Doing an on-line search is a little like being an explorer; you never know where your surfing will take you.

On-line resources are becoming more popular by the day and will almost certainly be an integral part of most job seekers' strategy within the next several years. If you neglect this area of job search simply because you are unfamiliar with it, you will be shortchanging yourself significantly.

# Strategies for Career Change

A complete analysis of career change requires a book of its own, but several basic steps will help point you in the right direction.

You're probably thinking of a change because you're bored beyond belief, are burned-out, are miscast, or just would prefer a different professional way of life after 10 or 15 years of doing what you're doing.

Jumping *from* is easy. You just quit, or—consciously or subconsciously—get or allow yourself to be fired. Jumping *to* is the tough part.

First, you need to make two lists. List A should contain all of the things you like about your existing function, company, position, and industry. List B should contain all of the things you can't stand about what you are doing, in these same categories. The ideal change, it will come as no surprise to you, will include all of the List A items and none from List B. This won't happen, of course. To come as close to this ideal as you can, though, is your reasonable goal.

If you're lucky, the adjustment will be a minor one: moving to a company that gives you a freer hand in the same function and industry, for example; doing what you do for an organization larger—or smaller—than yours, or in a different geographic setting.

Slightly more difficult, but manageable, are position changes other than "straight ahead." One of our clients who had risen through the commercial real estate and building management ranks to the vice-presidency of a large New York commercial

---

[1] *The names, addresses, and phone numbers of more than 20 database resources (as well as a complete listing of on-line job-posting sources) are offered in a booklet titled* The Job-Seeker's Guide to On-line Resources, *published by Kennedy Publications, Templeton Road, Fitzwilliam, NH 03447.*

real estate concern said the fun had gone out of his work. His most challenging years, he said, were at the building management level, where he had to juggle working relationships with various unions and state and local regulatory bodies, as well as solve dozens of variegated day-to-day problems. His more elevated executive position gave him considerable policymaking power and paid extremely well but bored him to the point that he hated to come to work in the morning. He wanted to return to where the action was, even if it involved a pay cut.

His problem was to find such a job without appearing to have lost his drive and ambition. It might seem to some, for example, that he had peaked professionally and was willing to settle for fewer responsibilities and less challenge—when in fact the opposite was true. With the appropriate résumé, cover letter, and list of targeted prospects, he reached his goal. (His résumé appears on pages 212–213; his cover letter on page 263.) Within three months he was appointed building manager of the Empire State Building.

More difficult, and impossible to cover in a book of this scope, are changes that involve function or—in many cases—industry. If you realize after working with data or "things" for ten years that you would prefer to work more with people, you may have to complete additional necessary training or appropriate courses in your spare time. Plan to spend a year or more making this happen, including enough networking and information interviewing to be sure you remain on the right track.

# Putting It Together

You've heard of the hidden job market? No need to pay thousands of dollars to the large career service companies that advertise access to the "90 percent of job vacancies...available that the average job searcher does not know about." Their claims of inside information from corporations that for some reason share this knowledge with them but don't get the word out to "the average job searcher" are false.

The hidden job market is simply the wealth of positions that don't get advertised, because they are filled first by individuals who have done the homework outlined in this chapter and are tapped into the networks we've mentioned. There is no need to advertise, after all, if one or more qualified candidates for a position are known to exist and be available.

Be that candidate. In any company you'd like to work for, find one or more people in a position to provide inside information. To help you determine whether an opening exists or might be coming up, get answers to the following questions and any others you can think of:

- Is there an impending merger or acquisition?

- Is expansion a probability—or the addition of one or more product or service lines?

- Are sales up—and staying there?

- Is activity scheduled that leads to one of your strengths?

- Have you identified a problem area that your background would help solve?

Set up an interview with your contact person if you need additional information, then send your résumé and an appropriate cover letter to the line officer or department head who will be doing the hiring.

# 6

# Cover Letters That Sell

A cover letter is a personal letter in the sense that it introduces you *personally*—whether it is addressed to a box number in answer to an ad or sent to an individual who has personally requested it. As such, each must appear to have been written solely for the eyes of the addressee, even if it is but one of 500 you have sent out.

This is important because it gives you the opportunity to neutralize the impersonally written résumé by introducing you in more human terms. Each cover letter should highlight your strengths speciflcally in light of the opportunity you are addressing.

No better model exists for constructing your cover letter than the four paragraph sales letter prescription offered in business English classes decades ago:

1. Command attention,
2. Sustain interest,
3. Ensure conviction,
4. Incite action.

Whether you do this in more or fewer than four paragraphs will depend on the circumstances. Those four components, however, should all be there.

## Command attention

The most effective way to get the reader's attention is to state your business in as forceful and succinct a way as you can. Are there exceptions? Of course. An advertising copywriter, for example, expected to write winning copy every time she turns on the computer, might start off with her best headline, followed by a couple of sentences telling how well it sold the product. Other situations will vary with the purpose of the letter, as described later in this chapter.

## Sustain interest; ensure conviction

Consider these not as discrete paragraphs but rather as two inherent elements often combined in the body of the letter. Those of your credentials—accomplishments, responsibilities, skills, professional record, and education—that you know to be of particular importance to your reader should be laid out with the appropriate emphasis and in the appropriate sequence, with specific examples as they apply. See the samples included later in this chapter for varying kinds of circumstances.

## Incite action

Notice in all of the sample letters that follow (except for replies to blind newspaper ads) that the writer requests an interview—and, further, indicates his or her intention to follow up with a phone call to personally petition for an interview.

This is important. First of all, with the number of résumés hitting the desks of hiring line executives or institutional supervisors, it is unlikely your letter will trigger an immediate return call unless the opening is current and you are right for it. Essential as it is for an organization to seek out the best people, the press of day-to-day responsibilities often pushes this need down the list of professional priorities.

Saying you will call to request the interview increases your chances of getting it. The absence of a reply to your letter is of itself a negative response, obviously. By calling, you force a *direct* negative response (if this be the case) and eliminate the possibility of *passive* rejection. No chance now that the addressee lets your letter work its way down to the Pleistocene level of his or her In box and dooms it to inaction.

# Cover Letter Situations

Most of your mailings will fall under one of the five following categories, so the remaining pages of this chapter consist of specific tips for each situation, followed by sample letters written for Career Clinics clients under the same circumstances:

- Newspaper ad replies
- Executive recruiter/employment agency inquiries
- Corporate/institutional cold calls
- Slight-career-change cold calls
- "I'm back in the job market" reintroductions

## Newspaper ad replies

Not all ads will require an equal measure of your attention. When you see one you think you are perfect for, though, give it an extra effort.

Go over the ad's requirements thoroughly. Assume they have been rank-ordered, and deal with each as sequenced in the ad. Write and rewrite a description of those accomplishments, skills, and responsibilities that relate specifically to each requirement, until you have eliminated all excess words. Communicate your strengths clearly and succinctly. Work on your transitions until each idea flows effortlessly to the next. Below is an ad from the business section of the *Sunday New York Times* that was of particular appeal to a client. His reply can be found on pages 246–247.

---

## DIRECTOR OF
## MARKETING & SALES

### (Highly Competitive Compensation with Significant Incentives That Could Lead to an Equity Position)

Stickum Adhesives Corp. is an international environmentally friendly, specialty products company that manufactures both water based and hot melt pressure sensitive adhesives and coatings for the Nonwoven Disposables and Tape and Label Industries. We also manufacture a full line of laminating, cold seal and heat seal patented adhesives for the Flexible Packaging Industry.

Requirements to qualify are as follows: significant, solid, sales track record; well-established personal relationships with many potential customers; in-depth understanding of the markets; ability to provide corporate direction for new product development; technical undergraduate degree and graduate business degree required; excellent communication skills; and, profit and loss responsibility reporting directly to the president.

This position is located in Lexington, Kentucky and initially requires extensive travel and customer contact. We offer a highly competitive compensation package and a competitive benefits package including a 401(k) plan. If you qualify for this important position, please send your résumé and a letter in confidence that would demonstrate your knowledge of the above markets. Please, no phone calls or replies from employment agencies. Respond to:

President's Office
Stickum Adhesives Corp.
4181 Shasta Avenue
Lexington, KY 43080

Y 7427 TIMES 10108
*An Equal Opportunity Employer M,F*

---

The second letter is written in response to the *Wall Street Journal* ad reprinted below, and appears on page 249. It isolates and deals directly with three of the top criteria listed in the ad and thus significantly improves the candidate's chances for an interview. This style and approach are particularly effective when answering ads, because they will hold up well against the hundreds of conventional responses to the same job. You'll get good marks not only for being original but also for making the respondent's job easier. The first person in the target company to see your response—whether it happens to be your prospective boss (in a small company) or a personnel department "first reader" (in a larger company)—will select for further review only those responses that best match the carefully defined requirements of the job. By writing such a letter, you've made the reader's job as easy as possible. As a consequence, your readily identifiable strengths for the position will classify you immediately as a candidate worth a second look.

---

### DIRECTOR OF ECONOMIC DEVELOPMENT
### $57,694 - $80,782

The City of Albuquerque is establishing a new Department of Economic Development and is seeking a responsible individual with initiative and creativity to lead this new department.

Promotes economic development within the City of Albuquerque and investment in major economic and real estate development. Meets with business leaders and developers to promote specific projects. Chairs staff groups and task forces. Manages staff and administers departmental budget.

Master's Degree in business finance or economics and ten years of professional experience in urban development, including some supervisory experience. A Bachelor's Degree in one of the above fields and fifteen years of professional experience in urban development, including supervisory experience, will be considered.

Resumes should be submitted no later than Monday, July 31, 1995 to: Personnel Department, City of Albuquerque, 550 Main Street, Albuquerque, NM 74190.

***Equal Opportunity Employer***

---

Finally, don't send your ad response off immediately. Letting it sit for a few days will give you a chance to read it with a fresh eye and make improvements at leisure. The first week or so after the ad's publication, it will attract bagfuls of replies. Wait until the first wave subsides, in about a week or so. Your letter and résumé will get more attention and be more carefully read.

## Executive recruiter/employment agency inquiries

Get in touch with the best of each (the quality and quantity of jobs they list is a good clue), keeping in mind that few employment agencies handle many jobs above the $70,000 salary level. To check out recruiters who are likely to have something at your level and in your field, write or call the American Management Association (1601 Broadway, New York, NY 10020; (212) 586-8100; (212) 903-7812; FAX (212) 903-8163) for a copy of its *Executive Employment Guide*. For $20.00, you'll receive a list of more than 125 executive recruiters nation-wide (several with offices world-wide), including names; phone numbers; special fields covered, if any; minimum salaries of positions handled; and an indication as to whether each accepts résumés or will accede to an interview regarding opportunities in general. The entries are cross-referenced both by city and state, and by job specialty. Another source is *The Directory of Executive Recruiters*, from Kennedy Publications (Templeton Road, Fitzwilliam, NH 03447; (800) 531-1026; FAX 603/585-9555). At $39.95 it's twice the price of the AMA guide, but it does list more than 2,800 search firms in the U.S., Canada and Mexico, and the entries are as inclusive as those in the AMA guide. If you have access to a well-stocked public library, of course, you may be able to avoid buying either book.

Make the principal purpose of your letter to set up a conversation with one recruiter in each firm—best, in person; second best, by phone. Reconcile yourself to the reality that your chances of matching the specifications of any current search assignment are probably one in a thousand. What you want is information, as well as the opportunity to favorably impress an individual with the power to call you about a client opening six months from now.

Start by calling each target search company within visiting distance, and talk with—or get the name of—the highest-ranking individual available. Just get a name and title and "permission" to send in a résumé. Make your cover letter brief, highlighting major strengths, and follow with a phone call in ten days to set up an interview if you can. On page 250 is a sample letter sent to a recruiter for this reason.

## Corporate/institutional cold calls

If your universe of prospects is large, it will be impossible to include a paragraph or more tailored to the express needs of every organization. Decide first how much research on individual companies you are willing to undertake.

Let's say there are 10 companies you are extremely interested in and another 50 you want to contact because a real possibility exists that there is a spot for you—or soon will be. Thoroughly research the top 10 companies and write letters indicating your awareness of a particular—and recent or imminent—expansion, merger, acquisition, or market repositioning and your ability to help the company implement or maximize it. On page 251 is an example of this type of letter.

For the remaining 50 or more organizations, it may be enough to simply address each letter to the appropriate person and then mention the company's name once or twice during the body of the letter. More effective, if you can take the time, is to rank-order the companies, complete in-depth research on them, ten at a time, and write your letters as you would for the top ten. Most letter houses with word processing equipment can do this for you for about $1 per letter, including addressing the envelopes. Obviously it is important to have the letters typed individually rather than printed, even if you do go to a word processor. Form letters get thrown out before they're read. On pages 252–259 are some corporate cold call letters for the two situations described above.

## Slight-career-change cold calls

If you are making a transition between two related fields, your résumé obviously should be written to minimize the differences between your current and future professions or positions—and indeed use the terminology of the field you are working to get into. The letter you write to accompany the résumé, similarly, should pick up on accomplishments valued equally by current and future employers and stay away from the differences.

The closer your new career is to the old one the easier your task is, obviously. There will be more to draw from your past, and less to hypothesize about your future. In any case the format of the letter accompanying your résumé, is basically the same as for any other cover letter. On pages 260–265 are a few examples.

## "I'm back in the job market" reintroduction letters

Most executives and professionals make at least one dreadful career mistake during their forty or more years of ladder climbing and tightrope walking. Now and then the greener grass wilts without warning. A pre-employment promise goes unfilled; an unanticipated personality or workplace conflict sours an otherwise promising venture. These things happen.

Many of them, sadly, don't have to happen. Sometimes asking the right question in the final interview will uncover a potential stumbling block large enough to change an acceptance to a rejection. But that's another story, touched on in a bit more detail in Chapter 7.

If you find yourself in an untenable position, get out as gracefully and as quickly as you can—in a way that doesn't arouse your current employer's suspicions in the process, obviously. Don't bite the bullet and do a miserable three to five when you could be advancing professionally and happily elsewhere. Re-establish your network and get the word out subtly that you'd rather be somewhere other than where you are. The letter on page 266 is one way to do this.

October 21, 1996

Mr. Alex Agase
President
Stickum Adhesives Corporation
4181 Shasta Avenue
Lexington, KY 43080

Dear Mr. Agase:

Your ad in the October 14, 1991, *Sunday New York Times* could have been written specifically with me in mind. Over the past 20 years, I have built a distinguished career in the sales and marketing of adhesives for the nonwoven disposables and tape and label industries. I have also developed a large number of professional relationships that last to this day, including many individuals who can attest to the accuracy of this letter and accompanying résumé.

Let me address the principal requirements for your Director of Marketing and Sales position:

- **Significant, solid sales track record**

  I offer 20 years of unparalleled adhesives industry sales and marketing experience, including the growth of a personal products line from $60,000 to $7 million in four years (see attached record of achievements).

- **Well-established personal relationships with many potential customers**

  I can discuss in considerable detail my close relationships with key executives at companies such as Kimberly-Clark (Bob Underhill), Johnson & Johnson (Pete Turso), Pope & Talbot (Andy Urban), and Weyerhauser (Tom Dahl), to mention a few.

- **In-depth understanding of the markets**

  My on-the-job experience, as well as my participation as moderator at Insight conferences, has kept me abreast of all applicable market situations.

- **Ability to provide corporate direction for new product development**

  In various situations over the course of my tenure at H. B. Fuller, particularly as Business Manager of Nonwovens, I set the corporate direction for product development (including the decision to bring Fullastic to the marketplace for Kimberly-Clark and Procter & Gamble after four years of product testing and development).

- **Excellent communications skills**

  There are two kinds of communication at which I excel—verbal communication and communication as a management tool. Examples in each area are as follows:

  1. I have written numerous strategic business plans that have led to successful sales penetration in nonwoven markets and will be happy to provide nonproprietary examples upon request.

  2. My management style is to clearly communicate corporate and departmental missions to all individuals reporting to me and similarly to listen carefully to my employees. This philosophy has resulted in effective performance by my subordinates and virtually no turnover of employees personally hired by me.

- **Profit and loss responsibility**

  I have held profit-and-loss responsibility in three of my last four positions: (1) as District manager at H. B. Fuller, managing both sales and manufacturing; (2) as Business Manager at Fuller; and (3) as Regional Manager at Swift, with P&L responsibility for manufacturing and sales in the northeast region. As General Manager for a joint venture in 1987, I had complete P&L responsibility (see attached résumé for details).

I look forward to discussing with you in person each of the above requirements, as well as other aspects of the position. I consider myself a problem solver for any combination of circumstances that might occur and will gladly accept any test you might devise that will cause you to view me the same way.

Sincerely,


Basil Langhart


Enclosures

# ROBERT M. SMICK

590 Mordeca Street • Silver Spring, MD 20850
Home: [301] 968-2402 • Office: [202] 747-9201

July 6, 1996

Z6322 TIMES 10108
C/O The New York Times
229 West 43rd Street
New York, New York 10036

Ladies/Gentlemen:

This letter is in response to your ad in the June 21 Business Section of The New York Times for someone to head up your Community Relations/Public Participation program.

For the past six years I have served as Executive Director for the Board on Minorities in Engineering & Sciences, National Academy of Sciences. In this position I am responsible for coordinating the efforts of 65 corporations, 15 federal agencies, and 112 universities to implement a science manpower policy utilizing $4,000,000 annually. I call upon the cooperation of prominent leaders from government, industry, academic institutions, and civic organizations to accomplish the Board's goals.

The public participation techniques I find most useful flow from an identification of the issues and the subsequent identification of competent, expert witnesses to present informed views regarding these issues. These data result in reports, symposia, and news conferences to inform the public. I have worked closely with the print media, and have appeared on television and radio talk shows in support of various issues espoused by the Board.

My background in chemistry and the Board's relationship with other divisions of the Academy have provided me with the basic tenets of hazardous waste management. A short time ago, in fact, I brokered a contract between DuPont and a small environmental engineering firm for an environmental impact study on waste disposal that resulted in a mutually satisfying relationship.

My résumé is enclosed. I look forward to hearing from you so that we may take the discussions of this challenging position one step further.

Sincerely,


Robert M. Smick
RMS/mg

## Steven Harley Wilson

1830 Saranac Boulevard • Prescott, AZ 83477
Phone: (602) 562-3275     Fax: (602) 773-1314

July 11, 1996

Personnel Department
City of Albuquerque
550 Main Street
Albuquerque, NM 74190

Re: Director of Economic Development position

Ladies/Gentlemen:

This letter and my enclosed résumé are submitted in response to your June 26, 1996 ad in the *Wall Street Journal* regarding the Director of Economic Development opening. I believe that my background matches very well with the requirements of the job, as I understand them from the *Journal* ad. Here are a few examples (I can provide many more during a personal interview):

| *Requirements* | *My Qualifications* |
| --- | --- |
| Ability to promote metropolitan economic development | Promoted economic development throughout the state of Arizona (including Phoenix) as an officer of the Arizona Development Authority |
| Sense of responsibility | Seventeen-year tenure with same organization (including several promotions of increasing responsibility) over 20-year financial career |
| Initiative and creativity | Organized and developed UrBank, a program to provide funding and structure for loans to Arizona inner-city businesses and residents |

I would welcome the opportunity to discuss this position with you in more detail, including specific contributions I can make to this new and exciting opportunity. Please let me know if there is additional information I can provide that would lead you to schedule an interview.

Sincerely,

Steven H. Wilson

Enclosure

14 Panther Place
Stamford, CT 06814
August 15, 1996
(203) 352-4108
FAX (203) 352-9432

Mr. Willis Black
Vice President
Kory Ferry International
50 Park Place
Westport, CT 06880

Dear Mr. Black:

Among your clients may be one or more who are contemplating entry into the export market or have limited experience in this area.

As founder and managing director of Tremont International, I currently represent or distribute for dozens of manufacturers who until our relationship had never sold overseas. My intention is to take this expertise—together with more than 20 years of financial and investment management background—to a manufacturer ready to begin exporting.

My concept of exporting is designed to minimize cost and red tape, and at the same time maximize profit. You can see by the attached résumé that my specific accomplishments in this area are considerable, and range over a variety of consumer and industrial product areas.

Within the next few days, I will call to see when you might be available to discuss with me what prospects exist for meeting principals of firms you now represent.

Thank you for your consideration.

Sincerely,

Jarvis Henry

JH/nn

10 Tyrolia Lane
Lawrence, NY 11559
September 3, 1996

Mr. Paul Bergeson
President
Acme Stores, Inc.
655 Fifth Avenue
New York, NY 10036

Dear Mr. Bergeson:

Your recent acquisition of the Bandow chain would indicate an intent to pursue Southeastern market opportunities more vigorously than you have in the past several years. I believe that my retail management background would complement your long-range strategy for Acme very effectively.

For the past ten years, I have put together a record of which I am quite proud, including six years at Loud & Schwartz, culminating in a senior vice-presidency and membership on both the Executive Committee and the Management Board.

As you will see on the enclosed résumé, most of my accomplishments are quantifiable, including sizable volume and gross margin increases in every position of leadership I have held. In a single year at Loud & Schwartz, for example, the profit ranking of the division I led improved from tenth to first.

These are far from single-handed achievements, obviously. One of my strengths is the ability to recognize and utilize the best talent available and to extend the decision-making process so as to offer middle managers—and sometimes even those below them—a stake in determining or refining company policy.

I will call within the next week or so to see if you agree that our mutual interest would be served by a personal meeting and, if so, to see when your schedule permits it.

Sincerely,

Douglas Frisk

Encl.

859 Hobart Street
San Francisco, CA 94110
(415) 875-0922
November 11, 1996

Ms. Marcia J. Shin
Senior Vice-President
Florida State Bank at Orlando
801 North Lemon Avenue
Orlando, FL 32800

Dear Ms. Shin:

In approximately three months I am moving to Orlando with my family, and am bringing with me 15 solid years of banking experience—the last 8 in branch operations management. I would like particularly to utilize this experience with the Florida State Bank at Orlando.

As Branch Manager I currently surpervise 20 employees, including 9 tellers, at the largest branch of the Federal Mutual Savings Bank, in San Francisco. I serve as an officer of this bank as well.

As you will see from the enclosed résumé, I am well rounded in the workings of NOW and money market accounts, and am extremely strong in the use of systems to reduce overtime and increase both efficiency and customer relations.

I am in the process of planning an exploratory trip to Orlando sometime in late May and would like very much to meet you and learn of any opportunrities that may exist at the Florida State Bank at Orlando for someone with my background and potential. I look forward to hearing from you. Because the precise timing of my move is not certain, I have not yet informed my employer of my intention to move. I would therefore appreciate your confidentiality in this regard.

Sincerely,

Kenneth Rivera

Encl.

24 West 65th Street
Brooklyn, New York 11020
September 12, 1996

Mr . R. B. Ashton
Vice President for Merchandising
Loud & Schwartz
1821 Broad Street
Philadelphia, PA 20171

Dear Mr. Ashton:

For the past four years I have assumed positions of increasing responsibility for both domestic and import retail furniture buying, and am now ready for additional challenge.

At G. Dixon and Company I supervise all aspects of retailing from product purchase to merchandising for bedroom, dining room, occasional and lifestyle furniture. Revenues in this department run in excess of $2 million annually. In the Lifestyle Department alone I increased volume from $400,000 to more than $1 million in one year.

I have a particularly strong color and design sense and am able to identify a potentially successful product with a high degree of accuracy. As you will see from the enclosed résumé, another of my strengths is in the area of effective and creative merchandising.

It is my hope to bring these qualifications to Loud & Schwartz. Toward this end I will call you within the next week or so to see when your calendar permits a personal interview.

Sincerely,

Phyllis Sublett

Enc.

---

**FRANCIS C. HOLLAND**        P.O. BOX 663        NORTHPORT, CT 06490

---

October 29, 1996

Mr. Frederick R. Gloeckner
Vice President & General Manager,
    Export Sales & Services
General Electronics
3135 Weston Turnpike
Northfield, Connecticut 06431

Dear Mr. Gloeckner:

I would like the opportunity to put my nine years of marketing and sales experience to work for General Electronics.

My years with the Learning Corporation of America have been marked by consistently increasing levels of responsibility and achievement. In each of the three positions I have held, departmental sales have increased dramatically. Moreover, I have been responsible for opening market areas previously unknown to the company. The problem is that my current product line—educational films—is not in a growth stage, nor is it likely to be so in the foreseeable future.

For this reason I am seeking new challenges, and have selected General Electronics as one company whose dynamic marketing position is unparalleled. Within the next few days I will be calling you to determine when your schedule will permit us to discuss a sales or marketing management position with your firm.

Sincerely,


Francis C. Holland

43 Racine Avenue
Skokie, Illinois 60076
January 3, 1996

Ms. Roslyn Hendrickson
Executive Vice President
Thatcher and Thatcher
48 Greenwich Avenue
Greenwich, Connecticut 06830

Dear Ms. Hendrickson:

The enclosed résumé summarizes my background as follows:

> Extensive experience working directly with heads of Fortune 500 corporations,
> federal agencies and the Congress. Skilled in assessing importance of specific
> issues and designing successful issues-oriented actions.

This is the strongest two-sentence case I can make toward convincing you of my potential value
as a key public affairs or government relations manager for Thatcher and Thatcher.

What I do best is to analyze problems accurately, and then marshal the appropriate resources
to solve them. The arena in which I am most effective is in the protection and fostering of corporate interest—either as a spokesman to the public, or in influencing the passage of legislation
or regulations best reflecting that corporate interest. One of my major responsibilities as Executive Director, Board on Minorities in Engineering and Sciences is to work with Cabinet and federal agency heads, as well as with members of Congress, to formulate and influence the
passage of laws and regulations regarding issues affecting the Board's objectives and policy.

On both a day-to-day and long-range basis I direct the planning, organization and administration of the Board. I organized a national symposium that included 800 prominent leaders from
government, industry, academic institutions, and civic organizations. I plan and chair semi-an-
nual meetings for 35 corporate leaders to address national manpower problems.

I am particularly interested in working for a company like Thatcher and Thatcher because it will
allow me to use all of my background—technical, scientific, educational, and public and legislative affairs.

I look forward to discussing with you the possibility of a position with Thatcher, and will call
within the next week or so to see when your schedule might permit a personal interview.

Sincerely,

Harry K. Ellis

Enc.

35 Lyndon Way
Cromwell, New Jersey 07841
November 10, 1996

Mr. Wade King
Vice President, Finance
Alliance Imaging, Inc.
3111 S. Tustin Ave.
Orange, CA 92655

Dear Mr. King:

Within the next six weeks I will be moving to Orange County, where I intend to put to use my 20 years of financial management experience in the health care field.

I am writing to see if there is an opening—either now or in the immediate future—for a professional with the skills and achievements I have to offer.

My strengths include a heavy background in grants application and analysis, budget forecast and maintenance, staff supervision, and problem solving.

Upon my arrival in California I will call to see if you believe our mutual interest might benefit from a personal meeting. Enclosed is a copy of my résumé for your information.

Sincerely,

Barton R. Nelson

Encl.

455 Ocean Parkway, Apt. 1C
Brooklyn, New York 11218
September 15, 1996

Ms. Irene Seanor
Executive Director
Foster Labs, Inc.
Anderson Blvd.
St. Charles, IL 60134

Dear Ms. Seanor,

With more than ten years clinical chemistry experience as a graduate biochemist in hospital settings, I am seeking a position as a technical representative or specialist. I am thoroughly familiar with the chemicals used for general and special tests in hospitals and doctors' offices and all of their applications. I am also expert in the use and promotion of testing equipment.

My résumé can only highlight my qualifications. A personal interview will assure you of my potential value to your company. I will call you in a few days to request an appointment.

Sincerely yours,

Harry Martinez

Enc.

310 West 30th Street
New York, New York 10001
April 20, 1996

Ms. Claire Weber
Director of Marketing
Worthington Electronics
Manheim Road
Secaucus, N.J. 02471

Dear Ms. Weber:

The state of the art in the electronics market changes at such a rapid pace that aggressive marketing and astute product management are essential if high profitability is to be achieved. I offer a background of more than twenty years in the field of electro-mechanical products.

My ability encompasses concept and design and includes complete product management through the entire production process. In addition, I have worked with engineers, designers and product managers in U.S. and foreign manufacturing plants to bring in production schedules for high volume sales of most profitable items.

The enclosed résumé hits the high points. Perhaps we can get together and talk in detail of my potential value to your organization. I will call you in a few days to arrange an appointment for a personal interview.

Sincerely yours,

Phillip Mitchell

Encl.

19 Wingate Road
Cleveland, Ohio 44113
February 1, 1996

Mr. Charles Close
Executive Vice President
T. Clark and Company
Sugar Grove, IL 60134

Dear Mr. Close:

The enclosed résumé highlights significant accomplishments during my 11 years of sales and marketing management. I am looking now for a greater challenge, and believe you will agree that my record justifies such an expectation.

In seven years with Foraldo Corporation I rose from western regional manager of the Epcraft Division to vice president of a group overseeing all five of the firm's tool divisions. This position involved the development and management of a nationwide organization of 92 manufacturers' rep firms and 10 direct sales managers, and supervision of a staff of 250.

The sales incentive program I established at Foraldo resulted in a 13% increase in annual sales and helped set new corporate records in gross profit levels. I have a keen sense of cost control, and am particularly strong in the structural reorganization of profit centers to increase efficiency and productivity.

My goal is to join a firm that requires the immediate use of these skills whether to increase a rate of established growth or to effect a turnaround situation.

Within the next week or so I will call to see whether you agree that our mutual interests would be served by exploring this matter further, and if so, when your calendar might permit time for a personal interview.

Sincerely,

John A. Larson

Encl.

411 Market Place
Boston, MA 09296
May 12, 1996

Mr. Samuel Insull
Vice-President for Corporate Affairs
Sunco Oil Carpany
60 West 42nd Street
New York, New York 10042

Dear Mr. Insull:

After four years of public affairs and press work with both the White House and as an aide to the Governor of Massachusetts, I am eager to return to corporate life once again.

I offer a unique combination of public and private sector experience. Most recently, my work as lead advance for Vice President Gore, Hillary Clinton, and Mrs. Gore has given me the opportunity to handle press and protocol matters both domestically and abroad. My charge has been to manage the sensitive—and potentially inflammatory—relationships when representatives from different cultures, societies and religions meet and mix. This calls for a high order of organizational skills, tact, and attention to detail.

As special assistant to the president of Arnoco Industries I single-handedly organized a Government Relations Conference at which were set industry standards that ultimately influenced crucial federal legislation. My corporate experience also includes five years with Dean Witter as both a registered representative and Executive Assistant to the President, and a customer service position with Merrill Lynch.

This combination of public and private sector experience has been excellent preparation for a position in corporate communication/public affairs—possibly involving legislative liaison at federal, state and local levels. I look forward to discussing this prospect with you, and will call within the next few days to see when your schedule permits such a conversation to occur.

Sincerely,

Martha Buchanan

Encl.

43 Crescent Lane
Port Washington, New York 11050
June 5, 1996

Ms. Alberta Magnus
Editor-in-Chief
The Viking Press
16 E. 46th Street
New York, New York 10077

Dear Ms. Magnus:

Is one of your new publications being delayed in startup for lack of qualified editor-ship? Is one of your existing periodicals foundering, or not running at peak efficiency or quality for a similar reason?

If the answer is "yes" in either case, I think it would be to our mutual advantage to talk. I have a solid 20 years' writing and editing experience to draw on—all in the areas of business, finance, and insurance. I have conceived new magazine ideas, managed the gestation periods, and brought inaugural issues to the black of print.

Moreover, as you'll see from the enclosed résumé, my current freelance client base is both varied and prestigious.

I have considerable talent and commitment to offer some very special and specialized audiences, and would appreciate the opportunity to discuss this with you personally. I'll give you a call within the next week or so to see when it might be convenient for us to meet.

Sincerely,

Jake Smith

Encl.

2803 Chesapeake Street
Washington, D.C. 20008
April 3, 1996

Mr. James Clark
Vice President for Programming
Extension Cablevision, Inc.
1007 Post Road East
Westport, CT 06880

Dear Mr. Clark:

For the past three years I have been involved in television programming and production at Hayden Lurch Associates, part of my job as Manager of the Audio-Visual Department. My immediate goal is to apply this valuable background—as well as my current freelance video-tape producing experience—to the needs of station WXYZ.

While at Hayden Lurch I have coordinated productions from start to finish for such clients as Sun Company, Inc. and Burroughs, including budgeting, scripting, editing, production work, and talent coordination. In addition I prepare departmental budgets, develop concept proposals for client selection, and supervise both creative and administrative personnel.

I have the respect of both colleagues and clients for overall effectiveness, on-schedule and under-budget performance, and quality of final product. My reason for wanting to leave Hayden Lurch—and public relations in general—is an intense desire to focus my skills and expertise full time in the field of television.

Within the next few day I will call to see if you agree that it would be advantageous for us to meet and discuss a position with WXYZ, and if so, to schedule a time that is convenient for you. My résumé is enclosed.

Sincerely,


Rollin Ashton


Encl.

975 E. 44th Street
Brooklyn, New York 11234
January 23, 1996

Mr. Richard Fairbank
Vice President for Operations
Ackroyd and Fisher
369 Lexington Avenue
New York, New York 10010

Dear Mr. Fairbank:

Over the past ten years I have grown at Dakota Realty from Building Superintendent of a single building to Vice-President and Director of Operations for six commercial buildings—including the ICC Building on Fifth Avenue and the MCA Universal Building at 445 Park Avenue. My accomplishments over this period are considerable, as you will see from the enclosed résumé, and include responsibility for a 55% increase in revenue for the 445 Park building during my tenure there as building manager.

My purpose for writing is to acquaint you with my background and indicate my availability for a building management position—for either a prestigious office building or a corporate headquarters. My credentials are impeccable, and I am willing to discuss any current or imminent openings with you at your convenience.

I will call you over the next week or so to see when you might be available for a personal interview.

Sincerely,

Juan S. Geisler

Encl.

62 Marsh Street
Chicago, Illinois 60602
December 7, 1996

Mr. Verner Anderson
President and General Manager
WGBW TV
14 Rockville Plaza
Detroit, Michigan 51073

Dear Mr. Anderson:

For the past 15 years I have co-directed Datus Productions, a film, television and audio/visual production company I co-founded to serve clients in publishing, advertising, and other manufacturing and service industries. As you will see on the enclosed résumé, my clients include McGraw-Hill, Young & Rubicam, Amerada Hess, and American Express.

My interest at this point of my career is to devote fewer energies to building a business and more to developing product. I have determined that the way to do this is to work with one "client" only—and do it full time.

This decision is reached from a position of strength: I have eight active clients and a number of additional projects under development. The point is, I have product development skills I am not utilizing as much as I want to.

Please look over my résumé to see if any of my skills and accomplishments match your current or imminent needs. I'll call you in a week or so to see when your calendar permits a personal meeting.

Thanks for your time.

Sincerely,

Tilden Meyers

Encl.

15 Cayaka Street
Los Angeles, CA 90057
December 29, 1996

Dear_____ :

For more than twenty years I have built a record of solid accomplishment in the business of education—as a financial officer, a human resources manager, and as a senior operating executive. I would like to offer this experience to the executive management or human resources operation of (name of company) .

At two colleges in the past twelve years, I devised a considerable number of bold, innovative management programs. They improved efficiency, reduced costs, eliminated problems, and unsnarled administrative tangles. At the same time, the academic programs were maintained and improved. My competencies range from administering complex federal programs to negotiating labor contracts and disputes; from supervising the revision of a school's complete legislative structure to instituting and administering a collegewide energy conservation and deferred maintenance program.

I look forward to discussing with you the several ways in which my experience, talents, and services could be of use to (name of company). I will call next week to see when your calendar permits scheduling an appointment.

Sincerely,

Robert O. Levinson

45 Hunter Lane
Grand Rapids, MI 49505
April 18, 1996

Mr. Clarence Halter
President
Animated Industries, Inc.
4641 Boardwalk
Dallas, Texas 41414

Dear Mr. Halter:

Four months ago you and I discussed an opportunity at Animated, and you were kind enough to set up meetings with Jack Conde and Ernest Soderstrom. Shortly thereafter, as you know, I accepted a position with Springborn & Son's, where I am now.

For reasons I will go into later, I would like to re-open our discussions. If you think such a conversation would be mutually beneficial, I'll call next week to see when you have a half hour or so of free time.

Sincerely,


Jerry Lake

227 Jefferson Street
Geneva, IL 60134
March 13, 1996

Ms. Mary Pearson
Director of Marketing
Follett Publishing Company
433 N. Michigan Avenue
Chicago, IL 60607

Dear Ms. Pearson:

Thank you for considering me for the Director of Marketing Services position we discussed on Monday. By way of verifying my continued interest in this opening, I'd like to review those of my responsibilities and accomplishments I feel would insure a level of performance fully meeting your needs.

Division-wide responsibilities, carried out by a staff of nine reporting to me:

- Sales training and sales information
- Advertising and promotion
- Professional services, including speakers' bureau
- Conventions and exhibits
- Controlled circulation magazines
- Software service center
- Telemarketing

Relevant recent accomplishments:

- As senior marketing manager, developed marketing action plans for all state and city adoption campaigns for past three years
- Developed marketing action plans for Texas high school biology adoption, netting more than $3.5 million in textbook sales—a 30% market share
- Total marketing responsibility for elementary school product in adoption situations, as well as open market
- Continuing supervision of marketing efforts for software, basic skills, and titles for the learning disabled—the company's three most profitable product lines

Some of these accomplishments came out during our meeting; others did not. In any case, I thought you should know the full range of my qualifications as you deliberate your selection of a Director of Marketing Services.

Thanks again for the opportunity to meet with you.

Sincerely,

Philip Chapman

# 7

# Winning Interview Techniques

You were asked to be interviewed because an executive, personnel director, or other representative of the employer felt that the company's interest would be served by knowing more about you. Your résumé indicates to them that you are qualified; now they are trying to determine if you are the *best* qualified.

With this in mind, you must now convince them that it is in their best interest to hire you. You must present yourself in such a manner that the interviewer will feel that your assets and abilities are superior to those of any other candidate.

Surprisingly, and sadly, the job does not always go to the most qualified. It is possible to predict with some reliability which candidates will receive not just one, but many job offers. We have analyzed the common denominator each of these "winners" possesses: It is a first impression that projects honesty, sincerity, and enthusiasm. Given two or more candidates with virtually indistinguishable credentials, the job will almost invariably go to the individual projecting the more positive and enthusiastic image.

## Creating the Right Impression

Because the first impression you make will carry through the entire interview and greatly determine its outcome, it is of vital importance to create the most positive image possible. Your physical appearance, mannerisms, vocabulary, attitude, and nonverbal communication all contribute to the impression you make.

How does one convey sincerity? By being honest, open, and real. Be yourself. Take the attitude that the company needs you, and feel confident. This starts the self-fulfilling prophecy. *Feel* successful and chances are better that you *will* be successful.

Any form of role-playing that projects a personality other than your own will likely lead to a disastrous interview. There is no way to predict what kind of person the employer is looking for, and if in fact you knew, it is highly unlikely you could keep up the charade for the duration of the interview.

## Do Your Homework

Because the interview is such a crucial part of the hiring process, take the time to prepare yourself completely. This preparation will add to your feeling of self-confidence and generate a positive, successful interview with the best chance of a job offer.

Learn as much as possible about your prospective employer—who the officers, directors, or partners are and what the firm's complete product or service line is. Be sure of the company's reputation, and get as much information as you can about past and upcoming mergers, acquisitions, and new market possibilities.

Any library can offer a wealth of information. Use such directories as *Standard & Poor's*, *Dun & Bradstreet*, and *Moody's*. (Names of additional business directories can be found on pages 277–278.) The business periodical Index will help you find any recent press coverage.

Try to read both current and back issues of any trade journals that deal with your industry and the company or companies you are interested in.

# Handling Tough Questions

Though every interview is different, all will include one or more questions you'd just as soon not have to answer. The interviewer will be listening not only for content, but sincerity, poise, and ability to think quickly as well.

Spend some time before the interview developing answers to those of the following questions you think might give you trouble. Some of them are tough and fair. Some of them are tough and unfair.

Be mindful of the fact that everyone has an "obnoxious question threshold" past which he or she cannot, *should* not go. A question you consider opprobrious calls for an appropriate response. For example, if you find it offensive to take a lie detector test, say so. Never compromise strongly held values to make interview points. It may be that your resolve, not your honesty, is being tested. But if it is your honesty that is being tested, feel perfectly comfortable to politely end the interview forthwith, on the appropriate grounds that you prefer not to work for a company whose values obviously differ so markedly from your own.

With a friend, your husband or wife—or even a tape recorder—go through questions you think you might be asked. Prepare answers you can give extemporaneously. The wording and substance of these questions will vary to reflect your particular set of circumstances. Review them in light of potential trouble spots in your background, and prepare for those few that may cause you problems in an interview.

1. What did you enjoy most about your last position?

2. What did you like least about your last position?

3. What do you consider your most outstanding achievement?

4. Describe the way you work under pressure.

5. Describe your relationships with your peers.

6. What did you do to prepare for this interview?

7. Give an example of the way you motivate other people.

8. What kinds of problems do you enjoy solving?

9. What do you think you could contribute to the company (or association, hospital, etc.)?

10. What is the most useful criticism you've received? What did you learn from it?

11. Are you willing to take a drug test?

12. Are you willing to take a series of personality (intelligence, aptitude) tests?

13. Are you willing to take a lie detector test?

14. What do you consider your greatest strengths?

15. What do you consider your greatest weaknesses?

16. In what ways do you think your weaknesses would interfere with the position we're trying to fill?

17. Why do you want to change jobs?

18. Were you ever fired? If so, why?

19. Would you consider relocating?

20. How do you explain the gaps (if any) in your employment record?

21. How do you spend your free time?

22. Are you active in community affairs? If so, describe your participation.

23. What were the last three books you read?

24. What newspapers do you read?

25. To what magazines do you subscribe?

26. What is your definition of success?

27. Where do you expect to be with your career in five years?

28. What is your attitude about working for a woman (man, if female)? A younger person?

29. What did you learn from your last position?

30. How did you get along with your previous boss (or staff)?

31. Why do you want to work for this company?

32. What are your hiring techniques? Describe some of the people you've hired, their positions, and why you hired them.

33. What skills do you think you possess that would be beneficial to this company?

34. What motivates you?

35. Do you work better alone, or as part of a team? Examples?

36. What are your long-range career objectives?

37. What are your short-term objectives?

38. Would you describe yourself as creative? What are some examples of your creativity?

39. Which of your bosses was your favorite? Why?

40. Which of your bosses was your least favorite? Why?

41. What was the toughest problem you've had to solve on the job? How did you solve it?

42. What are the three most significant business decisions you've made in your career? What factors led to your decisions, and what did you learn as a consequence?

43. What goals have you set for yourself (or for others), and what criteria were involved in setting them?

44. What was the most challenging team leadership situation you have faced, and how did you handle it?

45. What are some of the most significant examples of risk taking you have engaged in? What were the key factors in the situation, the process used to assess risk, specific actions taken, outcomes, and lessons learned from the situation?

46. Think of a time you took a position on an issue based on merit, over what was politically expedient. Describe the situation, and what you learned from it.

47. When have you felt like giving up on a task? Tell me about it.

48. What have you done to prepare yourself for a better job?

49. Give me an idea of how you spend a typical day.

50. In what situation did your persistence pay off in achieving a goal? In what situation did it not pay off?

# Other Interview Potholes

If you have sent out several different versions of your résumé, each targeting your achievements and experience to a particular kind of employer, review the appropriate version—and cover letter—to help you anticipate any tough questions as effectively as possible.

If you are between jobs, your reasons for leaving the last one will undoubtedly come up at the interview. Organize your thoughts on this subject before the interview. Preparing for the toughest possible questions will provide you with the confidence you need to do your best.

If you were fired, tell the simple truth. In these times of retrenchment, bankruptcies, mergers, relocations, and layoffs, firing is replacing baseball as the national pastime. Chances are that your prospective boss is no stranger to the experience and will find it easy to empathize if you deal with your situation honestly.

If you were fired because your performance was in question, answer truthfully and try to transmit the extent to which you made this a learning experience. Never offer unsolicited negative comments about any staff member, or about your former or present employer.

If you are presently employed, you will be asked why you want to change jobs, and specifically why you would like to work for the company you're visiting. Again, be brief, exact and direct. Wanting to move up, earn a higher salary, join a larger (or smaller) organization, a desire to relocate, or make a career change—all are appropriate reasons to be looking for a new job. The research you have done about the particular employer will help you point out why you feel positive about the interviewing company and how you think you can make a positive professional impact on it soon after coming on board.

To sum up, be as honest during your interview as you were writing your résumé. It is tempting to exaggerate, distort a little, tell a little lie or a half truth, but making yourself seem better or other than you are is a dangerous game. First of all, it's going to be virtually impossible for you to be consistent once you've injected a shot of fiction into your autobiography. Second, and more importantly, once you're caught in a lie—no matter how slight—you've lost your credibility; maybe even your reputation.

We remember referring a publicist to a major corporation. Her résumé was first-rate, and the interview good enough for her to accept a splendid offer. After six months she received a 20 percent salary increase. Several months later, however, the personnel department checked out the information on her résumé and on the company's application form. She had said she had worked for a certain employer for three years when in reality she had been there for only one year. Even though she was doing a fantastic job and her boss respected her work highly, she was fired. The company—not unlike many other employers—had a policy of terminating any employee found to be untruthful on the application form. The vice-president who had hired her was as upset as she, the irony being, he revealed, that he would have taken her on even if he had known she had worked for company X for only one year. And though he was a major decision maker, he couldn't change company policy.

# Nervous is Natural

If you experience a slight case of the jitters before and during your interviews, you're in good company. Though you've gone through the experience a dozen times or more, putting yourself in this vulnerable position can be an unsettling experience. We've found, as have colleagues all over the country, that an overwhelming majority of jobseekers view the interview as the most stressful phase of the job search.

Unfortunately, most job candidates experience the interview as an acid test of their abilities and self-worth. Such an attitude is extremely anxiety-producing and tends to create a negative reaction from the interviewer. If you're nervous, don't get more nervous about being nervous. (Easy for us to say, right?) But just go with it. The interviewer expects some nervousness on your part and usually he or she will try to help you through it.

It may help for you to view the interview as a meeting between two equals, a buyer and a seller, to explore what each has to offer the other. If you can convey the feeling early that you have something the company wants, you will establish parity in a hurry. Always keep in mind a feeling of equality between you and the interviewer. Being too humble or subservient is as bad as being arrogant. Be a good listener, but ask any questions that will help you find out how close you and the company are to a possible match—and what you can tell them that might tip the scales in your favor, if this is a job you want.

# Second and Third Interviews

As soon as you leave an interview for a job that interests you, get to a quiet place to record your impressions while they're fresh in your mind. Your objective now is to get a job offer—or at least a second interview. Be sure you ask for a business card from the interviewer so you can write a followup letter with an accurate title and address.

The best followup letter will:

- Indicate your continued interest
- Correct any mistaken impressions you may have left in the interview
- Volunteer any additional reasons for you to be hired
- Reinforce your strengths for the position that got you the first interview (For a sample letter, see page 267.)

Next, write down the attributes you have that match the description of the job for which you interviewed. Next to each of these indicate the degree to which you feel you transmitted these skills and accomplishments. Next to this identify the aspects of each attribute you feel you did not transmit to the interviewer.

Below these lists, identify your perceived weaknesses for the position in a similar way. First column: specific weakness. Second column: the extent to which you believe you neutralized this weakness in the interview. Third column: what you yet need to do.

If the negatives outweigh the positives, you probably won't need to complete your lists to realize it. If you still feel that this is the job for you, however, you have enough data for an action plan.

Your competition for the opening will consist of from one to five other candidates, so your task is to reinforce the positives and eliminate the negatives illuminated above, without overselling at either extreme. At one end, for example, you could convey an anxiety that knocks you out of the running. At the other end, a defensiveness could creep into your presentation and cause the same result.

At the end of the interview, it is a good idea to find out where you stand so you don't get lost among several other good candidates. Find out what is deterring an offer before you leave. Depending on the circumstances, this might be an appropriate time to volunteer a trial assignment for an area where you are perceived to be weak, but where you have confidence in you ability.

# Compensation

Never begin salary negotiations until you are relatively certain you have a job offer. When asked about your present or last compensation packages, answer concisely, including all bonuses and perquisites. If you feel you were or are underpaid, mention that as one reason for wanting to change jobs. Never, however, insinuate that you were exploited or victimized by an employer. Playing victim can backfire.

When discussing your present minimum salary requirements, stay flexible. If you know what salary range is being offered, put your salary expectations at the high end of that range. Remember, the interview is a screening process. If your minimum salary requested is considerably higher than the employer intends to pay, this alone could knock you out of the running.

Don't get boxed into a specific figure before you have to. Always talk in $5,000 to $10,000 ranges. If the interview has gone superbly, aim high and then negotiate. If you are in doubt about the range the employer is considering and are asked what your salary expectations are, answer the question with one of your own. "I'm glad you brought up the subject of compensation. What range do you see for this job?" Then negotiate from there.

Finally, never make a decision at the interview—whether it's the first, second, or third. Say: "I appreciate your offer, and will give it serious consideration. May I call you on Tuesday with my decision?" This gives you a chance to weigh any other serious offers, and also to reflect more thoroughly on this one. You may come up with a question that affects your decision—and even the composition of the job itself.

# 8

# Which Job Do You Take?

The tricky thing about handling your first job offer is knowing whether to hold out for a better one, or squeeze that bird senseless while it's still in your hand. Odds are you won't have to decide in isolation, unless this is the first solid opportunity you've had since severance pay ran out three weeks ago. And even then, unless you're down to zero cash reserves, you'll be better off saying no if the position is dead wrong for you and you realize it before the employer does. No point in reaching for this book again before you need to.

How to decide, then, supposing subsistence is not your number one problem? Even if you feel you've been offered a dream position, delay your final decision for a few days to provide some perspective. Thank your prospective boss for the offer, as we said in the last chapter, and tell him or her you'll call back by "Friday"—mentioning a specific day 48 to 72 hours from then. Unless the organization is in a crisis condition (which if you're hearing for the first time is an even better reason to stall), your request will be honored and you'll have a chance to weigh the offer both intrinsically and against any others you may have.

# What You Need to Know

## Complete your research

Any open questions about the organization and the position that are either hanging fire or to which you haven't received satisfactory answers should be resolved now. For example: Under what circumstances did your predecessor leave—if this is not a new position. If the reason was one of chemistry or personality conflict between him and your new boss, get to the bottom of it. Ask the person who held the job previously, if he is accessible. Any workways or points of view the two of you share that may have been inimical to his corporate health could serve you up the same fate. Decide which is more important to you, those particular values or the job.

Make sure you have a copy of the company's annual and 10-K reports (and know how to read them) and all pertinent product information, as well as any negative (or positive) coverage in the financial press the company has received within the past year. Your local librarian will help you.

## Dollar signs bedazzle

Look carefully at the flip side of your highest paying offer. Don't give up in potential and prestige what you might be gaining in a monthly paycheck. Analyze the entire compensation package, including benefits and perquisites, to be sure that a lower salary with excellent fringes may indeed not be more remunerative in the long run. Ask your accountant or lawyer to help steer you through the thornier issues.

If you view this position as a way station to greater professional advancement down the road, be sure the experience and accomplishments you stand to attain aren't clouded by accepting more money for a position that may weaken your next résumé.

## Trust your instincts

When all the evidence is in, count on your gut reaction to deliver a decision in your best interests. Maintain the professional ties that bind, however, so if you realize in six months that you've made a terrible mistake you can swallow your pride and announce your renewed availability (as in Chapter 6 "I'm back in the job market" re-introduction letters).

May the best possible position be yours.

# Appendices: Corporate Information Directories; List of Action Verbs

Most of these directories can be found in the reference section of any good library. Some may be available only in a business library.

## General Interest

Business Organizations, Agencies, and Publications Directory
Corporate 1000
Directory of Corporate Affiliations (Volume 1, U.S. Public Companies; Volume 2, U.S. Public Companies—Indexes; Volume 3, U.S. Private Companies; Volume 4, International Public and Private Companies)
Directories in Print (Volumes I and II)

Dun's Million Dollar Directory (Volumes I, II, and III)
Encyclopedia of Business Information Sources
International Corporate 1000
Macmillan Directory of Leading Private Companies
Small Business Sourcebook
Standard Directory of Advertisers

## Industry-Specific

American Architects Directory
American Hospital Association Guide to the Health Care Field
American Library Directory
Automotive News Market Data Book
Chemical Engineering Catalog
Commercial Real Estate Brokers Directory
Conservation Yearbook
Corporate Finance Bluebook
Design News
Directory of the Computer Industry
Dun & Bradstreet Reference Book of Transportation
Dun's Industrial Guide: The Metalworking Directory
Editor and Publisher Market Guide
Electrical/Electronic Directory

Electronic Design's Gold Book
Fairchild's Textile and Apparel Financial Directory
International Petroleum Register
Kline Guide to the Paper & Pulp Industry
Literary Market Place: The Directory of American Book Publishing
Magazine Industry Market Place
Moody's Manuals (for various industries)
O'Dwyer's Directory of Corporate Communications
O'Dwyer's Directory of Public Relations Agencies
Polk's World Bank Directory
Printing Trades Blue Book
Progressive Grocer's Marketing Guidebook

Standard & Poor's Security Dealers of North America
Standard Directory of Advertising Agencies
Telephony's Directory of the Telephone Industry
The Uncle Sam Connection, a Guide to Federal Employment
Thomas Register of American Manufacturers

Whole World Oil Directory
Who's Who in Advertising
Who's Who in Composition and Typesetting
Who's Who in Electronics
Who's Who in Insurance
Who's Who in Water Supply and Pollution Control
World Airline Record

# List of Action Verbs

The following list will help you identify verbs that reflect your job accomplishments, skills, or responsibilities. Use them in your résumé as appropriate.

| | | | |
|---|---|---|---|
| Preside | Report | Consider | Reconcile |
| Govern | Contact | Select | Update |
| Direct | Communicate | Revise | Upgrade |
| Administer | Service | Require | Arrange |
| Manage | Meet | Review | Modify |
| Supervise | Seek | Compare | Follow through |
| Control | Declare | Translate | Distribute |
| Execute | Promote | Justify | Sort |
| Authorize | Arrange | Interpret | Correct |
| Assume | Write | Appraise | Audit |
| Decide | Inform | Rectify | Account |
| Negotiate | Publicize | Implement | Collect |
| Represent | Persuade | Set up | Credit |
| Program | Harmonize | Maintain | Synthesize |
| Recruit | Moderate | Procure | Compute |
| Interview | Approve | Extend | Insure |
| Counsel | Disapprove | Anticipate | Secure |
| Guide | Appropriate | Forecast | Safeguard |
| Conduct | Contract | Render | Protect |
| Screen | Strengthen | Furnish | Store |
| Engage | Produce | Provide | Accept |
| Assign | Improve | Propose | Adhere |
| Delegate | Acquire | Prepare | Manipulate |
| Stimulate | Return | Recommend | Reshape |
| Train | Discharge | Test | Make |
| Teach | Disburse | Handle | Exercise |
| Motivate | Establish | Transfer | Design |
| Enhance | Conceive | Supply | Create |
| Process | Initiate | Issue | Invent |
| Enlarge | Plan | Submit | Research |
| Requisition | Organize | Receive | Activate |
| Ship | Operate | Reclaim | Formulate |
| Instruct | Allocate | Release | Develop |
| Terminate | Schedule | Systematize | Coordinate |
| Assist | Investigate | Index | Perform |
| Cooperate | Identify | Compile | Change |
| Serve | Define | Catalogue | Compose |
| Participate | Evaluate | Analyze | Continue |
| Employ | Measure | Examine | Expand |
| Contribute | Determine | Summarize | Qualif |

# More selected BARRON'S titles:

## BARRON'S ACCOUNTING HANDBOOK, 2nd EDITION
*Joel G. Siegel and Jae K. Shim*
Provides accounting rules, guidelines, formulas and techniques etc., to help students and business professionals work out accounting problems.
Hardcover: $29.95, Canada $38.95/ISBN 0-8120-6449-6, 880 pages

## REAL ESTATE HANDBOOK, 4th EDITION
*Jack P. Friedman and Jack C. Harris*
A dictionary/reference for everyone in real estate. Defines approximately 2000 legal, financial, and architectural terms.
Hardcover, $29.95, Canada $38.95/ ISBN 0-8120-6592-1, approx. 780 pages

## HOW TO PREPARE FOR THE REAL ESTATE LICENSING
## EXAMINATIONS SALESPERSON AND BROKER, 5th EDITION
*Bruce Lindeman and Jack P. Friedman*
Reviews current exam topics and features updated model exams and supplemental exams, all with explained answers.
Paperback, $12.95, Canada $16.95/ISBN 0-8120-2994-1, 340 pages

## BARRON'S FINANCE AND INVESTMENT HANDBOOK
## 4th EDITION
*John Downes and Jordan Elliot Goodman*
This hard-working handbook of essential information defines more than 3000 key terms, and explores 30 basic investment opportunities. The investment information is thoroughly up-to-date.
Hardcover $35.00, Canada $45.50/ISBN 0-8120-6465-8, 1392 pages

## FINANCIAL TABLES FOR MONEY MANAGEMENT
*Stephen S. Solomon, Dr. Clifford Marshall, Martin Pepper, Jack P. Friedman and Jack C. Harris*
Pocket-sized handbooks of interest and investment rate tables used easily by average investors and mortgage holders.
Each book: Paperback.
**Real Estate Loans, 2nd Ed.,** $7.95, Canada $10.50/0-8120-1618-1, 336 pages
**Mortgage Payments, 2nd Ed.,** $6.95, Canada $8.95/0-8120-1386-7, 304 pages
**Bonds, 2nd Ed.,** $5.95, Canada $7.50/0-8120-4995-0, 256 pages
**Canadian Mortgage Payments, 2nd Ed.,** Canada $8.95/0-8120-1617-3, 336 pages
**Adjustable Rate Mortgages, 2nd Ed.,** $7.95, Canada $10.50/0-8120-1529-0, 288 pages

Books may be purchased at your bookstore or by mail from Barron's. Enclose check or money order for total amount plus sales tax where applicable and 15% for postage and handling (minimum charge $4.95). Prices subject to change without notice.

**Barron's Educational Series, Inc.**
250 Wireless Blvd., Hauppauge, NY 11788
**In Canada:** Georgetown Book Warehouse
34 Armstrong Ave., Georgetown, Ontario L7G 4R9
www.barronseduc.com

(#11) R1/98

# BARRON'S

# Business Success Guides

For career-minded men and women, here are the facts, the tips, the wisdom, and the commonsense advice that will pave the way to success. A total to date of 30 short, pocket-size, entertaining and easy-to-read volumes advise on succeeding at all levels of management, marketing, and other important areas within the business and corporate world. They're written by the people who have been there, who currently hold top positions, who know the ropes—and know the facts *you* need to know!

## Each book: Paperback, approximately 96 pages, priced individually

0-8120-9893-5: **Conducting Better Job Interviews, 2nd Ed.**—$6.95, Canada $8.95
0-8120-4837-7: **Conquering Stress**—$4.95, Canada $6.50
0-7641-0403-9: **Creative Problem Solving, 2nd Ed.**—$6.95, Canada $8.95
0-8120-4958-6: **Delegating Authority**—$4.95, Canada $6.50
0-8120-9895-1: **How to Negotiate a Raise Without Losing Your Job, 2nd Ed.**—$6.95, Canada $8.95
0-8120-9892-7: **Make Presentations With Confidence, 2nd Ed.**—$6.95, Canada $8.95
0-7641-0400-4: **Maximizing Your Memory Power, 2nd Ed.**—$6.95, Canada $8.95
0-8120-9898-6: **Motivating People**—$6.95, Canada $8.95
0-8120-1455-3: **Projecting a Positive Image**—$4.95, Canada $6.50
0-8120-9823-4: **Running a Meeting That Works, 2nd Ed.**—$6.95, Canada $8.95
0-7641-0401-2: **Speed Reading, 2nd Ed.**—$6.95, Canada $8.95
0-7641-0071-8: **Successful Assertiveness**—$6.95, Canada $8.95
0-7641-0058-0: **Successful Computing for Business**—$6.95, Canada $8.95
0-7641-0127-7: **Successful Customer Care**—$6.95, Canada $8.95
0-7641-0074-2: **Successful Direct Mail**—$6.95, Canada $8.95
0-7641-0306-7: **Successful Environmental Management**—$6.95, Canada $8.95
0-7641-0072-6: **Successful Leadership**—$6.95, Canada $8.95
0-7641-0125-0: **Successful Negotiating**—$6.95, Canada $8.95
0-7641-0059-9: **Successful Networking**—$6.95, Canada $8.95
0-7641-0057-2: **Successful Purchasing**—$6.95, Canada $8.95
0-7641-0073-4: **Successful Team Building**—$6.95, Canada $8.95
0-7641-0060-2: **Successfully Managing Change**—$6.95, Canada $8.95
0-7641-0402-0: **Time Management, 2nd Ed.**—$6.95, Canada $8.95
0-7641-0069-6: **Understanding Business on the Internet**—$6.95, Canada $8.95
0-7641-0257-5: **Understanding Business Statistics**—$6.95, Canada $8.95
0-7641-0126-9: **Understanding Just in Time**—$6.95, Canada $8.95
0-8120-9897-8: **Using the Telephone More Effectively, 2nd Ed.**—$6.95, Canada $8.95
0-7641-0305-9: **Understanding the Virtual Organization**—$6.95, Canada $8.95
0-8120-9894-3: **Winning With Difficult People, 2nd Ed.**—$6.95, Canada $8.95
0-8120-9824-2: **Writing Effective Letters and Memos, 2nd Ed.**—$6.95, Canada $8.95

**Barron's Educational Series, Inc. • 250 Wireless Blvd., Hauppauge, NY 11788**
Order toll-free: 1-800-645-3476 • Order by fax: 1-516-434-3217
Canadian orders: 1-800-645-3476 • Fax in Canada: 1-800-887-1594

*Visit us at www.barronseduc.com*

Books and packages may be purchased at your local bookstore or by mail directly from Barron's. Enclose check or money order for total amount, plus sales tax where applicable and 15% for postage and handling (minimum $4.95). All books advertised here are paperback editions. Prices subject to change without notice.